The Slave Power

The Slave Power

*The Free North and
Southern Domination,
1780–1860*

Leonard L. Richards

Louisiana State University Press

)|(Baton Rouge

MM

Copyright © 2000 by Louisiana State University Press
All rights reserved
Manufactured in the United States of America
First printing
09 08 07 06 05 04 03 02 01 00
5 4 3 2 1

Designer: Amanda McDonald Scallan
Typeface: Trump
Typesetter: Crane Composition, Inc.
Printer and binder: Thomson-Shore, Inc.

Library of Congress Cataloging-in-Publication Data
Richards, Leonard L.
   The slave power : the free North and southern domination, 1780–1860 / Leonard L. Richards.
      p. cm.
Includes bibliographical references (p.) and index.
   ISBN 0-8071-2537-7 (alk. paper) — ISBN 0-8071-2600-4 (pbk.: alk. paper)
   1. Slavery—Political aspects—United States—History—18th century. 2. Slavery—Political
aspects—United States—History—19th century. 3. United States—Politics and
government—1783–1865. 4. Southern States—Politics and government—1775–1865.
5. Slaveholders—Southern States—Political activity. 6. Slavery—United States—Extension to
the territories. I. Title.
   E449 .R5135 2000

                                                                              00-008642

for Paige, Tyler, and Margot

Contents

Preface

This book grew out of two experiences: a short paper I presented back in the 1960s and an undergraduate writing seminar I taught for nearly a decade. The paper, which was on the well-known article by Chauncey Boucher mentioned in the first chapter, was memorable only in that it provoked an angry debate between two of my fellow graduate students over whether the federal government had been "designed" to enhance the power of the nation's leading slaveholders. In the exchange of rebuttals and counterrebuttals, one participant lost his temper; the other resorted to name-calling. Had this not happened, I might have forgotten the entire incident. But over the next thirty years, their angry words kept coming back to me whenever I studied the antislavery agitators whom Boucher disparaged in his article.

The writing seminar was on "power and slavery." In nine years of teaching that course, I read scores of essays on topics taken up in this book. At least ten students, for example, investigated what Gouverneur Morris said at the Constitutional Convention; another ten wrote about what James Tallmadge did during the Missouri crisis; and still another ten researched what happened to the Van Burenites at the 1844 Democratic convention. Thus, over the long haul, I undoubtedly learned more from the students who took the course than they learned from me. Unfortunately, I don't know which student to thank for which fact or which idea. But thanks are due to all of them. Every class raised questions that prompted further research.

I owe a very large debt to many archivists and librarians, especially those at the University of Massachusetts and the American Antiquarian Society, who repeatedly pointed me in the right direction. I am also in debt to my colleagues at the University of Massachusetts, especially to Ron Story, Bruce Laurie, and Mario DePillis for their encouragement when I first began wrestling with this book, and to Paula Baker, who is now with the University of Pittsburgh. Portions of several chapters, which were incorporated in papers given at the University of Hawaii, the Alexander Bracken Lecture Series at Ball State University, the Adams National Historical Site, and Old Deerfield's Presidential Series, benefited from the sound criticism I received from members of those audiences. Special thanks are due to Kevin Gilbert, who was my research assistant for one semester and who always went the extra mile to ferret out obscure bits of information, and to Bob Jones, who made Kevin available to me. Special thanks are also due to the anonymous reviewer who made several suggestions for improving the manuscript, and to Sylvia Frank, Lisa Sommers, and Gerry Anders of Louisiana State University Press, who shepherded the manuscript through publication. To Duane Gonzalez goes my sincere gratitude for his expertise in preparing the maps.

The Slave Power

1 | The Slave Power Thesis

On a warm March day in 1858, Senator James Henry Hammond of South Carolina lambasted a speech given the day before by William Seward of New York on the admission of Kansas as a slave state. No two men were farther apart on the issue before the Senate. To Seward, the South Carolinian was a hotheaded, unreasonable, proslavery firebrand. To Hammond, the New Yorker was a "Black Republican." Yet on one matter, the two old war-horses agreed. Neither had any doubt—none whatsoever—who ran the country. The New Yorker lamented the "fact." The South Carolinian was proud of it. Both agreed it was "the slaveholders of the South."[1]

Many in the audience undoubtedly agreed with them. The precise number is anyone's guess, but historians have long known that the notion that a slaveholding oligarchy ran the country—and ran it for their own advantage—had wide support in the years before and after the Civil War. It was the basic theme that Abraham Lincoln and his fellow Republicans used in the 1850s to gain political power.[2] Before that, it was deemed a self-evident truth by scores of prominent

1. *Congressional Globe*, 35th Congress, 1st session, 1857–58, p. 962.
2. For a full appreciation of how often Republicans relied on this theme, see the

northerners. John Quincy Adams, former president of the United States, was a true believer. So were Charles Sumner, senator from Massachusetts; Salmon P. Chase, senator from Ohio; Josiah Quincy, president of Harvard; Horace Greeley, editor of the *New York Tribune*; and Henry Wilson, future vice president of the United States. Oddly enough, many southerners also regarded the Slave Power thesis as a self-evident truth. Among the more prominent were Alexander Stephens, future vice president of the Confederacy, and the South Carolina hotspur James Henry Hammond.

The Slave Power thesis also enjoyed wide support among the lunatic fringe, and for that reason many discredited it. Of these eccentrics, probably the most determined was John Smith Dye. He published three histories of the Slave Power—one in 1864, another in 1866, and still another in 1868—all apparently at his own expense. He claimed that the Slave Power orchestrated the attempted assassination of Andrew Jackson in 1835, "assassinated by poison" both President William Henry Harrison in 1841 and President Zachary Taylor in 1850, and tried but failed to assassinate President James Buchanan in 1857, but so intimidated him that he became their tool.[3] Dye's books reflected rumors that had been around for years and would continue to be whispered long after his death.

It was not the Dyes of this world, however, that made the Slave Power thesis popular. That honor lay mainly with the Free-Soil Party of the late 1840s and early 1850s and the Republican Party thereafter. On most issues both the Free-Soilers and the Republicans had mixed messages. They condemned slavery as a "relic of barbarism" and a blatant violation of the Declaration of Independence's proclamation that "all men are created equal" and have inalienable rights to "Life, Liberty, and the pursuit of Happiness." Yet, often in the next breath, they denied that they had any right to interfere with slavery in the slave states—or any intention of doing so. And many went out of

---

massive collection of Republican newspapers, broadsides, and pamphlets at the American Antiquarian Society, Worcester, Massachusetts.

3. See the following works by John Smith Dye: *The Adder's Den; or, Secrets of the Great Conspiracy to Overthrow Liberty in America* (New York, 1864), *History of the Plots and Crimes of the Great Conspiracy to Overthrow Liberty in America* (New York, 1866), and *History of the Plots and Crimes of the Great Conspiracy to Overthrow Liberty in America* (Philadelphia, 1868).

their way to say they had no interest in the plight of black people. Indeed, many promised "to keep niggers out of the West" or to protect the North from "black pestilence."

Both Free-Soilers and Republicans, to be sure, had a sharply defined party line on at least one issue. They both vehemently opposed the expansion of slavery. But here, too, motivations varied. Some men and women clamored for free soil because they opposed slavery, or because they opposed its expansion. But others joined the free-soil ranks largely because they hated and feared blacks. "Free soil," in their minds, meant "white only." Still others supported free soil because they despised southern planters. To them the fight over free soil in the West was just part of the larger battle against the "slave oligarchs." It was a good issue—a fighting issue—because it had such wide appeal. Other than that, it had no special merit. If they could have found another fighting issue, one even more popular, they would have jumped on it.

Hostility toward slave oligarchs, in fact, provided common ground for the vast majority of Free-Soilers and Republicans. Men and women could differ on scores of issues, hate blacks or like them, denounce slavery as a sin or guarantee its protection in the Deep South, and still lambaste the "slaveocracy." It mattered not in the least where one stood on the other issues. One could still hate the slavemasters with a passion.

Free-Soil and Republican leaders, moreover, had a decisive advantage over earlier party leaders. In the past, northern congressmen had to exercise some restraint. Even if they repeatedly voted against the South on matters pertaining to slavery, they still had to cooperate with their southern colleagues to win national elections. Even Whig congressmen who repeatedly baited the South, men such as John Quincy Adams of Massachusetts and Joshua Giddings of Ohio, supported slaveholders for president or Speaker of the House when it was to their party's advantage.[4] Neither the Free-Soilers nor the Republicans had such restraints. Based entirely in the North, these parties had no need, much less desire, to placate the South.

4. *Congressional Globe*, 26th Congress, 1st session, 1839–40, pp. 51–4; Leonard L. Richards, *Life and Times of Congressman John Quincy Adams* (New York, 1986), 173–5; James Brewer Stewart, *Joshua R. Giddings and the Tactics of Radical Politics* (Cleveland, 1970), 96–7.

Thus the stock-in-trade of Free-Soil and Republican candidates was to attack the political influence of the slaveholding class at every opportunity. The Slave Power, contended one spokesman after another, had long ruled the nation. And now, said many, it was conspiring to add a covey of slave states to the Union by capturing the West, annexing Cuba, or extending slavery into the free states.

This became the heart and soul of the Slave Power thesis. It was not, however, a new argument. The contention that slaveholders had far too much power in national affairs had a long history. The same argument had been made at the time of Thomas Jefferson's election in 1800, at the time that Missouri was admitted as a slave state in 1820, and at the time that Texas was annexed to the United States in 1845. What the Free-Soilers and Republicans did was refurbish this old argument and relentlessly hammer it home.

The main victims of this pounding were northern Democrats. They were accused of being allies of the Slave Power, of complicitly allowing the slave oligarchs to run the nation, of selling out to their southern colleagues for a few measly positions in the national Democratic hierarchy. They paid dearly at the polls. Throughout the North, congressional districts that had been in Democratic hands for decades became Republican strongholds in the 1850s. Even New Hampshire, once the banner state of the Democracy, turned Republican. In 1853 the Democrats had won every district in the state by at least 1,200 votes. Four years later they lost every district in the state by 1,000 or more votes. That was not entirely because of Slave Power rhetoric. Other issues also took their toll. But every Republican candidate milked the Slave Power argument for all that it was worth.[5]

The triumphant Republicans never spoke with one voice. William Henry Seward of New York, the party's leading spokesman in the 1850s, had one story to tell. Abraham Lincoln of Illinois, Seward's challenger for the Republican presidential nomination in 1860, had another. One man's emphasis was on power. The Slave Power had

5. *Congressional Quarterly's Guide to U.S. Elections* (Washington, D.C.,1975), 597–603. For the effectiveness of the Republicans' crusade against the Slave Power in New Hampshire, see Thomas R. Bright, "The Anti-Nebraska Coalition and the Emergence of the Republican Party in New Hampshire: 1853–1857," *Historical New Hampshire* 27 (Summer 1972): 57–88.

too much power, and the slavemasters used it for their own advantage and to the disadvantage of northerners. The other man's emphasis was on conspiracy. The slavemasters, in conjunction with their northern lackeys, had conspired to extend slavery into the western territories, and in time into the free states.

William Henry Seward thought he understood political power better than any man of his generation. He had come to a position of prominence in the national Republican Party after a long apprenticeship in New York politics. Politics was his passion, and he had the brains, the capacity for hard work, and the stamina to be a master of it. He spent years hustling for votes, and as a result had a trunkful of political yarns, which he told with great wit. He also had a knack for working with difficult personalities, which oftentimes he put to good use. But he was incredibly vain and often too loquacious. These traits got him into trouble more than once. His worst trait, however, at least in the eyes of newsman Horace Greeley, was his penchant for "dexterity in politics," his love for political subtlety. As a result, some politicians thought he was duplicitous, totally lacking in any real convictions. But his critics were greatly outnumbered by his admirers, who overlooked his shortcomings, focused on his talents, and pushed him for higher office.[6]

Seward came into politics in the late 1820s with the rise of the Antimasonic movement. Born and raised in upstate New York, he was practicing law in the small town of Auburn when a large group of Masons in upstate New York decided to stop William Morgan from publishing their fraternal order's secrets. In late 1826 they botched several attempts to steal the manuscript and to burn down the publisher's print shop. Then, after having Morgan arrested on minor charges, they talked the jailer's wife into releasing him, promptly kidnapped him, and whisked him off in the night to Fort Niagara, some 150 miles by road to the west. On the road they received plenty of help—food, fresh horses, and carriages. After reaching Fort Niagara, no one knows for certain what they did to Morgan, but local sleuths concluded that they drowned him, weighted and tied, in the Niagara River. The kidnapping—and possible murder—attracted a lot of attention, but the wheels of justice barely moved

6. Glyndon G. Van Deusen, *William Henry Seward* (New York, 1967).

at all, or moved in strange ways. Of the fifty-four men who were indicted, only ten were convicted, and they received light sentences—ranging from thirty days to twenty-eight months.[7]

Law-abiding citizens were outraged. Justice, they said, had been blocked at every turn by Masonic sheriffs, Masonic judges, and Masonic officeholders. Many now saw themselves at the mercy of a powerful secret aristocracy that could literally get away with murder. Meeting in church halls and outside country stores, they pledged never to knowingly vote for a Mason for any public office. They formed a new party dedicated to driving Masons out of power. In 1827 the Antimasons carried fifteen assembly seats in central and western New York. To the dismay of seasoned politicians, the movement spread like wildfire to Vermont, Connecticut, Massachusetts, Pennsylvania, and the Michigan Territory. In 1828 William Henry Seward, age twenty-seven, began helping local Antimasons prepare speeches, addresses, and resolutions. Two years later he won a seat in the New York legislature as a zealous Antimason.

Seward and his fellow Antimasons in upstate New York were remarkably successful, virtually pounding local Masons into submission, forcing lodge after lodge to shut its doors. By 1834 local Antimasons no longer had real enemies to fight, and Seward and his colleague Thurlow Weed urged them to broaden their political program and join a new statewide coalition that would be dominated by Antimasonic leadership. The result was the New York Whig Party, largely a combination of Antimasons and National Republicans who were in general agreement on such national issues as supporting the Bank of the United States and federally sponsored roads and canals, and who were in complete agreement in their hatred of Andrew Jackson and his followers. Seward would lead the Antimasonic faction of the New York Whig Party for the next twenty years, serving both as governor and United States senator.

Seward was much like other former Antimasons in the Whig

7. For details on the Antimasonic movement and its influence on men like Seward, see William Preston Vaughn, *The Antimasonic Party in the United States, 1826–1843* (Lexington, Ky., 1983); Michael F. Holt, "The Antimasonic and Know Nothing Parties," in *History of U.S. Political Parties*, vol. 1, ed. Arthur Schlesinger, Jr. (New York, 1973), 575–93; and Ronald P. Formisano and Kathleen Smith Kutolowski, "Antimasonry and Masonry: The Genesis of Protest, 1826–1827," *American Quarterly* 29 (Summer 1977): 139–65.

coalition. He was less hostile to blacks than most northerners. While he assumed that blacks were inferior to whites, he was appalled by the race baiting that characterized Democratic Party politics in New York state. And, on more than one occasion, he supported black male suffrage. Also, like other former Antimasons, Seward was more hostile to slavery than most northerners. In 1850 he lambasted the Fugitive Slave Act, arguing that a "higher law" than the Constitution, the law of God, made slavery immoral. In 1854 he condemned the Kansas-Nebraska Act, which repealed the ban on slavery in the "Kansas country." Three years later he denounced as a conspiracy the chief justice's declaration in the Dred Scott case that Congress could not bar slavery from the territories. And just months after that, he told a Rochester, New York, audience that the North-South conflict over slavery represented an "irrepressible conflict."

In stump speeches about the Slave Power, Seward focused on power and privilege. In essence, he had the same complaint about slaveholders that he had years earlier about Masons. Both groups, he contended, were able to dominate their fellow citizens because they had special privileges or inordinate power that their fellow citizens lacked. Both constituted aristocracies "founded on the ancient principle of the inequality of men." Unless his listeners were "willing to see our republican system fail," they had no choice but to battle aristocracy "in every case, and throughout all hazards."[8]

The planters had one special privilege—"namely, personal dominion over slaves"—which "conscience and sound policy" forbade "all men alike." They also had been given "concessions" in the Federal Constitution, including the legal right to bring in additional slaves for another twenty years and the legal requirement that three-fifths of all slaves be counted in determining the number of seats that each state would have in the House of Representatives. Standing on these and similar privileges, slaveholders acted like every other aristocracy in history, expanding and aggrandizing their power.[9]

As a result, argued Seward, slaveholders now ran the country. They ran not only all the slave states but also the federal government. The president of the United States was no more than "a

8. *Works of William H. Seward*, ed. George E. Baker, 5 vols. (Boston, 1873–1884), 4: 226–7.

9. Ibid., 227–8, 258.

deputy of the privileged class, emptying the treasury and marshaling battalions and ships of war" to force northerners to obey the fugitive slave law, while firing governors and judges who attempted to resist the privileged class in the Kansas Territory. The vice president and Speaker of the House were "safe men, whom the privileged class can trust in every case." All the key committees in Congress were entrusted to "assured supporters of that class." Northerners couldn't even mention Canada, lest they "may lust after it." Meanwhile "millions upon millions" were "lavished in war and diplomacy to annex and spread slavery over Louisiana, Florida, Texas, Mexico, Cuba, and Central America."[10]

Seward provided his audiences with detail after detail. In Detroit he spent well over an hour describing the power structure of the United States Senate, the House of Representatives, the Supreme Court, and various executive offices. Who presided over the Senate? A slaveholder from Missouri. Who served as the presiding officer's secretaries, sergeants at arms, doorkeepers, pages? Either an "active or passive advocate" of the slaveholding class. Who chaired the committee on foreign relations? A Virginia slaveholder, the author of the Fugitive Slave Act. Who headed the committee on finance? Another Virginian. And so on through the power structure.[11] Numbers and names. Details and dates. After a while the "facts" are numbing, so numbing that one wonders how his listeners reacted. Did they really care who sat on the Senate committee on the District of Columbia? Or on the Senate committee on the Library of Congress? Halfway through his speech, Seward noted that his audience might be impatient with his theme, but he wasn't willing to "release" them "as yet" and continued in much the same vein.[12]

This was the approach not only of William Henry Seward but also of most spokesmen for the Slave Power thesis. Audience after audience was bombarded with "facts." Generally the focus was on two sets of facts. One was a simple record of congressional legislation. Who won the major sectional showdowns in the nation's history? Who prevailed in the congressional battle over admitting Missouri as a slave state? Over removing the great southern tribes to lands west of the Mississippi? Over denying abolitionists the

10. Ibid., 235–6.
11. Ibid., 258–75.
12. Ibid., 267.

right to petition against slavery in the nation's capital? Over the admission of Texas as a slave state? Over the new, tough Fugitive Slave Law of 1850? Over the repeal of the Missouri Compromise in 1854? In each case, it was easy to argue that the Slave Power prevailed.

Another standard argument was to point to federal officeholders. Who sat in the White House? The Speaker's chair? On the Supreme Court? The answer was that slavemasters had far more power than their numbers warranted. In the sixty-two years between Washington's election and the Compromise of 1850, for example, slaveholders controlled the presidency for fifty years, the Speaker's chair for forty-one years, and the chairmanship of House Ways and Means for forty-two years. The only men to be reelected president—Washington, Jefferson, Madison, Monroe, and Jackson—were all slaveholders. The men who sat in the Speaker's chair the longest—Henry Clay, Andrew Stevenson, and Nathaniel Macon—were slaveholders. Eighteen out of thirty-one Supreme Court justices were slaveholders.[13]

It was a powerful argument. Antebellum politicians of all stripes tried to make a case on the basis of simple head counts. South Carolina's John C. Calhoun, for example, kept track of the number of Connecticut Yankees sitting in Congress and at one point claimed that nearly half the national legislature had been born or educated in Connecticut. And someone clearly alerted the great French pundit Alexis de Tocqueville to Connecticut men in Congress. His tally showed five representing Connecticut and thirty-one representing western states.[14]

Yet there is little doubt that Seward and his associates had the better argument. For while Yankees had disproportionate power in

13. Information on officeholders other than president was computed from data in Gerald R. Lientz, "House Speaker Elections and Congressional Parties, 1789–1860," *Capitol Studies* 6 (Spring 1978): 63–89; DeAlva Stanwood Alexander, *History and Procedure of the House of Representatives* (Boston, 1916), 399–400; Cortez A. M. Ewing, *The Judges of the Supreme Court, 1789–1837* (Minneapolis, 1938), 58–61; and Albert P. Baustein and Roy M. Mersky, *The First One Hundred Justices* (Hamden, Conn., 1978), 104–5. Justice John Rutledge of South Carolina, who was appointed twice to the Court, was counted as one appointment.

14. Dixon Ryan Fox, *Yankees and Yorkers* (New York, 1940), 220; Alexis de Tocqueville, *Democracy in America*, ed. Phillips Bradley, 2 vols. (New York, 1958), 1: 304.

the national legislature and in northern state houses, they seldom controlled the higher offices of the national government. Slaveholders generally were in control.[15] Not only northerners but also southerners pointed to this fact. In 1850 the South Carolina Unionist Benjamin Perry made virtually the same numbers argument that Seward did. So did the North Carolinian Edward Stanly in the United States Congress, as did the Georgian Alexander Stephens on the eve of the Civil War. Southern hotspurs could dismiss such men as "traitors to the South." Harder to explain away, however, was the memorable speech of James Henry Hammond in 1858. The South Carolina firebrand was no Perry, no Stanly, no Alexander Stephens. He had been a devout follower of the great Calhoun. And in his famous "mudsill speech," which gained the attention of the entire nation, he not only agreed with Seward's contention that the South "ruled" the early Republic. He boasted about it.[16]

Seward invariably concluded his speeches with a call to arms. The fault, he said time and again, was not with the slaveholders. They were only acting in accordance with their training and self-interests. The fault was with the "non-slaveholding classes in the free states" who were "recreant to their own constitutions, and false to their own instincts and impulses, and even to their own true interests." It was their leaders who taught the "slaveholding classes that freedom, which could not be wholly conquered at once, could be yielded in successive halves by successive compromises."[17] What northerners had to do, then, was act in accordance with their true interests. First

15. Modern studies of the executive branch as a whole generally confirm the view held by Seward and his colleagues. In an analysis of the men appointed to some three hundred high government posts, Sidney H. Aronson found that 51 percent of John Adams's appointees were from the South, 56 percent of Jefferson's, and 57 percent of Jackson's. Similarly, in a study of every major cabinet and diplomatic appointment between 1789 and 1861, Philip H. Burch, Jr., found that exactly half went to men from the slave states. At the time, the free population of the North was nearly twice that of the South. See Aronson, *Status and Kinship in the Higher Civil Service* (Cambridge, Mass., 1964), 115; and Burch, *Elites in American History: The Federalist Years to the Civil War* (New York, 1981), 236–7.

16. Jesse T. Carpenter, *The South As a Conscious Minority, 1789–1861* (New York, 1930), 180–1; *Congressional Globe*, 31st Congress, 1st session, 1849–50, appendix: 339; 35th Congress, 1st session, 1857–58, p. 962.

17. Seward, *Works*, 4: 273.

they had to get well organized. Then they had to drive the Slave Power's northern lackeys out of office.

Abraham Lincoln was eight years younger than Seward. He lacked the schooling that Seward received as a youngster, never went to college, and by the 1850s had far less political experience. But like Seward he had been a small-town lawyer and an ardent Whig. The Antimasonic experience, which left a definite mark on Seward, had no effect on Lincoln. The movement barely touched Illinois. Lincoln came out of a political culture that caused him to see himself as a follower of Kentucky's Henry Clay. A strong national bank, protective tariffs, and federally sponsored internal improvements were a big part of that political culture. But the fear of conspiring Masons was not. Yet, oddly enough, while Lincoln lacked Seward's experience with conspiracy rhetoric, he made conspiracy more central in his telling of the Slave Power thesis.

Conspiracy was the focal point of Lincoln's famous "House Divided" speech, the opening salvo in his campaign against Senator Stephen A. Douglas in the 1858 Illinois Senate race. At the time, Douglas was the towering figure in Illinois politics, hailed far and wide by fellow Democrats as the Little Giant. Four years earlier, his actions in Congress had brought Lincoln back into politics. In 1854, in Douglas's anxiety to provide territorial government for the Kansas-Nebraska country, he agreed to the repeal of the Missouri Compromise, which had barred slavery in the northern half of the Louisiana Purchase, the land lying north of 36° 30′. In its place he substituted "popular sovereignty," which opened Kansas and Nebraska to slavery if the settlers so determined. With the help of President Franklin Pierce and presidential patronage, Douglas secured enough northern Democratic votes to get the measure passed. That outraged Lincoln. Previously, he had been a moderate on the slavery question. He had long hated slavery, but he had recognized the slave states' constitutional right to slavery and had supported the fugitive slave laws. He was content with what he regarded as Henry Clay's position—a national policy that treated slavery as an evil, set limits on its expansion, and looked forward to a day of its "ultimate extinction." In his mind the Missouri Compromise had reflected such a position. Its repeal was thus a giant step in the wrong direction. Indeed, the Little Giant's Kansas-Nebraska Act was a moral abomination.

Lincoln thus joined hundreds of thousands of northerners in vilifying Douglas for leading the country to an immoral position. And with them, he helped form a new party dedicated to stopping the expansion of slavery into Kansas and Nebraska. Events provided Lincoln and his fellow Republicans with plenty of ammunition with which to attack Douglas and other northern Democrats. In the Dred Scott decision of 1857, Chief Justice Roger B. Taney and the majority on the Supreme Court denied Congress's authority to prevent the spread of slavery into the territories. In essence the Court decreed that "slavery follows the flag." Meanwhile Douglas's alternative to the Missouri Compromise—allowing the actual settlers of the territory to vote slavery down or up—didn't work as planned. Douglas had hoped to "take the slavery question out of Congress—where it only kept everybody in an uproar—and banish the accursed problem to the frontier" so he could concentrate on "more important" issues such as railroads, river and harbor improvements, and a homestead act. Instead the Kansas frontier became the national symbol of political trickery, extreme partisanship, terrorism, guerrilla war, and fraudulent elections. In 1857 a notoriously unrepresentative convention at Lecompton drafted a proslavery constitution, and President James Buchanan, yielding to southern pressure, backed it to the hilt.

Lecompton provided Republicans nationally with a powerful issue. In Illinois, however, there was one hitch. Senator Douglas, along with several other northern Democrats fighting for political survival in their home districts, revolted against Buchanan and blocked the admission of Kansas as a slave state. Douglas, in fact, became a hero to many eastern Republicans, and Horace Greeley of the powerful *New York Tribune* urged Illinois Republicans to support his reelection. So did William Henry Seward. Some in Illinois took the same line. By and large, however, Illinois Republicans wanted no part of the Little Giant and resented Greeley and Seward's advice. "A penitent prostitute may be received in the church," noted one Illinois Republican, "but she should not lead the choir."[18]

Lincoln went further. In his "House Divided" speech, he por-

18. Robert W. Johannsen, *Stephen A. Douglas* (New York, 1973), 632–40; David Zarefsky, *Lincoln, Douglas, and Slavery: In the Crucible of Public Debate* (Chicago, 1993), 41–2.

trayed Douglas as part of the Slave Power conspiracy, along with former president Pierce, Chief Justice Taney, and President Buchanan. It was not just happenstance, Lincoln insisted, that Douglas's repeal of the Missouri Compromise was followed three years later by Taney's Dred Scott decision. Douglas and Taney were working from a common plan. The repeal was concocted with Dred Scott to follow. Hard evidence, Lincoln admitted, was missing. "But when we see a lot of framed timbers, different portions of which we know have been gotten out at different times and places by different workmen— Stephen, Franklin, Roger and James, for instance—and when we see these timbers joined together, and see they exactly make the frame of the house . . . we find it impossible to not *believe* that Stephen and Franklin and Roger and James all understood one another from the beginning, and all worked upon a common *plan* or *draft* drawn before the first lick was struck." Moreover, argued Lincoln, there was still a piece missing from the house—a future Supreme Court decision "declaring that the Constitution of the United States does not permit a *state* to exclude slavery from its limits."[19] Douglas and his coconspirators, therefore, had to be overthrown *now*.

Lincoln repeated the charge in a speech at Beardstown. He then introduced it into the first Lincoln-Douglas debate at Ottawa, a solidly Republican town in which the local congressman was best known as the brother of a famous abolitionist who had been killed some twenty years earlier defending an antislavery newspaper. Six days later at Freeport, another Republican stronghold, Lincoln devoted much of his rebuttal to the conspiracy charge against Douglas. After Freeport, among less friendly audiences, he softened the charge somewhat, sometimes portraying Douglas as an active agent of the Slave Power, sometimes as an unwitting tool, whose main service was in preparing the northern public to accept slavery as a matter of moral indifference.

Lincoln's basic argument was not unique. Scores of commentators had seen a link between the Kansas-Nebraska Act and what followed. Salmon P. Chase and Joshua Giddings, in their "Appeal of the Independent Democrats," also claimed that the bill repealing the Missouri Compromise was "part and parcel of an atrocious plot" to extend slavery into the West. The *New York Times* portrayed it as

19. *The Collected Works of Abraham Lincoln*, ed. Roy P. Basler, 9 vols. (New Brunswick, N.J., 1953–55), 2: 465–7.

"part of this great scheme for extending and perpetuating the supremacy of the Slave Power." The *New York Tribune* viewed it as the "first step" in "Africanizing" the American hemisphere. David Wilmot of Pennsylvania said it was the "precursor of a series of measures . . . to give the Slave oligarchy complete domination." Benjamin Wade of Ohio had "no doubt" that it was "but the first of a series of measures having for their object the *nationalization* of slavery."[20]

In Lincoln's hands, however, Douglas came across as the ringleader of the conspiracy. Douglas, according to Lincoln, had deliberately created "niches" in the Kansas-Nebraska Act to pave the way for both the Dred Scott decision and a second decision (yet to be written) that would open the free states to slavery. First, during the Senate debate on Kansas-Nebraska, Douglas engineered the defeat of an amendment that expressly would have permitted the people of a territory to exclude slavery. Why did he do that? "Plainly enough *now*, the adoption of it, would have spoiled the niche for the Dred Scott decision." Second, Douglas included superfluous language in the bill, language stating that the "true intent" of the bill was to allow the people of "any Territory or State . . . [to be] perfectly free to form and regulate their domestic institutions in their own way, subject only to the Constitution of the United States." Why did he include the word *state* in a bill dealing with territorial organization? What was the purpose? To create "another nice little niche"? To set the stage for a second Dred Scott decision, one that would prohibit the states from outlawing slavery?[21]

Equally important, argued Lincoln, was the Little Giant's role as a molder of public opinion. The Supreme Court, insisted Lincoln, needed the support or acquiescence of public sentiment to be effective. Without it, the Court's judgment would be nothing. Public sentiment was everything, and Douglas as "a man of vast influence" had an enormous role in shaping public sentiment. Indeed, many men would "profess to believe anything" as soon as they found out

20. Salmon P. Chase and Joshua Giddings, "The Appeal of the Independent Democrats in Congress to the People of the United States," *Washington National Era*, 24 January 1854; *Congressional Globe*, 33d Congress, 1st session, 1853–54, pp. 281–2; *New York Times*, 19 May 1854; *New York Tribune*, 15 May 1854; Charles Buxton Going, *David Wilmot, Free-Soiler* (New York, 1924), 459; Joseph P. Smith, ed., *History of the Republican Party of Ohio*, 2 vols. (Chicago, 1898), 1: 17.

21. Lincoln, *Works*, 2: 465–7, 550–1.

"that Judge Douglas professes to believe it." And what had Douglas done? For years he had denounced the Supreme Court for sanctioning the Second Bank of the United States and expressed more hostility toward the Court's decisions than "almost any living man." But when the Supreme Court expanded the rights of slaveholders in the Dred Scott decision, he reversed "his whole past life." He now unreservedly supported the Court's decision, not because of its merits, but because it had been propounded by the Supreme Court. In so doing, he was leading the northern public, and especially the young, to ignore right and wrong and quietly accept whatever the Supreme Court decreed. Indeed, Douglas himself would have no grounds to object to the next court decision. That decision, as much as the Dred Scott decision, "will be a *thus saith the Lord.*"[22]

Lincoln had no trouble making the case for a second Dred Scott decision. There was much talk about a "Dred Scott II" in 1858. The Buchanan administration's official newspaper, the *Washington Union*, had already laid out the logic for such a decision in November 1857 in an editorial entitled "Slavery Must Move North." Several senators, lawyers all, had already pointed out that such a decision would be entirely in keeping with the logic of Dred Scott. And there was already a case making its way through the courts, *Lemmon v. The People*, that many Republican jurists feared would provide the Taney court with an opening wedge.[23]

Finally, Lincoln pointed to Douglas's inconsistent commitment to popular sovereignty. The principle of local self-determination was widely regarded to be central to Douglas's thinking. He had said time and again that actual settlers in a community should determine their own institutions, their own government, their own way of life. Yet because the Mormon settlers in Utah sanctioned polygamy, he had insisted that the federal government should intervene and revoke Utah's territorial charter. Why, asked Lincoln, did the federal

22. Paul M. Angle, ed., *Created Equal? The Complete Lincoln-Douglas Debates of 1858* (Chicago, 1958), 128–9; Lincoln, *Works*, 2: 551–3.

23. *Congressional Globe*, 35th Congress, 1st session, 1857–58, pp. 385, 547, 617, 1089; *New York Tribune*, 8 March 1857; Don E. Fehrenbacher, *The Dred Scott Case: Its Significance in American Law and Politics* (New York, 1978), 60–1, 444–5; Paul Finkelman, *An Imperfect Union: Slavery, Federalism, and Comity* (Chapel Hill, 1981), 239.

government have the right to intervene in Utah but not in Kansas? How could the Little Giant justify this double standard? The answer, said Lincoln, was obvious. Popular sovereignty was not the neutral principle that Douglas claimed, but "a mere deceitful pretence for the benefit of slavery."[24]

Did Lincoln really believe that Douglas was part of a Slave Power conspiracy? One of Douglas's biographers, Gerald M. Capers, inferred that Honest Abe was just making political hay.[25] But most authorities have concluded that Lincoln was sincere. And Lincoln, in notes to himself, cited his fear of "a powerful plot to make slavery universal and perpetual" as his reason for running against Douglas in 1858. He admitted that he had not proven that a conspiracy existed. He had "only stated the evidence," and the evidence clearly indicated that Douglas was either a principle in such a conspiracy or a dupe.[26] And in Lincoln's mind, Douglas was too clever to be anyone's dupe.

In the end, Lincoln undoubtedly convinced many voters that he had Douglas dead to rights. At first Douglas just ignored the conspiracy charge or treated it like hogwash, but as the campaign continued he felt compelled to deal with the specifics. On Election Day Lincoln more than held his own against Illinois's foremost politician. His party outpolled Douglas's, 125,000 votes to 121,000, but the Democrats carried eight more legislative districts, and the state legislature reelected the Little Giant to a third Senate term.

After the Civil War, the Slave Power thesis became a formidable tool of historical explanation. That was partly because two of the leading histories were written by men who had been devotees of the Slave Power argument before the war. Horace Greeley had taken every opportunity to denounce the Slave Power in the *New York Tribune* in the 1850s. That he would use the same argument in his two-volume history of antebellum America, *The American Conflict*, thus came as no surprise. The same held true for Henry Wilson, who turned out a three-volume work entitled *History of the Rise and Fall of the Slave Power.* Like Seward and Lincoln, Wilson

24. Lincoln, *Works*, 2: 399.
25. Gerald M. Capers, *Stephen A. Douglas: Defender of the Union* (Boston, 1959), 177–8, 185.
26. Lincoln, *Works*, 2: 548–50.

had lambasted the Slave Power throughout the 1850s, first as a Free-Soiler, then as a Republican.[27]

The Slave Power thesis also came to enjoy wide support among academic historians. Of these the most important was the German-trained Hermann Eduard von Holst, who adopted it as a major theme in his seven-volume *History of the United States.* Von Holst had enormous prestige, and in 1889 a handbook for historians hailed his work as "unquestionably the ablest" on the nation's constitutional and political history. In doing so, the handbook took the Slave Power thesis as a given, a valid explanation for the course of events leading to the Civil War, virtually beyond dispute.[28]

The thesis lost ground thereafter. Frederick Jackson Turner and Charles A. Beard, the two giants of early-twentieth-century historiography, turned their backs on what they regarded as Civil War sentimentalism and focused instead on the conflict between northeastern capitalism and agrarianism. On their heels came the Civil War revisionists who clearly wanted no part of any thesis that undermined their "needless war" hypothesis. The death blow, however, undoubtedly came from the pen of Chauncey S. Boucher. In 1921, in a seminal article published in the *Mississippi Valley Historical Review,* Boucher contended that the claim that a powerful, well-organized Slave Power determined the course of the early Republic's history was simply antislavery polemics. The South was incapable of carrying out any well-organized conspiracy. The slaveholders were always hopelessly divided, with Andrew Jackson pitted against Henry Clay, John C. Calhoun against Thomas Hart Benton, Jefferson Davis against Andrew Johnson.[29]

Boucher, in effect, delivered a knockout punch and his victim has never fully recovered. For years historians simply belittled the thesis. Now it is more fashionable to dismiss the notion of a conspiring Slave

27. Horace Greeley, *The American Conflict,* 2 vols. (Hartford, Conn., 1864–66); Henry Wilson, *History of the Rise and Fall of the Slave Power in America,* 3 vols. (Boston, 1873–77).

28. Hermann Eduard von Holst, *The Constitutional and Political History of the United States,* 7 vols. (Chicago, 1876–92); Charles K. Adams, *A Manual of Historical Literature* (New York, 1889), 607.

29. Chauncey S. Boucher, "In Re That Aggressive Slaveocracy," *Mississippi Valley Historical Review* 8 (June–September 1921): 13–80.

Power as just one of many conspiracy theories that bedeviled the early Republic, part and parcel of a society in which the followers of Andrew Jackson envisioned a conspiring "Money Power" and spoke often of a "Monster Bank," and others railed about underhanded schemes and plots of the papacy, the Mormons, Federalist "monarchists," or British abolitionists. David Brion Davis, after a careful study of the literature of many of these supposed plots and intrigues, concluded that the Slave Power thesis reflected the larger dynamic of antebellum life, the "paranoid style" that seemed to dominate political and social thinking.[30]

A handful of well-known historians, it is true, have given some credence to the Slave Power thesis.[31] But usually they have paid homage to Boucher's highly touted article. Russel B. Nye, for example, cited the value of Boucher's essay, while including enough details in his own account to indicate that the abolitionists had ample grounds for suspecting the planter aristocracy. Eric Foner, while giving full credit to the findings of Boucher and the "paranoid style" argument, raised the question of why so many antebellum northerners accepted the Republican charge of slaveholder domination. The reason, he

30. David Brion Davis, *The Slave Power Conspiracy and the Paranoid Style* (Baton Rouge, 1969).

31. This is especially true of Russel B. Nye, *Fettered Freedom* (East Lansing, Mich., 1963), 314–5, and Lee Benson in "Explanations of American Civil War Causation," *Toward the Scientific Study of History* (Philadelphia, 1972), 307–26. More circumspect are Larry Gara, "Slavery and the Slave Power: A Crucial Distinction," *Civil War History* 15 (March 1969): 5–18; Eric Foner, *Free Soil, Free Labor, Free Men* (New York, 1970), 99–102; Richard H. Sewell, *Ballots for Freedom: Antislavery Politics in the United States, 1837–1860* (New York, 1976), 301–4; Michael F. Holt, *The Political Crisis of the 1850s* (New York, 1978), 184–5, and *The Rise and Fall of the American Whig Party* (New York, 1999), passim; William E. Gienapp, "The Republican Party and the Slave Power," in *New Perspectives on Race and Slavery in America*, ed. Robert H. Abzug and Stephen E. Maizlish (Lexington, Ky., 1986), 74; and Jonathan Halperin Earle, "The Undaunted Democracy: Jacksonian Antislavery and Free Soil, 1828–1848" (Ph.D. dissertation, Princeton, 1996). More skeptical yet is Davis, *Slave Power Conspiracy and the Paranoid Style*. Generally speaking, ferreting out the twists and turns of the Slave Power argument, or tracing it back to its roots, has not been a primary concern of recent scholarship. Instead the main goal of those who have written about Slave Power rhetoric has been to explain something else—the rise of antislavery politics, the origins of the Republican Party, the antislavery wing of the Democratic Party, the political crisis of the 1850s, the scientific approach to history, or the paranoia of antebellum America.

said, was that there was "much truth" in such charges. Richard H. Sewell, in his study of antislavery politics, agreed that "Free Soil apprehensions, while at times exaggerated, were by no means baseless." And William Gienapp, in his recent study of the origins of the Republican Party, in effect argued that Boucher and other critics concentrated on the most extreme Slave Power rhetoric. More realistic, contended Gienapp, were the statements of Lincoln and Seward, who spoke loosely of the plans and tendencies of the planter elite and never invoked the image of a tightly knit, well-disciplined conspiratorial group.[32]

What Boucher did, in fact, was attack a straw man. He did not square off against the arguments of Seward and Lincoln. He did not deal specifically with the speeches of Charles Sumner or Salmon

32. Nye, *Fettered Freedom,* 282–315; Foner, *Free Soil, Free Labor, Free Men,* 99–101; Sewell, *Ballots for Freedom,* 200; Gienapp, "The Republican Party and the Slave Power," 52–77. Of these accounts, probably the most influential has been Eric Foner's *Free Soil, Free Labor, Free Men.* In that subtle and far-ranging book, Foner argued that the idea of free labor was the centerpiece of Republican ideology and that the Republicans' fear of an arrogant Slave Power stemmed largely from their determination to protect and extend the North's free labor society and to stop the extension of slavery. This argument has been faulted for failing to explain the behavior of northern Democrats. Didn't they also believe in a free labor society? Why, then, did they mock Republican rhetoric? Why weren't they also worried about an all-powerful, menacing Slave Power? See, for example, Bruce Collins, "The Ideology of the Ante-Bellum Northern Democrats," *Journal of American Studies* 11 (April 1977): 103–5; and Gienapp, "The Republican Party and the Slave Power," 52.

In a much different interpretation of the period, one that challenges Foner on several fronts, Michael Holt, in *The Political Crisis of the 1850s,* disputed the notion that extension of a slaveholding society at the expense of a free labor society was the Republicans' prime concern. Instead, said Holt, the central issue was the survival of republican government, and for Republicans the embodiment of antirepublicanism was the Slave Power. Also taking issue with Foner, and to a lesser extent with Holt, William Gienapp in a significant article, and later an influential book, contended that historians had understated the importance of the Slave Power argument. He termed it the "essential key" to understanding Republican ideology in that it "united a number of diverse themes" including their hatred of "white planters," their fear for "white liberties," and their belief in conspiracy. Noting that the concept had been formulated in the 1830s, Gienapp insisted that it became truly significant only in the 1850s. The reason, he argued, was not "rapid change" or "social unease and popular anxiety," but the "brewing political crisis of the 1850s." (Gienapp, "Republican Party and the Slave Power," 53, 71, and *The Origins of the Republican Party, 1852–1856* [New York, 1987], 358–65.)

P. Chase, George Julian or Charles Francis Adams. Nor did he confront the writings of Joshua Leavitt or anyone else who wrote extensively about the Slave Power. What he tore apart was a composite
view which he himself constructed, a picture embracing the views
of abolitionists, Free-Soilers, and Republicans. And this picture was
far less nimble and far more vulnerable to attack than the men of
the 1840s and 1850s. Thus, blows that Lincoln and Seward had
fended off easily hit home.

Boucher's specialty was southern history, and he was an editor of
the John C. Calhoun papers when he wrote his seminal article.
From this experience, he knew that the South was never united on
the big questions of policy and action. He knew that Calhoun never
came close to achieving his dream of a united South. He knew that
Calhoun was blocked by Andrew Jackson, blocked by Thomas Hart
Benton, blocked even by some of his fellow South Carolinians. And
he had no trouble proving it. He had the details. He could provide
plenty of citations.

In making this argument, moreover, Boucher was careful. He anticipated many potential critics. He indicated that the congressional
record, which the great German scholar von Holst had relied on, distorted southern unity. There was more unity among southerners in
Congress, said Boucher, than among constituents at home. He also
indicated that there was more unity among southern Democrats
than among southern Whigs. And he freely admitted that southerners boasted of unity. Such talk, he counseled historians, was just
wishful thinking. In only one instance did he leave himself vulnerable to easy counterattack. He insisted that the South was as divided
as the North, that as many southern congressmen voted with the
North as northern congressmen voted with the South, and that—to
use the language of the time—"southern traitors" were as common
as "northern doughfaces." This argument has fared poorly. Historian
after historian has demonstrated that the South was more likely
than the North to hold firm in sectional battles.

But generally speaking, Boucher was surefooted in documenting
southern disunity. Apparently that was not the case, however, when
it came to explaining the Slave Power thesis. In that part of his long
essay, Boucher provided no documentation whatsoever, not even a
single footnote. He merely claimed that there was a unified view of
a conspiring Slave Power and that that view was sheer nonsense.

In fact, Boucher's claim was nonsense. Most men and women who used the term Slave Power were anything but precise. Did the term include all slaveholders or just the wealthy planters? Did it include the Border States or just the Deep South? The Jackson men or just the Calhounites? All southern Whigs or just the Tyler Whigs? Usually it was impossible to tell. And what about northern politicians who voted with the South? Northern newspapers that "truckled" to the South? Northern clergymen who defended the planters? Were such "doughfaces" part of the Slave Power? Again, usually it was impossible to tell.

Those who attempted precision, moreover, were hardly of one mind. Take, for example, the simple question of who was a member of the Slave Power. With the 1850 census at his fingertips, Seward defined the Slave Power as the 350,000 owners of slaves. But, cautioned Seward, if one added parents, children, immediate relatives, and dependents, the number would be closer to two million. Using the same census, Charles Francis Adams of Massachusetts defined the Slave Power as 350,000 men "commanding the political resources of fifteen states" and all "official strongholds" in the federal government. Indiana's George W. Julian, using the same census figures, defined the Slave Power as 1/25th of the white South and 1/100th of the nation. All three men clearly included small slaveholders as well as the great planters, and the Border States as well as the Deep South, in their calculations.[33]

In the eyes of Horace Greeley and many others, however, the inclusion of small slaveholders was unrealistic. And Greeley, in his *Tribune*, reached a far larger slice of the electorate than Seward, Adams, or Julian ever reached with their comments or speeches. In his count, Greeley eliminated the small slaveholders, as well as women and children, and defined the Slave Power as the 60,000 owners of more than ten slaves. Following the same procedure in an article in the *Atlantic Monthly*, Edmund Quincy defined the Slave Power as "not much more" than 50,000 "voting men." That number was way too big for Quincy's father, Josiah Quincy, the former president of Harvard. He maintained that no more than 1,000 decided policy. Meanwhile, an-

---

33. Seward, *Works,* 2: 236–7, 57; Charles Francis Adams, *What Makes Slavery a Question of National Concern?* (Boston, 1855), 27; George W. Julian, *Speeches on Political Questions* (New York, 1872), 67–8.

other Massachusetts champion of free soil, Charles Sumner, spoke of the "Slave Oligarchy" as consisting of 92,000 slaveowners.[34]

There was also sharp disagreement about specific individuals. Generally speaking, George Washington was always excluded from the cast of Slave Power villains and John C. Calhoun was always included. But what about the other political giants of the early Republic—men like Thomas Jefferson, Andrew Jackson, and Henry Clay? Were they members of the Slave Power? The answer usually depended entirely on the speaker or author's political background. Charles Sumner and William H. Seward, for example, were careful to exclude Jefferson along with Washington. But Edmund and Josiah Quincy, who had strong Federalist antecedents, left no doubt that both Jefferson and Jackson were part of the slaveocracy. Men who came out of the Jacksonian tradition, however, went out of their way to exclude Jackson from their lists of villains.[35]

Most revealing, perhaps, was John C. Hamilton's definition of the Slave Power. The son of Alexander Hamilton, he was true to his father's memory in his hatred of Thomas Jefferson and Jefferson's Virginia followers. But like his brother James, he had become a follower of Andrew Jackson. Accordingly, in his hands, the Slave Power included Jefferson in its ranks but not Jackson. Indeed, Jefferson and his Virginia followers were the heart and soul of the Slave Power, and John C. Calhoun and his South Carolina nullifiers merely followed in their footsteps. And just as the "noble" Washington temporarily blocked the aggressions of Jefferson and his "strict construction" followers in the 1790s, so did the "Patriot Soldier" Jackson temporarily halt Calhoun and the "arrogant" heirs of the Jefferson's Virginia school in the 1830s.[36]

*　*　*

34. *New York Tribune,* 25 June, 1 July 1856; [Edmund Quincy], "Where Will It End?" *Atlantic Monthly* 1 (December 1857): 243; Josiah Quincy, *Address Illustrative of the Nature and Power of the Slave States, and the Duties of the Free States* (Boston, 1856), 25; Charles Sumner, *Recent Speeches and Addresses* (Boston, 1856), 532–3.

35. Sumner, *Recent Speeches,* 528; Seward, *Works,* 2: 227; Quincy, "Where Will It End?" 242; Quincy, *Power of the Slave States,* 11–8; *Congressional Globe,* 25th Congress, 1st session,1838–39, appendix, 167–75; B. F. Morris, *The Life of Thomas Morris* (Cincinnati, 1856), 176–202; Francis P. Blair, *To My Neighbors* (New York, 1856); *Congressional Globe,* 35th Congress, 2d session, 1858–59, p. 1267.

36. John C. Hamilton, *The Slave Power: Its Heresies and Injuries to the American People* (New York, 1864).

Boucher was dead wrong, then, when he claimed that there was a unified view of the Slave Power. He was also dead wrong when he claimed that its advocates had a common history to tell. Just as men drew on their own political past in defining the Slave Power, so too did they draw on their political heritage in telling its history.

Generally speaking, those who came out of the Jacksonian tradition purveyed a short history of the Slave Power, noting some events of the 1830s but emphasizing those of the 1840s and 1850s. A key figure for free-soil Democrats, especially those from the Ohio Valley, was "old Tom Morris." A Democratic Party regular who had served in the Ohio legislature for fifteen terms and battled the "Bank Power," Morris was elected to the United States Senate in the early 1830s. There, to the chagrin of the Ohio politicians who elected him, he became alarmed by the South's influence in national politics, defended the abolitionists, and thundered against the annexation of Texas. Then, in a memorable speech, he called on "the people" to wage war against the Slave Power just as they had against the "Bank power." This was too much for "regulars" in the Ohio Democratic caucus, who stripped Old Tom of his Senate seat and later "lopped" him off as "a rotten branch" from the state party.[37]

Morris, although driven out of national politics, became a folk hero to the men who formed the Liberty Party, an avowed antislavery party that took root in the late 1830s. And later Salmon P. Chase, who became one of the key figures in popularizing the Slave Power thesis, credited Old Tom with alerting him to the nation's plight. The pattern that Morris followed, first focusing his wrath on the "monstrous Money Power" and then shifting to a "monstrous Slave Power," also became somewhat common among free-soil Democrats. James Doolittle of Wisconsin, after taking the same path, claimed that the same men who organized to put down the Second Bank of the United States when it tried "to enforce its

37. *Congressional Globe,* 25th Congress, 1st session, 1838–39, appendix, 167–75; Morris, *Morris,* 176–202; Francis P. Weisenburger, *The Passing of the Frontier, 1825–1850* (Columbus, Ohio, 1941), 378–9, 384–5; and John A. Neuenschwander, "Senator Thomas Morris: Antagonist of the South, 1836–1839," *Cincinnati Historical Society Bulletin* 32 (June 1974): 123–39. For another excellent study of Morris and other antislavery Democrats, which unfortunately appeared too late to be of much help to me, see also Earle, "Undaunted Democracy."

recharter" were now organizing "to put down a similar despotism" that "seeks today" to control the federal government.[38]

The trouble with Doolittle's analysis is that at best it accounted for only a small percentage of the men who organized against the Slave Power. By and large, most of the men who clamored against the Slave Power were not former Bank haters. They were former Bank supporters. Typical of many was Joshua Giddings, an Ohio congressman, who helped Salmon P. Chase popularize the concept of the threatening Slave Power. Giddings hardly shared the political tradition of Tom Morris, Chase, or Doolittle. A staunch Whig who vehemently opposed Jackson and his anti-Bank coalition, Giddings was far more impressed with the speeches of John Quincy Adams, William Slade of Vermont, and other antislavery Whigs. And these men, it is clear, had been complaining about the power of slavery in national politics at least a decade before Tom Morris. Particularly important, Giddings explained to his wife, was the leadership of Adams. The former president, said Giddings, showed "the manner in which the Slave interest . . . assiduously crept into our whole policy, subsidized our presses, affected our Literature, invaded the sanctity of the Post office, degraded our Patriotism, taxed the free labor of the north, frightened our Statesmen, and controlled the nation."[39]

Adams, in turn, was partly indebted to Benjamin Lundy, an antislavery Quaker who, in the late 1820s, began assembling material regarding a "pro-slavery plot" to acquire Texas. Among Lundy's papers were documents indicating that Senator Thomas Hart Benton of Missouri had once trumpeted the idea of acquiring Texas so that the South could add "NINE" more slave states to the Union, that Abel Upshur of Virginia had touted the acquisition of Texas as a means of driving up the price of Virginia slaves in the interstate slave trade, and that the slippery Aaron Burr was part of a Galveston land company that hoped to make a fortune in Texas lands and slaves. Lundy passed on these details to Adams in 1836. And Adams, it is clear, was very thankful for them.[40]

38. *Congressional Globe*, 35th Congress, 2d session,1858–59, p. 1267.

39. Stewart, *Giddings*; Joshua Giddings to his wife, 6 February 1842, Giddings Papers, Ohio Archaeological and Historical Society (microfilm).

40. Richards, *Adams*, 156–9; Merton L. Dillon, *Benjamin Lundy and the Struggle for Negro Freedom* (Urbana, Ill., 1966); 222–3; [Benjamin Lundy], *The Origin and True Cause of the Texas Revolution . . .* (Philadelphia, 1836).

Yet it is also clear that Adams was not surprised by what Lundy told him, that Adams had long expected the worst of Benton, Burr, and other associates of Andrew Jackson and the great slavemasters of the South. Indeed, Adams had blamed his defeat at Jackson's hands in the 1828 presidential election on the "Sable Genius of the South." He had also spoken of slaveholder domination at the time of the Missouri crisis in 1819. He had written a speech, one that he never delivered, denouncing the planters' excessive power in 1804. And like every one in his family, he blamed his father's defeat at the hands of Thomas Jefferson in 1800 on the inordinate power of the slavemasters.[41]

Those, like Adams, who came out of the Federalist tradition, and particularly the New England Federalist tradition, had a different view of the Slave Power than the Jacksonians. They traced it beyond the last years of the Jackson era, the movement to acquire Texas, the election of James K. Polk in 1844, and the Mexican War in 1846. They usually went back to the days of Thomas Jefferson, at least to the Louisiana Purchase in 1803 or the establishment of slavery in the nation's capital, but sometimes as far back as the election of 1800, sometimes to the Constitutional Convention of 1787, and sometimes to the very foundation of the new nation in 1783.[42]

The Slave Power thesis was thus more unruly than Chauncey S. Boucher made it out to be. Not only were most of its spokesmen vague and elastic, but the few who attempted precision never spoke with one voice. Still, if Boucher had chosen to engage actual statements rather than the picture that he himself had constructed, he would have found much to criticize.

Boucher, in fact, was basically right in insisting that Lincoln, Seward, and their colleagues had a common story to tell. It was not the story Boucher focused on. Nor was it usually their primary story; sometimes it was buried deep in their narratives. But it emerged whenever they took on the fundamental question of why slaveholders had the whip hand in the national government.

---

41. Richards, *Adams*, 9, 102–4, 156–7; Worthington C. Ford, ed., *Writings of John Quincy Adams*, 7 vols. (New York, 1913–17), 3: 46–77, 87–100.

42. Cf. William Jay, *Miscellaneous Writings on Slavery* (New York, 1853), 217; Hamilton, *The Slave Power*, 3; Quincy, "Where Will It End?" 242; John G. Palfrey, *Papers on the Slave Power* (Boston, 1846), 11–2; Sumner, *Recent Speeches*, 536; Seward, *Works*, 4: 228–31; Quincy, *Power of the Slave States*, 17.

One explanation, championed by James Henry Hammond among others, was that the plantation system was so adept at training men to command, to dominate, and to carry themselves with what the army today calls command presence that it naturally produced the nation's ablest leaders. Only a few advocates of the Slave Power thesis accepted this explanation.[43] Most rejected it. Generally, they had no quarrel with the claim that the plantation South produced strong leaders, and they certainly insisted that slaveholders were a domineering lot. Yet, as they saw it, the real underpinnings of southern power were regional unity, parity in the Senate, and the three-fifths clause of the Constitution. Alone, each was important; together, they were a formidable combination. In one instance the three-fifths rule might prove decisive, in another Senate parity, and in still another northern disunity; but usually it was two or three working together that gave the great planter-politicians the edge. Would they lose that edge if one prop were removed? That question lay behind the Republicans' drive for power and many a heated debate in Congress.[44]

Boucher was also basically right in insisting that Lincoln, Seward, and their colleagues had a distorted view of the world. That they did. They focused on some facts while ignoring others. They caricatured northern opponents. They minimized divisions in the plantation South. They exaggerated differences between North and South. They often failed to see the whole picture, often failed to put events into a larger context, often failed to see the world about them as later generations of historians would see it. They were, in short, no different than scores of other groups historians have studied.

The real problem, however, is why so many antebellum Americans came to share their perspective. Usually, conspiracy arguments have limited appeal, inspiring a handful of true believers but not a wide audience. The Slave Power thesis, in contrast, attained the status of conventional wisdom in Republican circles and had wide ap-

43. Joseph Stevens to Horace Mann, 15 August 1850, Horace Mann Papers, Massachusetts Historical Society.

44. Cf., for example, *Liberty Standard*, 1 December 1841; *Tocsin of Liberty*, 5 October 1842; *Emancipator Extra*, 21 September 1843; *Boston Daily Evening Star*, 28 August 1849; Quincy, "Where Will It End?" 244–5; Jay, *Miscellaneous Writings*, 218–30; Palfrey, *Papers on the Slave Power*, 4–6, 10–1; Quincy, *Power of the Slave States*, 5, 18, 25, 27, 31; Seward, *Works*, 4: 239, 256–7, 273–4; Lincoln, *Works*, 2: 246–7.

peal across the North. In the Illinois senatorial campaign of 1858, for example, Lincoln's claim that Stephen A. Douglas was part of a secret conspiracy to spread slavery across the country undoubtedly energized his core supporters[45] and probably helped his party win a plurality of the popular vote.

Elsewhere, Republicans linked their opponents to the Slave Power and won handily. Why was that the case? If the true believers in the Slave Power thesis were merely crackpots and eccentrics, or obvious sufferers from paranoia and status anxiety, it might be easy to dismiss their concerns. But the men who ran the *New York Times* hardly belonged to the lunatic fringe. Nor is there any evidence that they were being left behind in a rapidly changing industrial world. And the Harvard Fellows and Overseers, who chose Josiah Quincy to be their president, scarcely thought of him as a harebrained radical. Yet as early as 1804 Quincy insisted that the planter elite ran the country. And in 1856 he declared that every president since 1800 had been a tool of the Slave Power except John Quincy Adams.[46] How did he come to think in such terms? And why did others who had reputations for being staid and circumspect believe in the Slave Power thesis? What precisely went into the making of their world view?

45. Zarefsky, *Lincoln, Douglas,* 80–93, 228–9.

46. *Boston Repository,* 21, 25 September 1804; Edmund Quincy, *Life of Josiah Quincy of Massachusetts* (Boston, 1867), 65–6, 308–16; Quincy, *Power of the Slave States,* 17.

2 | Morris's Prophecy

The men and women who first called attention to the inordinate power of slavemasters generally came from two distinct camps. In one camp were the most conscientious opponents of slavery, disproportionately Quakers, who lambasted the United States Constitution as an immoral covenant that rewarded slavemasters for doing wrong. In the other camp were northern aristocrats like Josiah Quincy. They tended to be keenly aware of the benefits of power but resentful that others had more power than they did.

A few individuals embodied the views of both camps. Of these, probably the most perceptive was Gouverneur Morris of New York. At the Constitutional Convention no one came close to matching Morris in denouncing the immorality of slavery and the special privileges given slaveholders. He anticipated, moreover, one line of the Slave Power argument that would be repeated by thousands of others.

Morris was one of the more colorful of the fifty-five men who attended the Philadelphia convention in the summer of 1787. He is best known to historians as a good source for outrageous quotes and as the skilled stylist who wrote the final draft of the Constitution.

To his contemporaries he was known as a man with a gifted pen and a penchant for "saying things and advancing doctrines that no one else would,"[1] but also as a man of the world, tall and athletic in appearance, with a rich voice and great wit, a phenomenal memory and an uncanny ability to solve complicated math problems in his head, and "the great lover with the wooden leg."

Morris was the type of man that others liked to talk about. His enemies conceded that he had enormous talent but insisted that he was fickle and vain and misused his gifts. His friends conceded that he was too bold and fun-loving for his own good, but they seemed to admire him for his foibles and repeated tales about him that probably weren't true. One popular story had him, on a wager, slapping George Washington on the back and speaking to him intimately before a large gathering, only to have Washington, twenty years his senior, respond with an icy glare. Another story, even more popular among his cronies, had him losing his leg, not from falling under a carriage wheel or some such tragic event, but from jumping out of a lady's second-story bedroom window with her irate husband in hot pursuit.

This telling of Morris's life, however, misses a central feature of his character. Although he undoubtedly lived with gusto, and from all reports was generally congenial and lighthearted, he was also keenly aware of life's darker side and especially of the fact that some people had from birth far more privileges than others. That awareness stemmed largely from childhood slights. He was his father's fourth son and the son of a second wife in a family in which such facts were immensely important.

Morris's father was a rich, well-educated, landowning aristocrat with extensive legal and mercantile connections. His manor occupied about 2,000 acres ten miles outside downtown Manhattan in what is now the Bronx. It had a commanding view of Long Island Sound and was worked by forty-six slaves.[2] Here he sired two families, one much younger than the other. He had been a widower for fifteen years when he married Morris's mother, and by the time Morris was born the older children had grown up and moved away.

1. Max Farrand, ed., *The Records of the Federal Convention of 1787*, revised edition, 4 vols. (New Haven, 1937), 3: 534.

2. Max M. Mintz, *Gouverneur Morris and the American Revolution* (Norman, Okla., 1970), 3, 7.

Indeed, the three older sons were approaching middle age, the youngest one thirty-two years older than Morris.

The older children heartily disapproved of their father's second marriage, especially the fact that he had married a woman roughly their own age, and they battled her constantly for the rest of her life. Relations were so bad that Morris's father included a plea for reconciliation in his will, virtually begging his oldest son to bury his second wife at his side and not in some remote place, and apologizing for not providing a larger inheritance for each of his offspring. He also insisted that his youngest son, Gouverneur, not be educated at Yale, where the older brothers had gone, "lest he should imbibe in his youth that low Craft and cunning so incident to the People of that Country."[3]

One major source of cleavage in the family was the father's estate. Half of the land was turned over to Morris's oldest half brother before his father's death. The other half was willed to his mother for her lifetime, after which it was to go to another half brother, who was to pay his landless siblings various sums of money upon inheritance. Morris was to get 2,000 pounds and "a Negroe boy named George." Meanwhile, the estate was in his mother's hands for nearly twenty-five years. During that time, his half brothers and half sisters filed suit against her for mismanaging their inheritance. By the time she died, the half brother who was designated to inherit the land had become a British subject and was serving in Parliament. He eventually sold his patrimony to Morris.[4]

These experiences were never far below the surface in Morris. As a youth he rejected revolutionary rhetoric about the brotherhood of man and overcoming vice with virtue. Greed and shortsightedness, he concluded at an early age, governed all human behavior, and a wise man had to act accordingly, acquire a fortune on his own, not depend on the goodwill of others. This he set about to do and succeeded with relative ease. According to James Madison, by the time Morris reached his mid-thirties, he talked incessantly about the "political depravity of men, and the necessity of checking one vice and interest by opposing to them another vice & interest."[5]

3. Howard Swiggett, *The Extraordinary Mr. Morris* (New York, 1952), 12; Mintz, *Morris*, 13–5.

4. Mintz, *Morris*, 14–5, 171–5.

5. Farrand, *Records of the Federal Convention*, 1: 584.

As time passed, Morris became best known as an archconservative. He championed the institution of private property, saying that it fostered commerce, which gave a "mighty Spring" to the "progressive Force" of society. He thought governments were better run by aristocrats than by democracy and by men schooled in the "Busy haunts" of cities rather than in the "remote wilderness." At the Constitutional Convention, he favored a strong central government with both the president and the Senate having lifetime tenure, and he supported a national polity in which the eastern seaboard states would always have more power than frontier states which would later be admitted to the Union. He wanted only men who owned a freehold (that is, a substantial farm or its equivalent) to have the vote. "Give the vote to people who have no property," he said, "and they will sell them to the rich who will be able to buy them."[6]

The poor and rustic, however, weren't the only victims of Morris's barbs. He had an equally contemptuous view of men and women of his own social class. "The Rich," he told the Constitutional Convention, "will strive to establish their dominion & enslave the rest. They always did. They always will." The remedy was to set the rich off in the Senate and give the House to the small property owners, so that they could watch and control the rich.[7] Morris was especially scornful of aristocrats without brains or proven ability, men and women who had vast estates only because of hereditary privilege. During the Revolution, he fought to outlaw entailed estates and quitrents in New York. He also fought to commit New York to abolish slavery after the Revolutionary War "so that in future ages every human being who breathes the air of this State shall enjoy the privileges of a free man." He lost both battles.[8]

Ten years later, at the Constitutional Convention, Morris opposed giving Congress the power to pass sumptuary legislation, arguing that such laws "tended to create a landed Nobility, by fixing in the great-landholders and their posterity their present possessions."[9] He also continued his battle against slavery, especially when it became obvious that the new Constitution was to provide

6. Mintz, *Morris*, 73; Farrand, *Records of the Federal Convention*, 1: 583; 2: 202–3, 207–8, 209–10.

7. Farrand, *Records of the Federal Convention*, 1: 512, 517.

8. Mintz, *Morris*, 76, 78.

9. Farrand, *Records of the Federal Convention*, 2: 344, 351.

southern aristocrats with more power and more privileges than northern aristocrats. No one matched his scathing indictment of the convention's decision to forbid Congress from outlawing the African slave trade for at least another twenty years and to prohibit any tax of over ten dollars on an imported slave. Nor did anyone match his denunciation of the "three-fifths compromise."

Much has been written about the three-fifths compromise, whereby five slaves were to be counted as three whites in determining the number of seats each state would have in the House of Representatives and the amount each state would owe in direct taxes. The traditional view is that the five to three ratio was a legacy from the 1783 Congress and that most delegates to the Constitutional Convention knew beforehand that it was the "minimum price" for southern acceptance of any new constitution.[10] The evidence for this claim, however, is shaky. The ratio, to be sure, first emerged in the 1783 Congress, but then it applied only to taxes, not to representation. It was part of a proposal for assessing taxes among the states, which Congress first toyed with, then rejected, then resurrected and sent to the thirteen states as an amendment to the Articles of Confederation. Like many other congressional proposals, it failed to achieve the support of all thirteen states and thus legally died. Three years later, Congress again used the ratio when trying to raise money from the states.[11]

What about 1787? Was the ratio still on the minds of most of the fifty-five delegates who attended the Philadelphia convention? Did most assume from the outset that it was the price of southern acceptance of the Constitution? That is not clear. What is clear is that Charles Pinckney of South Carolina came to the convention determined to get such a ratio incorporated, not so much into any tax assessment scheme, but into any scheme of representation. The South had to have seats in Congress for three-fifths of its slaves. But

10. Cf. Max Farrand, *The Framing of the Constitution of the United States* (New Haven, 1913), 108; Clinton Rossiter, *The Grand Convention* (New York, 1966), 148; and Donald L. Robinson, *Slavery in the Structure of American Politics, 1765–1820* (New York, 1971), 156, 187–8. For a more recent update of the traditional argument, see also Earl M. Maltz, "The Idea of a Proslavery Constitution," *Journal of the Early Republic* 17 (Spring 1997): 48–9.

11. Worthington C. Ford et al., eds, *Journals of the Continental Congress, 1774–1789* (Washington, D.C., 1904–37), 24: 214–6, 223–4; 25: 948–52.

Pinckney didn't introduce the ratio. Instead, he had it introduced by James Wilson of Pennsylvania, who wanted to foster harmony at the convention between delegates from the major slave states and the most heavily populated northern states. Once Wilson introduced the ratio, Pinckney promptly seconded it. Thereafter, it surfaced in one debate after another.[12]

Morris attacked the three-fifths compromise from all angles. The idea that it was a compromise, he said, was nonsense. How could there ever be a direct tax? It was "idle to suppose that the Genl. Govt. can stretch its hand directly into the pockets of the people scattered over so vast a Country." In reality, the only way the federal government could raise money was through excise taxes and import duties—and these would fall heavier on northern freemen than on southern slavemasters. Indeed, more taxes would be collected on "the bohea tea used by a Northern freeman" than "the whole consumption of the miserable slave, which consists of nothing more than his physical subsistence and the rag that covers his nakedness." In essence, therefore, all the three-fifths clause did was give slavemasters extra representation in Congress.

What made this clause doubly wrong, said Morris, was that it rewarded slavemasters for importing more slaves. When "fairly explained," it all came down to this: "that the inhabitant of Georgia and S. C. who goes to the Coast of Africa, and in defiance of the most sacred laws of humanity tears away his fellow creatures from their dearest connections and damns them to the most cruel bondages, shall have more votes in a Govt. instituted for the protection of the rights of mankind, than the Citizen of Pa or N. Jersey who views with a laudable horror, so nefarious a practice." If this was not bad enough, added Morris, the three-fifths clause also enhanced "the most prominent feature in the aristocratic countenance of the proposed Constitution," the "vassalage of the poor," which was always "the favorite offspring of the Aristocracy."

Yet in support of this aristocratic abomination, the northern states were expected to sacrifice "every principle of right" and "every im-

12. Howard A. Ohline, "Republicanism and Slavery: Origins of the Three-Fifths Clause in the United States Constitution," *William and Mary Quarterly*, 3d series, 28 (October 1971): 568–71; Paul Finkelman, "Slavery, the Pennsylvania Delegation, and the Constitutional Convention: Two Faces of the Keystone State," *Pennsylvania Magazine of History and Biography* 92 (January 1988): 49–71.

pulse of humanity." They were also to "bind themselves to march their militia for the defence of the S. States; for their defence agst those very slaves of whom they complain." He "would sooner submit himself to a tax for paying for all the Negroes in the U. States than saddle posterity with such a Constitution."[13]

Morris moved to amend the three-fifths clause so that only "free" inhabitants would be counted in determining representation in the House of Representatives. The convention overwhelmingly rejected his amendment. All the northern states except New Jersey voted with the South. Yet, in the end, after the delegates finished with all the particulars and the final Constitution came up for approval, Morris supported it and put it into lean, crisp prose. In the eyes of James Madison, he was more than a good loser. He was exceptional in his "readiness to aid in making the best of measures in which he had been overruled."[14]

Once Morris put his name to the final document, he turned his attention to making money and played virtually no part in the ensuing battle over the Constitution's ratification. The arguments he made at the convention, which was held in secret, remained largely unknown until many years later when James Madison's notes of the convention were published. At the state ratifying conventions, scores of delegates attacked the three-fifths clause and even more assailed the provision forbidding Congress from outlawing the African slave trade for at least another twenty years. Only a few, however, repeated the central lines of Morris's argument.

Oddly enough, many delegates censored Morris's wording of the final document. The Philadelphia convention had decided not to use the word *slave* in order to make the Constitution more palatable to the North and more humane in the eyes of the world. As a result various euphemisms had to be found, such as a "Person held to Service or Labour." The three-fifths clause, in particular, was a masterpiece of circumlocution. It called for "adding to the whole number of free persons, including those bound to servitude for a term of years, and excluding Indians not taxed, three-fifths of all other persons." Many during the ratifying process, and especially in

13. Quotations for this and the two preceding paragraphs from Farrand, *Records of the Federal Convention,* 2: 221–3.

14. Ibid., 3: 500.

New England, found the wording hard to stomach. What "a strange collection of words," exclaimed the owner of Maine's only newspaper. "Who, in the name of God, but the *majority* of that honl. body, would ever have tho't of expressing like ideas in like words!"[15]

In New England, more than elsewhere, the supporters of the Constitution had their hands full selling the document's proslavery provisions. Ordinary citizens had no idea what was said or done in Philadelphia, but distrust of the governing elite was widespread. The previous winter whole towns in Massachusetts had rebelled against Boston's silk-stocking leadership. Angry citizens, led by Daniel Shays and other Revolutionary War officers, had closed courts, opened jails, and tried to seize the federal armory in Springfield. In the end, they had been badly defeated by an army of mercenaries hired by Boston's wealthiest citizens. They had also been forced to humble themselves and take an oath of allegiance to the state and its elected leaders. Seething with resentment, many now questioned the motives of the New England delegates to the Constitutional Convention. Indeed, many assumed that the proposed Constitution was just another aristocratic weapon to crush the "little people."

Winning support for the Constitution in New England was thus an uphill battle. To buy time and to keep the opposition from trashing the entire document, the Constitution's supporters maneuvered to have it debated line by line. Each step of the way, they had to ward off hostile comments from rural delegates with old grievances to settle, as well as from community leaders with an ingrained fear of centralized power. In this atmosphere, the Constitution's slavery provisions came under attack. Why, critics asked, had the New England delegates to the Constitutional Convention granted so much to the slavemasters of the South?

In truth, most of the New England delegates had not put up much of a fight. Only Elbridge Gerry of Massachusetts had consistently attacked the three-fifths clause. "Blacks are property," Gerry had argued, "and are used to the southward as horses and cattle to the northward." Why should they be counted, any more than northern "horses or oxen"? Counting them was blatantly unfair. It would give four southern voters more power than ten northern voters. Moreover, it would degrade northern freemen by equating them

15. Thomas B. Wait to George Thacher, 8 January 1788, Thacher Papers, Boston Public Library.

with slaves.[16] In the end, Gerry had refused to sign or support the Constitution.

In contrast to Gerry, the other New England delegates to the Constitutional Convention had readily accepted the Constitution's proslavery provisions in exchange for commercial concessions. They also had worried less about enhancing the South's political power at the expense of New England. They had behaved like Gerry in only one respect: they had displayed no interest in the moral questions surrounding the slavery provisions.

Had all these facts been known to their constituents, they may have had even more trouble getting their handiwork approved. Only in Connecticut did the Constitution pass by a comfortable margin. In Massachusetts, which stood second or third nationally to Virginia in total population, the final vote of the state ratifying convention was 187 to 168; in New Hampshire, 57 to 46; and in Rhode Island, the voters, in a popular referendum, initially rejected the Constitution by an eleven to one margin. Two years later a state convention endorsed it by a 34 to 32 vote.

The most persistent complaints about the Constitution's slavery provisions came from Rhode Island and Massachusetts Quakers. Not only did they repeatedly "give testimony" against the "cruel and barbarous" African slave trade, which the Constitution protected for at least another twenty years, they also complained about the impact of the Constitution's fugitive slave clause. In the early 1780s the Massachusetts Supreme Court had ruled slavery illegal, and as a result the Bay State had become a safe haven for runaway slaves from Rhode Island and other nearby states. Because the proposed Constitution decreed that all fugitive slaves had to be returned to their masters on demand, that would no longer be the case. A Nantucket man, well known in Quaker circles, had already been threatened with legal action once the Constitution went into effect. The Constitution, noted a Quaker acquaintance, rested not on "the Righteousness of God," but on "Slavery & Blood."[17]

16. Farrand, *Records of the Federal Convention,* 1: 205–6, 208; 2: 632–3; James H. Hutson, ed., *Supplement to Max Farrand's "The Records of the Federal Convention of 1787"* (New Haven, 1987), 69–70.

17. William Rotch, Sr., to Moses Brown, 8 November 1787, Austin Collection, Brown University; John P. Kaminski, ed., *A Necessary Evil? Slavery and the Debate over the Constitution* (Madison, Wisc., 1995), 67–8, 75.

Also of concern to some New Englanders was the three-fifths rule. The argument Gerry had made at the convention was heard time and again. "Tell me, if you can," wrote a Maine newsman, "why a southern negro, in his present debased condition, is any more entitled to representation, than a northern Bullock? Both are mere pieces of property—and nothing more!" Slaves are "the property of their masters," echoed a future Maine congressman, and therefore "ought to be taxed but *not represented,* any more than our *oxen or horses.*"[18]

To counter this argument, Rufus King, the floor leader for the Constitution at the crucial Massachusetts ratifying convention, insisted that the three-fifths ratio was well established, that it had been embraced by the Confederation Congress, and that it was indeed "the language of all America."[19] That argument fared badly. Two of the four New England states had voted against the ratio when it was proposed as an amendment to the Articles of Confederation, and few of the Massachusetts delegates had ever embraced it.

In denouncing the three-fifths clause, only a few echoed Morris's contention that the words pertaining to direct taxes were meaningless, that it was "idle to suppose" that the central government had the ability to "stretch its hand directly into the pockets of the people," and that all the clause really did was give slavemasters extra representatives in Congress. Most assumed that direct taxes were likely, just as they had been in Massachusetts, and that the three-fifths clause gave slaveowners a huge tax break. Time and again, delegates complained bitterly that under this provision a hardworking Yankee farmer would pay as much in taxes for "three infant children" as a wealthy Virginia planter would pay for "five sturdy, full grown negroes."[20] To counter this argument, supporters of the Constitution claimed that direct taxes would be levied only in times of crisis. Time would prove that they were right.

18. Thomas B. Wait to George Thacher, 8 January 1788, Silas Lee to George Thacher, 23 January 1788, Thacher Papers.

19. Jonathan Elliot, ed., *The Debates in the Several State Conventions on the Adoption of the Federal Constitution,* 2d ed., 5 vols. (Philadelphia, 1836), 2: 36.

20. Elliot, *Debates,* 2: 37–108; Massachusetts General Court, Commission on the Library, *Debates and Proceedings in the Convention of the Commonwealth of Massachusetts Held in the Year 1788* (Boston, 1856); Kaminski, *A Necessary Evil,* 77, 78, 102.

Along with worrying about direct taxes, delegates to the New England ratifying conventions also fretted about how the three-fifths rule would affect representation. Many were confused on this point. Indeed, some obviously thought that the slaves themselves were to be truly represented. Some talked incessantly about how the three-fifths ratio put southern blacks on the same footing as northern whites and how insulting this was to northern whites. Others were convinced that individual slavemasters would get extra votes for their slaves. That is, if a Virginia or South Carolina planter owned fifty slaves, he would have thirty-one votes to cast for a representative to Congress.

Rufus King and other supporters of the Constitution had no trouble countering such arguments. They simply pointed out that slaves were not to be truly represented, nor were individual slaveowners to be given additional votes. Instead, representation was to be "given to the state," and under another clause in the Constitution, whoever had the right to vote for the lower house in that state had the right to vote for Congress. This argument was factually correct, but why it satisfied any of the Constitution's critics is something of a mystery. For any way King and his colleagues chose to explain it, a southern white man's vote was going to be worth more than a northern white man's vote.[21] If the three-fifths clause were eliminated and only the free population were counted in determining seats in Congress, Massachusetts in particular would have more influence in national

21. In "The Idea of a Proslavery Constitution" (pp. 46–8), Earl M. Maltz disputes this point. He argues that Massachusetts had more stringent property qualifications for white male voters than did North Carolina, and hence the "voting power of the propertied class in Massachusetts" exceeded that of "the free whites in North Carolina." This argument, in my judgment, breaks down once states like New Hampshire, Pennsylvania, and Virginia are worked into the equation. Also, in both the port cities and the rapidly growing backcountry of Massachusetts, the property qualifications of the state constitution of 1780 seem to have been generally ignored. More serious was the *temporary* disfranchisement of over 4,000 men in western Massachusetts for participating in Shays' Rebellion, although the disfranchisement failed to stop Shaysites from being elected to the state ratifying convention. See David P. Szatmary, *Shays' Rebellion: The Making of an Agrarian Insurrection* (Amherst, Mass., 1980), 106, 131–2; Ronald P. Formisano, *The Transformation of Political Culture: Massachusetts Parties, 1790s–1840s* (New York, 1983), 408 n. 51; William Stickney, ed., *Autobiography of Amos Kendall* (Boston, 1872), 78–9; and Paul Goodman, *The Democratic-Republicans of Massachusetts: Politics in a Young Republic* (Cambridge, Mass., 1964), 136–45.

politics. While no one had exact population figures at his fingertips, there were estimates in circulation. At the Constitutional Convention, David Brearly of New Jersey had one set of numbers, Charles Pinckney of South Carolina another. If only the free population were counted, Brearly's numbers indicated that Massachusetts would have slightly more representation in Congress and the electoral college than Virginia, and Pinckney's numbers indicated that Massachusetts would have slightly less. With the addition of three-fifths of Virginia's slaves, however, Massachusetts would have no chance of matching Virginia's strength in Congress or the electoral college.[22]

Despite its apparent detriment to the power of Massachusetts in Congress, the three-fifths rule had a powerful ally in Rufus King. The thirty-three-year-old Harvard graduate and well-connected lawyer had told the Constitutional Convention in Philadelphia that the three-fifths ratio was "a most grating circumstance to his mind" and "would be so to a great part of the people of America." He had no doubt that the slave trade provision would aggravate his constituents. Like Gouverneur Morris, he also knew that the two provisions would increase the power of Virginia and the Deep South in the national legislature at the expense of the rest of the country. And like Elbridge Gerry, he worried about the potential impact on the four New England states. The main division in the young Republic, he contended, was not "between the great & small States; but between the Southern & Eastern."[23]

Nonetheless, at the Constitutional Convention, King was a voice of conciliation. Rather than strenuously opposing the three-fifths clause or the slave trade clause, he hoped that their acceptance would produce a readiness on the part of the South to "strengthen the Genl. Govt. and to mark a full confidence in it."[24] Like the other New England delegates, he never inveighed against the moral iniquity of slavery. His parents had owned slaves, and in the next fifteen years he would own one or two, sell one, try to buy another, and set one free. He prided himself, moreover, on being a prudent man, a

22. Winton U. Solberg, ed., *The Federal Convention and the Formation of the Union of the American States* (Indianapolis, 1958), 407–9.

23. Farrand, *Records of the Federal Convention*, 2: 220; 1: 562, 566.

24. Ibid., 2: 220.

well-trained lawyer who argued from carefully worded legal briefs, not a madcap like Gouverneur Morris, who delighted in being frank and audacious.[25]

At the Massachusetts ratifying convention, King continued in the same vein. He strongly defended the proposed Constitution, stressing the value of the three-fifths ratio for taxing purposes and minimizing its effect on the distribution of political power.[26] In effect, he came close to arguing that Morris's analysis of the three-fifths clause was dead wrong. Within fifteen years he would completely reverse that position, and fifteen years later he would create a national sensation by arguing, in effect, that Morris's analysis at the Constitutional Convention was dead right.[27]

Why the change of heart? First, over the long term the new political structure did not work out as King and many other New Englanders had hoped. Soon after the Constitution was ratified, King, along with most of New England's leaders, became a mainstay in the Federalist Party. As the party of George Washington, who enjoyed the unanimous support of all thirteen states, the Federalists appeared in the late 1780s and early 1790s to have a grand future. King moved to Long Island and was elected senator from New York. A few years later, he became the minister to Great Britain. His counterpart in France was Gouverneur Morris, who lived in Paris during and after the Reign of Terror and enhanced his reputation as a ladies' man thanks to a torrid love affair with Talleyrand's mistress. The 1790s were good years for both men, as they were for most of the Federalist elite.

The years of Federalist domination, however, came to a quick end. In 1796 the Federalist candidate, John Adams, almost lost the presidency. Four years later he was defeated by Thomas Jefferson in a close contest. In only four more years, the presidential election resulted in a landslide for Jefferson. Meanwhile the Federalist Party

25. Robert Ernst, "Rufus King, Slavery, and the Missouri Crisis," *The New-York Historical Society Quarterly* 46 (October 1962): 358–64; Joseph L. Arbena, "Politics or Principle? Rufus King and the Opposition to Slavery, 1785–1825," *Essex Institute Historical Collections* 101 (January 1965): 63–7.

26. Elliot, *Debates*, 2: 36–108; *Boston Independent Chronicle*, 24 January 1788.

27. Charles R. King, ed., *The Life and Correspondence of Rufus King*, 6 vols. (New York, 1894–1900), 4: 324–5; 6: 267, 697–700; *Niles' Weekly Register* 17 (4 December 1819): 219.

failed to take hold in the new states west of the Appalachians and lost support in most of the original thirteen. Even political blundering by the Jeffersonian opposition failed to restore Federalism's former glory. In 1807 the Jefferson administration, in an attempt to bring European belligerents to their knees, passed the Embargo, a drastic measure that closed American ports, deprived merchants and mariners of a livelihood, and caused thousands to avoid ruin only by flouting the law. In 1812 the Madison administration led the nation into a war that was popular in some quarters but detested in others, a war that led to one national embarrassment after another, with British redcoats marching unmolested through the countryside, virtually dividing the country in half, and burning the nation's capital to the ground. In these times of distress, the Federalists regained some lost seats in Congress, but not enough to control the nation's destiny.

The Federalist elite thus never regained what they considered their rightful role. Rufus King was one of the few to remain in the limelight, running for vice president in 1804 and 1808, for president in 1816, getting reelected to the Senate in 1813 and again in 1819. More typical was Gouverneur Morris, who served briefly in the Senate from 1800 to 1803 and as New York canal commissioner from 1810 to 1813. Both men fumed at the direction the Jeffersonians were taking the country, but as usual Morris was more blatant about it. He excoriated Jefferson's Embargo and "Mr. Madison's War," and in 1814 he cast his lot with the antiwar states' rights Hartford Convention. He unequivocally put his hopes in a separate northern confederation.

The Federalists lost power for many reasons. But one reason—the reason many Federalists chose to focus upon—was the three-fifths rule. The Jeffersonian opposition was from the beginning southern based, heavily dependent on a slaveholding leadership, with a growing, but largely subservient, northern wing. In 1796, when Jefferson barely lost to John Adams, he won 82 percent of the electoral vote in the slave states, only 19 percent in the northern states. Four years later he won the presidency by retaining his southern base and adding to his northern total, winning again 82 percent of the electoral vote in the slave states and 27 percent in the northern states.

Quick to pinpoint the source of Jefferson's strength, the *Connecticut Courant* in 1796 began running long disunion essays that blamed the three-fifths rule for the nation's troubles. The three-fifths rule, declared a writer signing his name "Pelham," gave an advantage to slavemasters like Thomas Jefferson. With additional seats for their "CATTLE" in Congress, and thus additional votes in the electoral college, the odds were stacked in Jefferson's favor.[28] Four years later, when Jefferson beat Adams by just eight electoral votes, this refrain gained a wide audience. Noted the *Gazette of the United States:* "There are above 500,000 negro slaves in the United States, who have not more voice in the Election of President and Vice-President . . . than 500,000 New-England horses, hogs, and oxen. Yet . . . their masters for them choose 15 Electors!"[29]

Disproportionate representation became the standard explanation for the Federalist loss of executive power in 1800. It was an easy argument to make. For there was little doubt that the three-fifths rule played a decisive role in John Adams's defeat. Adams's native Massachusetts had the largest free population in the nation but not the most electoral votes. Thanks to the three-fifths rule, Jefferson's Virginia had five more electoral votes than the Bay State. Virginia had six "slave" seats, the rest of the South, eight. In New England, Jefferson got trounced and lost the North as a whole by a margin of twenty electoral votes to fifty-six, but in the South he won fifty-three electoral votes to Adams's nine. In winning nationally by just eight electoral votes, he had the benefit of at least thirteen of the fourteen slave seats; some pundits thought he had all fourteen. In any event, without the so-called slave seats, he would have lost the election and John Adams would have served a second term. Many historians, celebrating the virtues of the master of Monticello, forgot this fact; New England Federalists never did.

Not every New England Federalist shed tears over Adams's defeat, however. He was anathema in some Federalist circles. The fact that Jefferson and the Virginians were in power was their major concern. That concern became more intense when it became clear that even more slave territory was to be added to the United States. In 1787 the last Confederation Congress had taken steps to bar slavery in the territories north of the Ohio River, but south of the river, slavery was quietly allowed to expand. Kentucky entered the Union as a slave state in 1792, Tennessee in 1796. Two years later Congress dealt with

28. *Connecticut Courant,* 21 November, 12 December 1796.
29. Quoted in the *Washington Federalist,* 14 January 1801.

the vast Mississippi Territory. Was it too to become slave country? George Thacher of Massachusetts led a small coterie of congressmen, including some Federalists, who were determined to bar slavery in the new territory. They were badly defeated.[30] Then in 1803 the Jefferson administration purchased Louisiana, a huge stretch of land that was several times the size of New England, with a well-established slave system in and about New Orleans.

The purchase of Louisiana, in the eyes of many New England Federalists, was the last straw. Federalist newspapers clamored for disunion and encouraged Federalist leaders in Congress deliberately to plan it. The Louisiana Purchase, they said, was a violation of the Constitution and destroyed forever the balance of power between the free states and the slave states. How many slave states did the Jeffersonians plan to carve out of Louisiana? Six? Eight? Nine? In 1804 a bill was submitted to establish territorial status for the southern portion of the Louisiana Purchase. Senator James Hillhouse of Connecticut, a staunch Federalist who had vehemently opposed the acquisition of Louisiana, proposed a series of amendments designed to strike a blow against the African slave trade and to curtail the growth of slavery west of the Mississippi River. All his proposals went down to defeat. Another slave territory—and at least one potential slave state—was added to the Union.[31]

It was against this backdrop that William Ely, a thirty-eight-year-old Yale graduate and state representative from western Massachusetts, fashioned an amendment to the Constitution. It called for the abolition of the three-fifths rule and for apportioning seats in Congress in accordance with a state's free population. Under the current system of "unequal representation," said Ely, the Union was in grave danger. It could not "harmoniously exist for a long period" unless "all free citizens" were given "equal political rights and privileges." Accordingly, in June 1804, he moved that the Massachusetts legislature instruct the Bay State's two senators to obtain an amendment of the Constitution abolishing the three-

30. *Annals of Congress*, 5th Congress, 2d session, 1797–98, pp. 1306–13, 1318.

31. Everett S. Brown, "The Senate Debate on the Breckinridge Bill for the Government of Louisiana, 1804," *American Historical Review* 22 (January 1917): 340–64. See also Everett S. Brown, *The Constitutional History of the Louisiana Purchase, 1803–1812* (Berkeley, 1920), 101–46.

fifths rule. Jefferson's supporters in the Massachusetts legislature tried to derail Ely's proposal, claiming that it was the work of alarmists and that it had no chance of gaining the support of either two-thirds of Congress or three-fourths of the states.[32] Nevertheless, the Ely amendment passed handily and in December, Senator Timothy Pickering, as instructed, laid it before the United States Senate, where it was quickly squelched. John Quincy Adams, the other senator from Massachusetts, prepared a ten-page speech in its behalf. He never had a chance to give it.[33] As was customary, copies of the Massachusetts resolution were sent to each of the states. Connecticut, New Hampshire, and Delaware postponed consideration, while the other states rejected it, several with a scathing condemnation.[34]

In the meantime, scores of speeches were given and dozens of pamphlets were published, arguing the merits of the Ely amendment.[35] It was at this point that Josiah Quincy, a thirty-two-year-old state senator, and John Quincy Adams, a thirty-seven-year-old United States senator, first became seriously involved in "the battle against the Slave Power."[36] Like most of the amendment's advo-

32. *Northampton Hampshire Gazette,* 27 June 1804; *New England Palladium,* 19 June 1804; *Resolves of the General Court of Massachusetts* (Boston, 1804–05), 20 June 1804; Samuel Eliot Morison, *Life and Letters of Harrison Gray Otis, Federalist,* 2 vols. (Boston, 1913), 1: 263.

33. *Annals of Congress,* 8th Congress, 2d session, 1804–05, pp. 20–1; [Octavius Pickering], *The Life of Timothy Pickering* (Boston, 1873), 4: 64–5; Worthington C. Ford, ed., *Writings of John Quincy Adams,* 7 vols. (New York, 1913–17), 3: 87–100.

34. *Philadelphia Aurora,* 3, 7, 17, 21 January, 20 February 1805.

35. *The Portfolio* 4 (18 August, 1 September 1804): 261, 274; *The Repertory,* 26 October, 6, 8 November 1804; *Boston Repository,* 21, 25 September 1804; *Defence of the Legislature of Massachusetts; or the Rights of New England Vindicated* (Boston, 1804); [William Plumer], *An Address to the Electors of New Hampshire* (Portsmouth, N.H., 1804); Samuel Taggart, *An Oration Delivered at Conway, July 4, 1804* (Northampton, Mass., 1804); Thomas Branagan, *Serious Remonstrances Addressed to the Citizens of the Northern States and Their Representatives* (Philadelphia, 1805); Linda K. Kerber, *Federalists in Dissent: Imagery and Ideology in Jeffersonian America* (Ithaca, N.Y., 1970), 36–9; James M. Banner, Jr., *To the Hartford Convention: The Federalists and the Origins of Party Politics in Massachusetts, 1789–1815* (New York, 1970), 101–9.

36. Edmund Quincy, *Life of Josiah Quincy of Massachusetts* (Boston, 1867), 65–6; *Boston Repository,* 21, 25 September 1804; Ford, *Writings of John Quincy Adams,* 3: 46–51, 69–77.

cates, Quincy and Adams knew very well that the proposal had no chance of passing. The task at hand was to educate northerners, to make them understand how national politics was biased against them, and to put Jefferson's northern supporters on the defensive. If "gentlemen do not now agree with us," said Quincy, "the time will come when all concur in this common cause."[37]

To accomplish this, Adams, Quincy, and their Federalist colleagues relied heavily on numbers. Adams was usually careful in his calculations. Most of the others simply took the census of 1800, calculated three-fifths of total number of slaves, and divided that number by the 33,000 people each congressman was suppose to represent. From these calculations they declared that there were fifteen slave seats in Congress, equal to the combined House vote of six whole states, one more than the combined vote of Connecticut, New Hampshire, and Rhode Island, and two less than the entire vote of Massachusetts. Their calculations were invariably off by one or two seats, mainly because the formula they followed was far simpler than the one Congress adopted to apportion seats.[38]

Yet, sloppy accounting or not, they all hammered away with their numbers. And while they suffered a crushing defeat in the battle over the Ely amendment, the numbers argument became a part of New England's political culture and, as the years passed, northern political culture. The same numerical arguments, updated to fit the year, would be repeated at the Hartford Convention in 1814, during the Missouri crisis in 1819, and again in the 1840s and 1850s. At first New England Federalists were the main purveyors of the message. By the time of the Missouri crisis, it had advocates in both parties and across much of the North. Rufus King, representing New York in the United States Senate, now joined the charge.

37. Quincy, *Josiah Quincy*, 66. See also John Quincy Adams to Abigail Adams, 3 December 1804, Adams Papers, Microfilms, Massachusetts Historical Society.

38. The congressional method was to find a common divisor—say, 33,000—and divide it into the state's population under the three-fifths rule, and then reject the remaining fraction. The rejection of the fraction always caused strife. In some states it meant that only a few hundred people weren't being counted, in other states, many thousands. This method was followed in 1792, 1802, 1811, 1822, and 1832. In 1842 Congress opted to count major fractions and in 1850 adopted a new method. For the hotly contested way Congress handled apportionment, see Michael L. Balinski and H. Peyton Young, *Fair Representation: Meeting the Ideal of One Man, One Vote* (New Haven, 1982), 16ff.

* * *

The Louisiana Purchase and the admission of new states, along with the numbers argument, escalated opposition to the three-fifths compromise, but it also brought into focus another clause in the Constitution—the clause popularly known as the Great Compromise, which provided each state with an equal number of seats in the United States Senate.

At first few regarded this clause as a victory for the South. Even Yankee leaders who were suspicious of the South failed to pounce on it. Throughout the 1780s they had battled with southern leaders over matters pertaining to state and regional power. Some had pushed for Vermont's admission to the Union to counter southern influence. Many knew that southern leaders had schemed to keep Vermont out of the Union until Kentucky or some other slave state was admitted. They had learned to expect the worst.[39] Yet, while the three-fifths clause immediately raised a red flag, the clause granting each state equal power in the Senate did not. In fact, the smaller New England states generally championed state equality in the Senate. They saw it as a necessity. They claimed that it would enable Rhode Island and other small states to protect themselves against mighty Virginia.

That was essentially the way that the framers of Constitution also saw it. James Madison and other southern spokesmen expected that the Senate would be the legislative bastion of the North rather than the South. With the exception of Maryland, the major slave states championed proportional representation rather than representation by states. Even Georgia, despite its small population, had no desire to merely offset a northern state in the Senate. Georgia was the largest state geographically, and according to conventional wisdom its rich acreage would soon attract hundreds of thousands

39. Edmund C. Burnett, ed., *Letters of Members of the Continental Congress,* 8 vols. (Washington, D.C., 1921–36), 7: 545, 547, 571, 573; 8: 708, 714, 724, 733, 741, 757; William T. Hutchinson and William M. D. Rachal, eds., *The Papers of James Madison,* 23 vols. (Chicago, 1965), 4: 200–3; Andrew A. Lipscomb and Albert Ellery Bergh, eds., *The Writings of Thomas Jefferson,* 20 vols. (Washington, D.C., 1903), 7: 146, 434; H. James Henderson, *Party Politics in the Continental Congress* (New York, 1974), 307–9; Peter S. Onuf, *The Origins of the Federal Republic: Jurisdictional Controversies in the United States, 1775–1787* (Philadelphia, 1983), 121, 168–72; James S. Leamon, "Revolution and Separation: Maine's First Efforts at Statehood," in *Maine in the Early Republic,* ed. Charles E. Clark et al. (Hanover, N.H., 1988), 97.

of farmers. Georgia boosters were certain of it. Expecting to be a major population center in a decade or so, they preferred to have the Senate as well as the House based on population.

In 1787, moreover, there was some confusion about how to categorize the various states. Legally, there were eight slave states and five states that had either outlawed slavery or taken steps to eventually eradicate it, but few lumped all eight slave states in the same category. Delaware was hard to categorize, sometimes classified with the South, sometimes not. New York and New Jersey had thousands of slaves, but they were not considered true slave states like South Carolina and Georgia. Nor were they regarded as eastern states like the New England states. They were usually termed middle states. Some of the confusion cleared when New York and New Jersey adopted gradual emancipation in 1799 and 1804. But words like eastern and middle did not vanish immediately. Only gradually did they give way to North and South, free and slave.

Only gradually, moreover, did politicians realize that equality in the Senate was more vital to the South than it was to the small states. In the early years following the Constitution, debate focused on the geographic size of various states as much as it did on population, and northerners seldom had the best of the argument. More often than not, New Englanders were on the defensive. Virginians hammered on the theme that they had made a great concession in giving tiny states like Connecticut, New Hampshire, Rhode Island, and Delaware an equal voice in the Senate. Rhode Island was likened to a pygmy state, a farm, a fragment of land, a little corner. The entire state, noted Mathew Carey of Philadelphia, had fewer people than Washington and Orange Counties in New York or Chester and Lancaster Counties in Pennsylvania. Why should it have an equal voice in ratifying treaties and approving presidential appointees?[40]

New Englanders at first were hard pressed to counter this argument. But in time the dynamics of western expansion and population growth provided them with plenty of ammunition to launch a counterattack. In the eyes of New Englanders, two facts became clear: the new slave states lacked the requisite number of freemen

40. Rosemarie Zagarri, *The Politics of Size: Representation in the United States, 1776–1850* (Ithaca, N.Y., 1987), 125–44; Mathew Carey, *A Calm Address to the People of the Eastern States* (Philadelphia, 1814), 8, 14–5.

to be true states, and Congress bent the rules to grant them state-hood.

In fact, Congress had no minimum population standard. The original benchmark of 60,000 free inhabitants, which had been established by the Northwest Ordinance of 1787, was dropped during Jefferson's administration. The new criterion that an incoming state must have at least the population required for one House seat had only limited support. The popular notion that a new state should have as many inhabitants as Delaware, the least populated of the original thirteen states, also had only limited support in Congress. It soon would be violated in the case of one northern state—Illinois—and four southern states—Mississippi, Missouri, Arkansas, and Florida.[41]

In the end the only standard was that the number of slave-state senators and free-state senators should be the same. From 1802 to 1850 the political balance was maintained by admitting alternately slave and free states. Whether this was intentional from the beginning is arguable. But after the War of 1812, paired admissions of free and slave states was definitely a hard-and-fast rule of politics. If a northern territory was ready for statehood, there had to be a potential southern state waiting in the wings or no action would be taken. For the sake of balance, Congress admitted four southern territories and one northern territory before they had the desired number of inhabitants. Almost invariably, however, the southern territories had far fewer free people than their northern counterparts—63,000 on average as compared to 160,000 on average.[42]

The tendency to admit slave states with tiny free populations became clear early in the century. With that knowledge Yankee spokesmen stopped focusing entirely on mighty Virginia, with its huge population, and started focusing on the other slave states with vast acreage but relatively few free people. Their argument was simple and easy to defend. Why should the slave states, with just over half the free population of the North, have the same number of Senate seats as the North? Why should the vote of a freeman in the Deep South be worth more than a hardworking northerner's vote in

41. Jack Ericson Eblen, *The First and Second United States Empires: Governors and Territorial Government, 1784–1912* (Pittsburgh, 1968), 230–1.

42. J. D. B. DeBow, *Statistical View of the United States* (Washington, 1854), 43–6, 63, 82; Eblen, *First and Second United States Empires,* 230–1.

both the House and the Senate? In fairness, wrote "Boreas" in 1812, the North should have thirty-one senators to the South's eighteen.[43]

Such complaints largely went unheeded in Congress. Following the War of 1812, the advocates of sectional balance had their way and paired admissions were the rule. Indiana and Mississippi were admitted as a pair, then Illinois and Alabama, Maine and Missouri, Arkansas and Michigan. But the fairness argument never died. In the 1840s a congressman from Ohio complained bitterly that if Florida were divided in two—as many slave-state politicians hoped—a free person's vote there would count forty times as much as a free person's vote in Ohio. That, he said, was grossly unfair to his constituents, and he wouldn't have it.[44] In the 1850s the abolitionist William Jay hammered away on an updated version of the old theme. He pointed out to his readers that six slave states—South Carolina, Georgia, Alabama, Mississippi, Louisiana, and Kentucky—had an "aggregate free population of 189,791 less than Pennsylvania." Yet the people of these states had six times as many senators as Pennsylvania. Why, he asked, should the vote of a free person in the Deep South be worth six times as much as a hardworking Pennsylvanian's vote?[45]

Rufus King had come around to Gouverneur Morris's viewpoint by 1803. He abandoned his old argument that the three-fifths clause was a compromise. He no longer pretended that the South gave as much as it got. He even admitted in private letters that he and the other northern delegates to the Constitutional Convention had been "injudiciously led" to accept this "unreasonable" clause.[46] In public, however, he remained the judicious statesman.

King maintained that posture until the Missouri crisis of 1819. By that time he was the Federalist Party's elder statesman, having run for vice president twice on the Federalist ticket, president once. He was now in his mid-sixties and for the past six years had represented New York in the United States Senate. With his term about to expire, he was up for reelection. He was well known for his force-

43. "Boreas," *Slave Representation* (New Haven, 1812), 16.

44. *Congressional Globe*, 28th Congress, 2d session, 1844–45, appendix, 331.

45. William Jay, *Miscellaneous Writings on Slavery* (New York, 1853), 218ff.

46. King, *Life and Correspondence*, 4, 324–5; Ernst, "King and the Missouri Crisis," 364–5.

ful stand on matters pertaining to foreign policy, commerce, banking, and public lands. He was not, however, widely regarded as an
antislavery man.

Missouri's petition for statehood changed all that. In late 1819
King gave two speeches against the admission of Missouri as a slave
state that infuriated Thomas Jefferson, James Madison, James
Monroe, and a host of southern leaders. President Monroe, who had
hated King for years, portrayed King as a fiend who wanted to either
rip the Union to shreds or make the South subservient to the North.
Jefferson and Madison agreed. A South Carolina senator accused
King of trying to inspire slave rebellions. So did a Virginia judge.[47]

The speeches were not reported in the *Annals of Congress*. But
parts were recast in the heated debates that followed, and King had
the substance of his speeches printed in *Niles' Register*, the weekly
news magazine with the widest national circulation. The printed
account, undoubtedly carefully edited, was largely devoted to proving that Congress had the constitutional right to set conditions on
the admission of Missouri to statehood. The tone was legalistic.
Moral arguments were generally avoided. But the three-fifths clause
was discussed at length.

In discussing the three-fifths rule, King basically reiterated
Morris's position of thirty years past without any of Morris's flair.
He also relied heavily on the numbers argument that New
Englanders had been perfecting for the last fifteen years. The present
House of Representatives, he argued, consisted of 181 representatives, apportioned among the states at the rate of one representative
for every 35,000 "federal numbers." The nation's slave population
was 1,191,364 according to the last census. Thus the slave states had
20 representatives and 20 presidential electors "more than they
would be entitled to, were the slaves excluded." Virginia benefited
most. It had 582,104 free persons and 392,518 slaves. In any state
without slavery, 582,104 free persons would be entitled to elect only
16 representatives, while in Virginia 582,104 free persons elected 23
representatives, "seven additional ones on account of her slaves." As
a result, five free persons in Virginia had as much power in the

47. James Monroe to George Hay, 5 January 1820, Spencer Roane to James
Monroe, 16 February 1820, Monroe Papers, New York Public Library; *Annals of
Congress*, 16th Congress, 1st session, 1819–20, p. 378; Glover Moore, *The Missouri
Controversy, 1819–1821* (Lexington, Ky., 1953), 252–3, 295.

choice of congressional representatives and presidential electors as seven free persons in any of the nonslaveholding states.[48]

It was an old argument, one that had been heard many times before. But King did not call for the repeal of the three-fifths clause, because it was an "ancient settlement" between the original thirteen states, and "faith and honor" dictated that it not be disturbed. But it was a concession made with the original slave states, not with slave states carved out of the wilderness, and to extend "this disproportionate power to the new states would be unjust and odious." The nonslaveholding states "whose power would be abridged, and whose burdens would be increased" should not be expected to consent to this extension, and the slave states should be "magnanimous" enough not to insist on it.[49]

King made no headway with Jefferson and his Virginia followers. Indeed, most of them saw another Federalist plot in the making. But they realized that that explanation was at best only partly true.[50] For King had not launched the crusade against Missouri, nor had his Federalist allies. And the Federalists in Congress numbered only about two dozen men. They were too few in number to stop Missouri from becoming a slave state. The men who lit the fuse that sparked what would become the Missouri debacle were northern members of Jefferson's own party. They were also the ones who provided most of the votes in 1819 that temporarily stopped Missouri from becoming a slave state. They too had come to worry about the inordinate power of the slave states. And they too had come to accept Morris's indictment of the Constitution.

48. *Niles' Weekly Register* 17 (4 December 1819): 219; King, *Life and Correspondence*, 6: 233, 698–700.

49. Ibid.

50. Homer C. Hockett, "Rufus King and the Missouri Compromise," *Missouri Historical Review* 2 (1908): 211–20; Moore, *The Missouri Controversy*, 179–80, 233, 252–3.

3 | Tallmadge's Challenge

To Thomas Jefferson, the Missouri crisis of 1819 was "like a fire-bell in the night" that awakened and filled him with terror. He immediately considered it the "knell of the Union" and lost no time blaming it on disgruntled Federalists,[1] but ironically the man who lit the fuse was one of his own followers, James Tallmadge, Jr., a forty-one-year-old freshman congressman from Poughkeepsie, New York.

Not only was Tallmadge a freshman congressman, he was a lame duck. He had not run for reelection in 1818 and thus had only a few more months to serve in Congress. For him and his family, life in the nation's capital had been a nightmare. Frequent bouts of diarrhea had left him prostrate, and early in 1819 his small son had died. He had just taken his wife back home to Poughkeepsie, buried their son, and returned to Washington to complete his term when a bill enabling Missouri to become a slave state came before the

1. Andrew A. Lipscomb and Albert Ellery Bergh, eds., *The Writings of Thomas Jefferson*, 20 vols. (Washington, D.C., 1903), 15: 249, 280–1; Paul Leicester Ford, ed., *The Works of Thomas Jefferson*, 12 vols. (New York, 1905): 12, 180, 186–9.

House.[2] To that bill, he proposed an amendment prohibiting "the further introduction of slavery" into Missouri and providing that slaves born in Missouri after it became a state "shall be free, but may be held to service until the age of twenty-five years."[3] Those words led to a congressional donnybrook that lasted the better part of two years.

What motivated Tallmadge? That has always been something of a mystery. Thomas Jefferson thought the lame duck freshman congressman was doing the bidding of DeWitt Clinton, the governor of New York and one of the kingpins of New York politics, who in turn was working hand in hand with the Federalists. And many historians have accepted Jefferson's assumption as the gospel truth.[4] But the archival evidence, which is skimpy, hardly supports this conclusion. According to one of Tallmadge's private letters, every faction in New York was angry at him—the Federalists for his defense of Andrew Jackson's invasion of Florida, Clinton for his backing of President Monroe, and Clinton's enemies for his support of Clinton. According to one of Tallmadge's political allies, Clinton opposed Tallmadge's amendment until he discovered how popular it was in New York.[5]

Moreover, to people who knew Tallmadge well, he was anything but the political puppet Jefferson imagined. In their eyes he was more a maverick who refused to play by the rules and who had an uncanny instinct for hitting the jugular. He was "politically eccen-

2. Laura Tallmadge to Mrs. M. B. Tallmadge, 22 January 1819, J. Tallmadge, Sr., to Matthias B. Tallmadge, 3 February 1819, Tallmadge Family Papers, New-York Historical Society.

3. For the exact wording, cf. *Annals of Congress,* 15th Congress, 2d session, 1818–19, p. 1170, and James D. Woodburn, "The Historical Significance of the Missouri Compromise," *American Historical Association Annual Report, 1893* (Washington, D.C., 1894), 255.

4. Others have treated Jefferson's assertions as nonsense. Cf. Glover Moore, *The Missouri Controversy, 1819–1821* (Lexington, Ky., 1953); Shaw Livermore, Jr., *The Twilight of Federalism: The Disintegration of the Federalist Party, 1815–1830* (Princeton, N.J., 1962), 88–95; and George Dangerfield, *The Awakening of American Nationalism, 1815–1828* (New York, 1965), 107–9.

5. James Tallmadge to John Taylor, 4 April, 4 September 1819, John W. Taylor Papers, New-York Historical Society; *Memoirs of John Quincy Adams, Comprising Portions of His Diary from 1795 to 1848,* 12 vols., ed. Charles Francis Adams (Philadelphia, 1974–77), 5: 203.

tric and wrongheaded," noted a contemporary historian of New York politics. He had a "talent for mischief," wrote one New York politician. "The truth is," explained a Poughkeepsie neighbor, that "in regard to political operations, Tallmadge is one of nature's *bad bargains*."[6]

In the end, whether Tallmadge was a maverick or the tool of DeWitt Clinton hardly matters. What is striking is the number of free-state politicians who quickly rallied to Tallmadge's side. In 1818 he had tried to block statehood for Illinois because the Illinois Constitution failed to completely outlaw slavery. Only thirty-four representatives voted with him then. Yet a year later, in calling for limitations on slavery in Missouri, he had the immediate backing of seventy-nine representatives. After a heated and often bloodthirsty debate, the House passed his amendment, with eighty-seven members voting to prohibit the further introduction of slavery into Missouri, and eighty-two voting to free all slave children born after Missouri became a state. On the first clause all but ten free-state representatives voted with Tallmadge, on the second, all but fourteen.

Most of these supporters were northern members of Jefferson's own party. They generally called themselves Republicans, a name that the followers of Lincoln and Seward would later appropriate because it had a nice Jeffersonian ring to it. But unlike their namesakes, these original northern Republicans were members of a party with deeper roots in the South than in the North. Nearly all were well aware of this fact. Many had little or no love for Clinton. Most detested Federalists. Yet, after Tallmadge left Congress and returned to Poughkeepsie, many of them teamed up with arch-Federalist Rufus King to fight the admission of Missouri as a slave state. So, for nearly two years, the most divisive issues of the day—the future of slavery and the inordinate power of the South in national affairs—dominated the political agenda. Why did that happen? And why were so many northern Republicans willing to allow that to happen?

The answer lies partly in the history of the three-fifths rule. Not only did Rufus King and the New England Federalists have a change

6. Jabez D. Hammond, *History of Political Parties in the State of New York*, 2 vols. (Albany, 1842), 2: 184; William L. Marcy to Martin Van Buren, 27 December 1826, Van Buren Papers, Library of Congress; Thiron Rudd to John W. Taylor, 27 February 1828, Taylor Papers.

of heart and accept Gouverneur Morris's indictment of the three-fifths rule, so did many northern Republicans.

Time had proved that Morris was basically right. The direct tax provision of the three-fifths clause turned out to be almost meaningless, and accordingly all the three-fifths clause really did was give the slave states more power. As Morris predicted, the new federal government under the Constitution depended on import duties for the lion's share of its income, and northerners paid the lion's share of the duties. Direct taxes, from the outset, were dismissed as unpopular, cumbersome, and impossible to enforce. For every dollar raised through direct taxes, it was argued, three or four could be raised through import duties for the same cost and three times as fast.

Only when the import trade was threatened by war did the federal government even consider direct taxes. In 1798 it appeared that the United States would soon be at war with France, and as a result many in Congress thought it dangerous for the federal treasury to be totally dependent on import duties. So Congress, with much grumbling, agreed to a direct tax of two million dollars. Similarly, during the War of 1812 the Madison administration desperately needed money, and Congress imposed direct taxes of three million dollars in 1813, six million dollars in 1814, and three million dollars in 1815. According to northern congressmen, the slave states were slow in paying their share of the bill, and in some cases they did not pay at all. Kentucky was accused of paying only one-tenth of the money it owed, and South Carolina and Georgia were accused of paying "not even a single cent."[7] All in all, Congress resorted to direct taxes only four times in the seventy-two years between Washington's election and Lincoln's. In the other sixty-eight years direct taxes were neither enacted nor even seriously discussed.

By 1800 the pattern was already clear. Not even Rufus King still pretended that the three-fifths rule was a compromise whereby direct taxation was proportioned to representation. Instead, he now claimed that no one at the Constitutional Convention had foreseen that the federal treasury's entire revenue would come from indirect

7. *Annals of Congress*, 7th Congress, 1st session, 1801–1802, p. 1073; Worthington C. Ford, ed., *Writings of John Quincy Adams*, 7 vols. (New York, 1913–17), 3: 71, 75; [William Plumer], *An Address to the Electors of New Hampshire* (Portsmouth, N.H., 1804), 11; *Annals of Congress*, 13th Congress, 3d session, 1814–15, pp. 423–4, 697–8.

taxes, and as a result the free states "were injudiciously led to accede to this unreasonable provision of the Constitution."[8] King knew better—or at least he should have known better—but he maintained this position for the rest of his life.

Others developed other compromise arguments. Some contended that counting "only" three out of five slaves, in itself, amounted to a compromise. And some went further and claimed that the three-fifths clause really amounted to a two-fifths penalty for the South, in that if all slaves were counted, the slave states would have much more power in Congress. This contention, which was generally dismissed as "just a lawyer's argument," was espoused from time to time not only by proslavery zealots but also by some abolitionists who insisted that the Constitution was at heart an antislavery document, not a proslavery document as Wendell Phillips and other abolitionists contended. Even Frederick Douglass, the most prominent black abolitionist, at one point adopted the two-fifths penalty argument. Later, during the secession crisis, a few South Carolinians tried to sell the penalty interpretation to their fellow secessionists. The Confederacy, however, also rejected it and incorporated the three-fifths formula into the Confederate Constitution.[9]

While the direct tax provision proved to be almost a nullity, the representation provision proved to have even more impact than Morris predicted. Morris had thundered against giving the South "extra" representatives for three-fifths of its slaves in every Congress and in every electoral college and for rewarding the Deep South with even more congressional seats for enslaving even more Africans. That of course came to pass. The slave states always had one-third more seats in Congress than their free population warranted—forty-seven seats instead of thirty-three in 1793, seventy-

8. Charles R. King, ed., *The Life and Correspondence of Rufus King*, 6 vols. (New York, 1894–1900), 4: 324–5.

9. For the checkered career of the two-fifths penalty argument, cf. Lysander Spooner, *The Unconstitutionality of Slavery* (Boston, 1845); Wendell Phillips, *A Review of Lysander Spooner's Unconstitutionality of Slavery* (Boston, 1847); John W. Blassingame, ed., *The Frederick Douglass Papers*, 5 vols. (New Haven, 1979–92), 2 (1982), 197; Philip S. Foner, ed., *The Life and Writings of Frederick Douglass*, 4 vols. (New York, 1950), 2, 472; Laura A. White, *Robert Barnwell Rhett, Father of Secession* (Gloucester, Mass., 1965), 191–2, 197–9, 203–4; and Charles Robert Lee, Jr., *The Confederate Constitutions* (Chapel Hill, 1963) 83, 90–1.

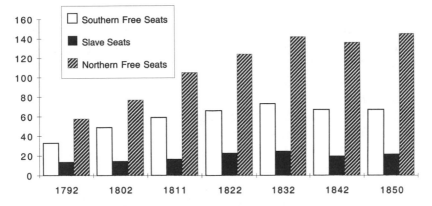

Impact of three-fifths rule on House of Representatives

six instead of fifty-nine in 1812, and ninety-eight instead of seventy-three in 1833—and that in turn affected the number of electoral votes they could cast. The Deep South also imported more slaves from Africa in the twenty years from 1788 to 1808 (the year the international slave trade was legally banned) than in any other twenty-year period.

What Morris did not anticipate, however, was that the three-fifths rule would also play a decisive role in every political caucus and every political convention. That was largely because he, along with most of the Founding Fathers, minimized the role political parties and party caucuses would play in the Republic. Once parties developed in the 1790s, the effect of the three-fifths rule on the party system gradually became clear. As we will see, it gave southerners an even larger voice in the nation's dominant party—first the Jeffersonian Republicans and then the Jacksonian Democrats—than they had in the House or the electoral college.

In the case of the Jeffersonian Republicans, the dominance of southerners became clear during Jefferson's eight years in the White House. At first northern Republicans grudgingly accepted their subordinate role. In time, however, many became restless. In 1808 and 1812 New York Republicans led a mini-rebellion against the inordinate power of Jefferson and his Virginia colleagues. In 1819 many of them joined James Tallmadge in taking the battle a step further, challenging both the expansion of slavery and twenty years of southern domination.

* * *

From the inauguration of Jefferson in 1801 to the end of Monroe's second term in 1825, Virginians dominated national politics. Not only did they hold the presidency for twenty-four straight years, they also shaped the rules of national politics to ensure their preeminence and to reflect their ideas.

Jefferson and his Virginia colleagues had unusual political resources. Thanks to the three-fifths rule, Virginia had the most electoral votes in 1800 and was second only to New York in 1820. In Virginia the great planter-politicians had a hammerlock on state politics. That was partly because they were masters of magnificent estates such as Gunston Hall, Montpelier, and Monticello, prominent slaveholders who had been chosen by their neighbors to serve in the county court and state legislature before being elevated to positions of national power, men who had achieved national distinction by the time of the Revolution.[10] It was also partly because the Virginia Constitution grossly favored the tidewater aristocracy at the expense of the western part of the state. The system of representation in the House of Burgesses (two delegates for each county) took no account of population. So Warwick on the coast, with 620 free whites, had the same power as Shenandoah County with 17,000. Farmers from west of the Blue Ridge howled about the unfairness of this situation. One reformer after another demanded that Virginia's leaders, who fancied themselves as the foremost spokesmen for republicanism nationally, live up to the basic republican tenet of majority rule. But the Virginia elite gave ground slowly and grudgingly.[11]

10. Probably the best-known and most influential study of Virginia leadership is Charles S. Sydnor, *Gentlemen Freeholders: Political Practices in Washington's Virginia* (Chapel Hill, 1952). See also Dumas Malone, "The Great Generation," *Virginia Quarterly Review* 23 (1947): 108–22.

11. Cf. Norman J. Risjord, "The Virginia Federalists," *Journal of Southern History* 33 (November 1967): 507–8, 514–6; Merrill D. Peterson, ed., *Democracy, Liberty, and Property* (Indianapolis, Ind., 1966), 271ff.; and Alison Goodyear Freehling, *Drift toward Dissolution: The Virginia Slavery Debate of 1831–1832* (Baton Rouge, 1982), 36ff. Virginia, it should be noted, was not the only slave state to favor the planters in apportioning seats in the state legislature. In various ways, so did Maryland, North Carolina, South Carolina, Georgia, Louisiana, and Florida. In some of the new states in the Southwest, the planters had less power—additional voting power in the Senate but not the House, a slight edge in both houses, or no

The Virginia aristocracy also took a step in 1800 that partly muffled western dissidence and gave the tidewater elite an even stronger voice in national affairs. In the previous presidential election, Virginia had followed the district system in choosing presidential electors. Under this system each district in the state could act independently, and one dissident district had chosen a presidential elector pledged to Adams rather than Jefferson. In 1800 Jefferson and his colleagues made sure that this would not happen again. In place of the district system, the state legislature established the general-ticket system, whereby the people of the entire state chose a slate of electors. Thus the dominant party could control the state's entire electoral vote and make it appear that mighty Virginia spoke with just one voice.[12]

Not only did the Virginia aristocracy completely dominate the state, but they also suffered from less internal discord than their counterparts in other states. They had to cope with internal strife between 1806 and 1810, but not with the persistent factionalism that disabled Jeffersonian Republicans in New York and Pennsylvania. They shared too much in common. They had the same kind of estates, the same dependence on the plantation economy, the same interest in the price of slaves and land. They were less divided socially and economically than Republicans elsewhere. And since they spent less energy fighting among themselves, less time on the factional and partisan contests common elsewhere, they had the time and energy

---

edge whatsoever. In each case, the advocates of slave representation drew analogies between the position of the great plantation counties in the state and the southern states in the nation. How, they asked, could southerners insist on counting slaves in congressional apportionments if they were to disregard slaves in state legislature apportionments? And in each instance, the dissidents fired back that slave representation violated the hallowed concept of majority rule and made them second-class citizens. Cf. Charles S. Sydnor, *The Development of Southern Sectionalism, 1819–1848* (Baton Rouge, 1948), 278–9, 284–7; Barbara Jeanne Fields, *Slavery and Freedom on the Middle Ground: Maryland during the Nineteenth Century* (New Haven, 1985), 21; Edwin Arthur Miles, *Jacksonian Democracy in Mississippi* (Chapel Hill, 1960), 33–4; Malcolm Cook McMillan, *Constitutional Development in Alabama, 1798–1901* (Chapel Hill, 1955), 36–7; and Lonnie J. White, *Politics on the Southwestern Frontier: Arkansas Territory, 1819–1836* (Memphis, Tenn., 1964), 185–9.

12. Norman J. Risjord, *Chesapeake Politics* (New York, 1978), 554–6.

to amplify Virginia's voice in national politics, especially in Republican caucuses.[13]

The Republican caucus was an outgrowth of congressional party politics. In the 1790s, once Federalist and Jeffersonian legislators realized that they were at loggerheads over both men and issues, they began to meet separately to formulate strategy and tactics. These caucuses were less apt than a British caucus to force a legislator to vote one way or another on highly publicized issues. The members of the caucus knew very well that a congressman was dependent on his constituents for reelection, rather than the party, and had no desire to lose good party men. But the caucus did thrash out questions of organization and procedure, shaped the political agenda, and good party men went along whether they got their way or not.

In 1800 both parties used the congressional caucus to confer the party's stamp of approval on presidential and vice presidential candidates. Thereafter, the Republican congressional caucus chose the party's leaders and, significantly, every presidential aspirant sought its endorsement, even those who later denounced the caucus as an undemocratic cabal. More importantly, the caucus was the party's only national organization for some twenty years.[14]

The inherent structure of the caucus, along with the three-fifths rule and Senate parity, gave the planters the edge. To be in the caucus, one had to be a party member in the national legislature. That meant, in turn, that a state or section's potential power in the caucus depended on how many Jeffersonian Republicans it elected to

13. Harry Ammon, "The Richmond Junto, 1800–1824," *Virginia Magazine of History and Biography* 61 (October 1953): 395–418; and Hammond, *Political Parties in New York,* 1: 405–6.

14. The power of the Jefferson caucus has been much debated. Earlier studies generally agreed that the caucus was decisive, that it nominated presidents, that it was indeed the king maker. More recently, however, some historians have suggested that King Caucus's power has been grossly overrated, that dozens of Jeffersonian Republicans boycotted nominating caucuses, and that many congressmen ignored their caucus when it came to controversial votes in Congress. All this is true. Party bolters and mavericks were commonplace, but so too were politicians like Martin Van Buren and his New York Bucktails who held the caucus in high regard, indeed treated it as the one true church and sacrificed their own opinions and sometimes their own political careers following its dictates. Cf. Mosei Ostrogowski, "The Rise and Fall of the Nominating Caucus, Legislature and Congressional," *American Historical Review* 5 (January 1900): 253–83; Ralph V. Harlow, *The History of the Legislative Methods in the Period Before 1825* (New Haven, 1917), 184–9, 194–5,

Congress. A state like Connecticut, which in the early years elected only Federalists to the House and the Senate, thus had no say in the Jeffersonian caucus, whereas a state like Kentucky, which elected only Republicans, always had a voice. At times, moreover, a sparsely populated state like Georgia was entitled to more votes in the caucus than a heavily populated state like Massachusetts.

Since the North was the majority section in the House as well as in the nation, historians have often assumed that it was the majority in the caucus. That was not the case. From the party's birth in the 1790s until 1816, the slave states always elected more Republicans than the free states. In the sixth Congress, which served from 1799 to 1801, for example, the ratio was thirty-five to twenty-one; eight years later, seventy-three to seventy-one; eight years after that, seventy-nine to sixty-six. Northern Republicans enjoyed a majority only after the War of 1812, when their Federalist rivals for the most part dropped out of national politics, and their own party split into warring factions.[15]

What this meant, of course, was that in the formative years of the party's development the southern wing was always in control. This was true even when ambitious and contentious slaveholders fought one another for preeminence, as when Jefferson stripped his fellow Virginian John Randolph of power, Monroe tried to wrest the presidential nomination from Madison in 1808, and William Crawford of Georgia almost took the nomination from Monroe in 1816. In

---

200–7, 249–51; Noble E. Cunningham, Jr., *The Jeffersonian Republicans* (Chapel Hill, 1957), 90–1, 162–6; idem, *The Jeffersonian Republicans in Power* (Chapel Hill, 1963), 99–123; James Sterling Young, *The Washington Community, 1800–1828* (New York, 1966), 112–7, 124–7, 138–41; James S. Chase, *Emergence of the Presidential Nominating Convention, 1789–1832* (Urbana, Ill., 1973); and Michael Wallace, "Changing Concepts of Party in the United States: New York, 1815–28," *American Historical Review* 74 (December 1968): 461–5.

15. Computed from data in Kenneth C. Martis, *The Historical Atlas of Political Parties in the United States Congress, 1789–1989* (New York, 1989), 73–86. I have relied on Martis throughout this book concerning the party affiliation of members of Congress. As historians of the period know, both the primary and secondary sources often disagree concerning the party affiliation of some congressmen. According to Martis, the standard sources that most historians have used in determining party affiliation for the first fifty years of Congress have "a low reliability factor," especially for the years 1815 to 1825 (see p. 21). For details on the various conflicts and the final determination reached by Martis, see pp. 247–317.

such contests the rivals always looked to northern members for help, and on occasion northern Republicans received a few plums from the table. The Speaker's chair went twice to a northerner and the chairmanship of Ways and Means went once. Otherwise, real power was in the hands of slaveholders, the Speaker's office for 79 percent of the time, Ways and Means for 92 percent, the White House for 100 percent.

The only position that consistently went to a northerner was the vice presidency. That office had some stature before 1800, but after 1800 the Virginians turned it into a dead-end job and made sure that it always went to a political has-been. Under the Constitution, the vice president was supposed to be the nation's second-best-qualified presidential candidate, the man who finished second in the electoral college's balloting for president. In 1800 that system had created a deadlock when the Jeffersonian electors had cast an equal number of ballots for Jefferson, their intended presidential candidate, and Aaron Burr of New York, their intended vice presidential candidate. To prevent a similar situation in the future, Jefferson and his associates shepherded through Congress and the states the Twelfth Amendment to the Constitution. It provided for separate balloting for president and vice president.

Under the old electoral machinery, the vice president had always been a man who was in his political prime. Adams and Jefferson subsequently became president, and Burr had plenty of followers who saw him as a potential president. In their eyes he was anything but a has-been. That was not the case with the men chosen under the new system. In 1804 the Virginians backed DeWitt Clinton's uncle George for vice president. George Clinton had once been a power in New York politics, serving as governor for nearly twenty-five years and presiding over the state's ratification of the Federal Constitution. But in 1804, when the caucus selected him as Jefferson's running mate, he was well past his prime. He was sixty-five, but an old sixty-five, slowing down mentally as well as physically. He was, noted a sympathetic New Hampshire senator, "too old for the office" and "altogether incapable" of discharging its few duties. In 1808 the caucus again selected Clinton, this time as Madison's running mate, and he died in office. In 1812 the caucus first chose seventy-two-year-old John Langdon of New Hampshire to be Madison's running mate. When he declined because of the infirmities of old age, the caucus turned to Elbridge Gerry, who had been a signer of the Declaration of Independence, a member of the Constitutional Convention, and governor of Massachusetts. He was now seventy years old, in poor health, and died within two years of taking office. In 1816 the caucus turned to another New Yorker, Daniel Tompkins, who had served as governor for four terms and taken steps in 1812 to temporarily block DeWitt Clinton's bid for the party's presidential nomination. He was only fifty-two, but a physical wreck thanks to his efforts to bolster New York's defenses during the War of 1812, his desperate financial straits, and his fondness for the bottle. Seldom sober, he spent most of his vice presidency back home in New York. Nonetheless, the caucus nominated him for a second term in 1820.[16]

Some northern Republicans undoubtedly accepted this state of affairs. In exchange for patronage and dead-end jobs in the national hierarchy, they muffled whatever antislavery or antisouthern feeling they might have, voted with the South on crucial measures, and converted a southern minority position in the House and the nation at large into a majority political position. Others, however, bristled at Virginia's overweening power. Especially combative were New York Republicans, who after Jefferson's eight years in office thought their time had come. In their eyes they had won the battle against Alexander Hamilton and the Federalists in 1800; they had taken New York City out of Federalist hands, provided Jefferson with the state's twelve electoral votes, and thus had made him president. The New Yorkers, however, were divided into three warring factions, which the Virginians, through the use of federal patronage, were able to exploit. These divisions proved to be a major stumbling block to consolidation of power, but the Clinton faction made the

16. Everett S. Brown, ed., *William Plumer's Memorandum of Proceedings in the United States Senate, 1803–1807* (New York, 1923), 450; Cunningham, *Jeffersonian Republicans in Power*, 104, 114; Richard P. McCormick, *The Presidential Game: The Origins of American Presidential Politics* (New York, 1982), 87–8, 96, 105; Arthur Schlesinger, Jr., and Fred L. Israel, eds., *History of American Presidential Elections, 1789–1968*, 4 vols. (New York, 1971), 1: 187, 191, 305–6, 342–3; Ray W. Irwin, *Daniel D. Tompkins: Governor of New York and Vice President of the United States* (New York, 1968), 205–10.

effort.[17] With assistance from other elements in the party, they backed George Clinton for president in 1808 and DeWitt Clinton in 1812.

The force behind the New York drive for power was DeWitt Clinton, who in 1808 orchestrated his uncle's effort to topple Virginia dominance. Tall and handsome, regal in bearing, he rose in the tough school of New York politics working for his uncle. Never much of a team player, his youthful good looks and colossal ego had earned him the nickname Magnus Apollo. According to a recent biographer, he had been a loyal supporter of the Virginians until 1803. At that time he became mayor of New York, just when the Anglo-French war again heated up, and became deeply troubled by the Virginians' defense policies. As he saw it, the nation's Virginia leadership had a duty to protect the port of New York and the state's commercial farmers from abuse by British and French frigates, a duty which they never made even a halfhearted attempt to fulfill. He asked for four federal forts, at one million dollars each, only to get sympathetic letters in return. He asked for three or four frigates and got more letters.

Then, in 1807, after the British frigate *Leopard* attacked the American frigate *Chesapeake* off Norfolk Roads, Clinton thought the time had finally come for the Virginians to provide for the nation's defense. He and his followers called for a national program of military preparedness. Instead, to their horror, Jefferson pushed through the Embargo, which outlawed nearly all American exports and virtually closed the port of New York. To make matters worse, the Jefferson administration threatened to cut off federal patronage from Republican leaders who criticized this policy.[18]

Losing patronage was a serious matter for Clinton. He did not invent the spoils system in New York, as some historians later claimed, but even his admirers admitted that he was "more radical" than his predecessors in using it.[19] So for a season he pretended to be a sup-

17. For details on how the Virginians used federal patronage to keep the New Yorkers divided, see Solomon Nadler, "Federal Patronage and New York Politics, 1801–1830" (Ph.D. dissertation, New York University, 1973).

18. Steven E. Siry, *DeWitt Clinton and the American Political Economy: Sectionalism, Politics, and Republican Ideology, 1787–1828* (New York, 1990), 2, 57–122.

19. Howard McBain, *DeWitt Clinton and the Origin of the Spoils System in New York* (New York, 1907), 158.

porter of the president's policy. However, with 537 vessels standing idle in New York's harbor, and the revenues of the New York Customs House falling from $4.5 million to nothing, that pretense was impossible to sustain. Then the Jefferson administration began bestowing patronage on Clinton's enemies. At that point, Clinton abandoned pretense, openly broke with the administration, and advocated his uncle's nomination for the presidency.

Uncle George was more than willing to go along. After serving four years as Jefferson's vice president, he had completely soured on Virginia dominance. He had concluded that the Virginians would never provide New York, or any of the free states, with adequate defense. All they wanted, he wrote his nephew, was a military force "sufficient to keep their slaves in awe & prevent their cutting their Masters throats." He later characterized the Jefferson administration's management of national affairs as visionary, feeble, and corrupt. As a result, he argued, "the cause of republicanism" was in grave danger.[20]

The insurgents, however, were one step behind James Madison's managers. To forestall all potential challengers, notably James Monroe of Virginia and Clinton of New York, the Madison camp decided to hold the congressional nominating caucus early in the year. Accordingly, 89 of the 144 Republicans in Congress met in January 1808 and selected Madison for president and Clinton for vice president.[21] Three of the New York congressmen refused to support Madison, and most of the others boycotted the meeting. In all, only one New York Republican supported the caucus's presidential nominee. After that, the Clintonians denounced the caucus as an undemocratic cabal and conducted a feeble campaign in behalf of George Clinton. In the end, he received 6 electoral votes for president, 113 for vice president.

Over the next four years, the bad feelings between the Clintonians and the Madisonians worsened. By 1810 DeWitt Clinton, now forty years old, decided to challenge Madison himself. The president, in his eyes, was not only a threat to New York's commercial interests

20. George Clinton to DeWitt Clinton, 13 February through 10 April 1808, Clinton Papers, Columbia University Library.

21. In determining what happened in this and other caucuses, I have followed the standard historical source. In this case, the sources are Cunningham, *Jeffersonian Republicans in Power*, 114, concerning the actual vote, and Martis, *Historical Atlas of Political Parties*, 24, concerning the number of eligible caucus members.

but incompetent as well, a mere shadow of a man, barely fit to hold Clinton's boots. Frequently demonstrating his anti-British and pro-commerce sympathies, Clinton tried to win support from the West as well as the East, especially from Henry Clay and the Kentuckians. But above all he had to prove that his New York base was solid. To do that, he needed to secure the New York legislature's endorsement before the congressional caucus met in Washington. Governor Tompkins, whom the Madison men had been courting, blocked this strategy by proroguing the state legislature.[22] While the New York legislators were back home, the congressional caucus in Washington met and renominated Madison, but the number of absentees—55 of 137 eligible congressmen—was striking.[23] Shortly thereafter, the New York legislature reconvened and ninety-one of the ninety-five Republicans caucused to consider challenging the incumbent president. With members of the New York congressional delegation egging them on, they voted unanimously against Madison's candidacy and nominated Clinton for president.[24]

The Clinton camp immediately went on the attack. "It must rejoice the heart of every good man," declared one Clinton newspaper, ". . . to find that the democratic-republicans of the FIRST STATE OF THE UNION, have dared to make a stand against the usurpation and overbearing aristocracy of Virginia." And then in June, when Congress declared war against Great Britain, anti-Virginia rhetoric skyrocketed. The country was unprepared for war, argued the Clintonians, and the idea that the Madison administration wanted to protect northern commerce was pure nonsense. The Virginians had never shown any concern for northern commerce; indeed, they had gone out of their way to cripple it. With this largely sectional appeal, the Clintonians worked hard to court the vote of northern Federalists. Gouverneur Morris joined the cause, but many Federalists, including Rufus King, refused to support a Clinton-Federalist coalition, and the thought of such a coalition alienated many northern Republicans.[25]

22. Hammond, *Political Parties in New York*, 1: 297–311; Siry, *Clinton*, 159–60.

23. *Niles' Weekly Register* 2 (30 May 1812): 192–3; and Schlesinger and Israel, *American Presidential Elections*, 1: 252–3, for those participating. See Martis, *Historical Atlas of Political Parties*, 24, for those eligible.

24. Hammond, *Political Parties in New York*, 1: 315–6; Siry, *Clinton*, 160.

25. Siry, *Clinton*, 161; King, *Life and Correspondence*, 5: 266; Schlesinger and Israel, *American Presidential Elections*, 1: 252–5, 287–91.

In the end, Clinton needed another nineteen electoral votes to win the presidency. The votes of Pennsylvania would have sufficed. As it was, he carried the free states by a margin of eighty electoral votes to forty but got trounced in the slave states, winning only nine electoral votes to Madison's eighty-eight.

Throughout these electoral battles, the Clinton camp complained bitterly about how the three-fifths rule gave the Virginians an additional edge. In 1808 the once-notorious Citizen Genet, whom the Federalists had vilified in the 1790s for interfering in American affairs on behalf of the French government, wrote an election pamphlet on behalf of his father-in-law, George Clinton. In denouncing the Virginia oligarchy and in claiming that his father-in-law was "an old fashioned American statesman and warrior," friendly to commerce as well as agriculture, hostile to all visionary and hazardous experiments such as Jefferson's Embargo, he also lambasted the South's slave representation. It guaranteed rule by the minority, he contended, and deprived the country of able leadership. The *American Citizen*, a Clinton newspaper, echoed Genet's concerns.[26]

In 1812 the argument was repeated, both by northern Republicans and by Federalists who joined Clinton's coalition. "On this subject," declared the *Connecticut Journal*, "all the North have a common interest." For too long the North had allowed "the *slave country* to triumph in this palpable fraud." For too long had the nation's commerce, agriculture, finances, and glory been "trampled in the dust, by the very man whom Southern slaves have lifted to office."[27]

In actual fact, Clinton probably would have lost the general election in 1812 even if Madison had not had the benefit of slave representation. In 1811 Congress was reapportioned, and the new apportionment provided the South with eighteen slave seats. Madison undoubtedly won sixteen of these, but Clinton needed an additional nineteen electoral votes to win the presidency. Perhaps

26. A Citizen of New-York [Edmond Genet], *Communications on the Next Election for President of the United States* (New York, 1808), 10–2; *New York American Citizen*, 14, 20 January 1808.

27. "Boreas," *Slave Representation* (New Haven, 1812), 22. Also quoted in William C. Fowler, *The Sectional Controversy* (New York, 1863), 62–3. See also *Connecticut Courant*, June 30, 1812.

in a closer contest he could have won the support of Pennsylvania's Republican leaders. And perhaps in a closer contest he could have picked up a handful of electoral votes elsewhere. He was adroit, a wheeler-dealer of the first order.[28] But even a savvy politician can accomplish only so much. Thus, despite the wailing of the Clintonians and the Federalists, the only time that slave seats clearly determined the outcome of a presidential election was in 1800.

Where slave representation was clearly more decisive was in the Republican caucus. There, it changed the dynamics of national politics. In the House of Representatives, congressmen from the slave states were always in the minority and in the Senate they were usually evenly matched. But in the Republican caucus, where many of the key decisions were made, the men from the slave states were in the majority, and the three-fifths rule assured that. Take, for example, the 1808 caucus, the one that initially chose James Madison to head the ticket. Of the 144 men eligible to attend that caucus, 73 came from the slave states, 71 from the free states. Without the three-fifths rule, which at that time provided the South with fifteen slave seats, the men from the slave states would definitely have been in the minority, potentially outnumbered by as many as twelve votes if all party regulars attended the caucus.[29]

Or consider the 1812 caucus, the one that renominated Madison. Of the 137 congressmen eligible to attend that caucus, 71 were from the slave states, 66 from the free states. Without the three-fifths rule, which accounted for at least sixteen of the slave-state Republicans, southerners again would have been in the minority.[30] Would a northern majority have looked as favorably on Madison's nomination for a second term? Would they have abided by the Virginians domination of party policy? Would they have allowed the Virginians to use federal patronage to exploit the divisions among northern

28. On Clinton's political skills, see Craig Hanyan and Mary L. Hanyan, *DeWitt Clinton and the Rise of the People's Men* (Montreal, 1996). This book has nothing to do with the 1812 election. It deals only with the last few years of Clinton's life. It is very helpful, however, in explaining how Clinton operated, how he put together coalitions, and how he tailored his message to fit what most voters wanted.

29. Computed from data in Martis, *Historical Atlas of Political Parties.*

30. Ibid.

Republicans? The Clintonians thought the answer to all these questions was "no."

There was one oddity in all this. Anytime there was a Federalist resurgence in the North, the power of the slave states in the Republican caucus was enhanced. Federalists, for the most part, were not the masters of their own destiny. A feeble party in most places, with inept candidates and lackluster campaigns, the Federalists generally made comebacks only when the Jeffersonian leadership did something that outraged northern voters. The Embargo was one such incident. The War of 1812 was another. Following the Embargo, northern Republicans paid dearly. They went into the 1807–1808 elections with fifty-seven seats in the House, two fewer than their southern colleagues. They came out with forty-two seats, eight fewer than southern Republicans. They struggled to regain their former strength but lost further ground to the slave states when Congress was enlarged in 1811, and they did not surpass their former strength until after the War of 1812, when Federalists in many districts were portrayed as traitors for opposing the war effort and toying with the idea of secession at the Hartford Convention on the eve of Andrew Jackson's victory at the Battle of New Orleans.[31]

With the further decline of Federalism, northern Republicans finally were a match for their southern colleagues. In the Congress that

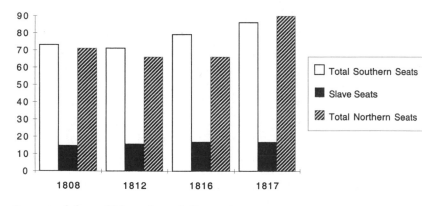

Impact of three-fifths rule on Jeffersonian caucus

31. Ibid., 24.

convened in December 1817, they had for the first time a majority in the Republican caucus.[32] But they were still hampered by the three-fifths rule. Without it, they would have had a nineteen- or twenty-vote majority in the caucus. With it, they had only a four-vote majority.

That was the winter that James Tallmadge, Jr., came to Congress. Was he aware of the numbers? The dynamics of slave representation? How it affected his party's caucus? There is no hard evidence one way or another, but given what happened over the next two years, and how he behaved, it is a safe bet that he was keenly aware of the numbers.

At first nothing changed with a northern majority. The caucus backed Henry Clay for another term as Speaker of the House, and he won the election handily. A South Carolina slaveholder, William Lowndes, was reappointed chairman of Ways and Means, the most powerful committee in the House. The only leadership position of any consequence that went to a northerner was the chairmanship of the Elections Committee. It too was a reappointment, and it went to Tallmadge's close friend John W. Taylor, who first came to Washington in 1813. At age thirty-three, Taylor was one of the youngest members of the twenty-seven-member New York delegation, but like Henry Clay he was a strong supporter of the War of 1812, the Second Bank of the United States, internal improvements, and a protective tariff. Clay held him in high esteem. That view would change in the next eighteen months.[33]

The two issues that Clay and other southern leaders never wanted to confront were slavery and southern domination of the young Republic. But the Congress that Tallmadge joined in December 1817 was destined to confront those issues time and again. The cotton kingdom was booming, expanding westward, and with it the inter-state slave trade had skyrocketed. No longer could Chesapeake planters pretend that plantation slavery was the moribund legacy of British rule. The cotton boom in western South Carolina and Georgia, in Alabama and Mississippi, was the talk of Washington.

32. Ibid.

33. Gerald R. Lientz, "House Speaker Elections and Congressional Parties, 1789–1860," *Capitol Studies* 6 (Spring 1978): 69; DeAlva S. Alexander, *History and Procedure of the House of Representatives* (Boston, 1916), 399f; DeAlva S. Alexander, "John W. Taylor: New York's Speaker of the House of Representatives," *Quarterly Journal of the New York State Historical Association* 1 (January 1920): 14–22.

And so were the slave caravans going west. All congressmen had to do, Tallmadge later noted, was look out "the windows of Congress Hall" and see "a trafficker in human flesh . . . on his way to the West" driving before him male slaves, handcuffed and chained together, and women and children in the rear "under the guidance of the driver's whip."[34]

The demand for slaves accentuated two old problems. One was the international slave trade. Nearly every humanitarian in the country, north and south, agreed that the trade in slaves between Africa and the New World was a despicable business that had to be destroyed. Yet when Congress outlawed the international slave trade in 1807, it refused to impose harsh penalties on the law's violators, and it allowed the individual states to decide what to do with Africans brought illegally into their ports. After the War of 1812, several southern states and territories passed laws whereby the Africans would be sold to the highest bidder. In addition, the federal government lacked the ships to police the illicit slave trade and would not accept the British navy's offer of help. Amelia Island and Galveston became notorious as places where Americans could get hundreds of Africans for ready money.

So obvious was the ineffectiveness of the 1807 law that President Madison in 1816 asked Congress to pass tougher penalties and President Monroe in 1817 called for the suppression of the Galveston and Amelia Island slave traders. Congress authorized more cruisers to suppress the trade in nearby waters and in 1820 declared that the illicit slave trade was piracy and thus punishable by death. But the federal government remained lax in enforcing the law, occasionally catching a slaver but never obtaining a death sentence until the Lincoln administration.[35]

The other old problem accentuated by the postwar demand for slaves concerned the federal fugitive slave law. The act of 1793 authorized a slaveowner or his agent to cross a state line, seize an alleged runaway slave, take the captive before any federal judge or local magistrate, and upon proof of ownership, receive a certificate

34. *Annals of Congress*, 15th Congress, 2d session, 1818–19, p. 1210.
35. *House Documents*, 15th Congress, 1st session, 1817–18, nos. 12, 46, 47; W. E. B. DuBois, *The Suppression of the African Slave Trade to the United States* (Baton Rouge, 1969), 108–17; Hugh G. Soulsby, *The Right of Search and the Slave Trade in Anglo-American Relations, 1814–1862* (Baltimore, 1933), 13–38.

entitling the pursuer to return home with his captive. The law provided fines for anyone who interfered with this process, but no legal protection whatsoever for the alleged slave. Nor did it inflict a penalty on a pursuer who returned home without bothering to get a certificate. The law thus invited kidnappings, and after the War of 1812, talk about free blacks being kidnapped by bounty hunters and whisked off to the slave markets of the Deep South multiplied enormously. In response, between 1816 and 1818 all the free states bordering the South passed antikidnapping laws with punishments ranging from jail time to whipping and cropping to the death penalty. This, in turn, infuriated many slaveholders, who demanded that Congress pass a more effective fugitive slave law. Congress responded in 1818 with a proposal that gave the pursuers of runaway slaves additional advantages and protection. The ensuing debates were bitter, involving both open attacks on slavery and open defenses of it. Freshman senator William Loughton Smith of South Carolina not only sang the praises of slavery and its expansion but also claimed that blacks were better off as slaves than as free men and women. The proposal eventually passed both houses, but with differences in detail. These were not resolved, and thus the proposal never became law.[36]

Although issues concerning the African slave trade and fugitive slaves caused heated debates, they were the kind of debates that Speaker Clay could control. That was not the case, however, when the House had to deal with such matters as the expansion of slavery and the extension of southern power. By the time Tallmadge reached Washington in 1817, the rapid rise of the West after the War of 1812, and the doubling of the population west of the Appalachians, had put these issues squarely on the House agenda. Just before his arrival, two rapidly growing territories had asked for statehood. Indiana had become a free state, Mississippi a slave state. Now, in late 1817, three more territories wanted statehood. Alabama and Missouri wanted to become slave states, and Illinois apparently wanted to nullify the Northwest Ordinance's prohibition against slavery.

It was clear to Tallmadge, among others, that slavery was not

36. Thomas D. Morris, *Free Men All: The Personal Liberty Laws of the North, 1780–1861* (Baltimore, 1974), 3–4, 35–40, 219–22; *Annals of Congress*, 15th Congress, 1st session, 1817–18, pp. 231–9.

dying by "imperceptible degrees" as Jefferson once predicted. It was expanding. It might even be expanding by leaps and bounds, not only gaining complete domination over the old slave country below the Ohio River and east of the Mississippi, but also making substantial inroads in lands across the Mississippi and north of the Ohio.

Illinois was the first problem. When the territory applied for statehood, more than 1,200 slaves and indentured blacks lived there. The Northwest Ordinance of 1787, despite the article banning slavery, had had little effect on their lives. Their masters had fought tenaciously to keep them in bondage, and territorial officials had sided with their masters. In fact, two territorial governors—William Henry Harrison and Ninian Edwards—were themselves slaveowners. These policymakers had circumvented the 1787 ordinance by maintaining that all blacks who had been brought into the territory before 1787 were still legally slaves, as were their children, and by pretending that all other blacks in the territory were indentured servants who had voluntarily contracted with their masters before entering the territory. It was next to impossible for black servants to prove otherwise, since Illinois law forbade blacks from testifying against whites.

The proslavery men, however, had to cope with other white residents who hated both slavery and blacks. These people wanted to keep all blacks out of the territory, and in 1813 Illinois passed a law that promised any black man who entered the territory thirty-nine lashes, repeated every fifteen days until he left. The following year, a new legislature made it clear that this law did not bar the owners of salt works and mills from hiring southern slaves on a yearly basis.[37]

In 1818 the founding fathers of Illinois presented Congress with a constitution that prohibited slavery, but with several loopholes. The document only prohibited slavery that might hereafter be introduced. Under this clause, slaves who had come to Illinois before the Northwest Ordinance, and the children of such slaves, were still slaves. The document also allowed the indenturing of black males

37. N. Dwight Harris, *The History of Negro Servitude in Illinois* (Chicago, 1904), passim; Paul Finkelman, *Slavery and the Founders: Race and Liberty in the Age of Jefferson* (Armonk, N.Y., 1996), 57–67, 72–4; and Eugene H. Berwanger, *The Frontier against Slavery: Western Anti-Negro Prejudice and the Slavery Extension Controversy* (Urbana, Ill., 1967), 8–29.

under twenty-one and black females under eighteen for periods longer than their childhood and of blacks of any age who entered "indenture while in a perfect state of freedom, or on condition of a bona-fide consideration received or to be received for their service." It also permitted the salt works near Shawneetown to hire slaves from other states until the year 1825. And it confirmed the bondage of all involuntary servants already in Illinois, promising to free their children only when the boys reached age twenty-one, the girls age eighteen. Finally, it gave masters four months to import and indenture as many additional servants as they wished.[38]

Tallmadge challenged the troubling document and tried to block Illinois's bid for statehood. Only thirty-four colleagues supported his effort.[39] Once admitted to statehood, the Illinois legislature passed an elaborate act, "respecting Free Negroes, Mulattoes, Servants, and Slaves," that in many ways resembled a southern slave code. The legislature also sent to the United States Senate two men who were certain to vote with the South, Jesse Thomas, who owned five servants, and Ninian Edwards, who not only owned slaves but "defended his right to do so in language that would have done justice to a Georgian or South Carolinian."[40] Their election, in effect, gave the slave states a majority in the Senate and assured that any attempt to block the expansion of slavery would depend entirely on the actions of the House. In the next several years, the widespread white desire to keep all blacks out of the Illinois, coupled with the heroic efforts of an antislavery governor, himself a former Virginia slaveholder, would thwart Edwards and his proslavery supporters. And in time Illinois would become a genuine free state. In 1819, however, the proslavery element seemed to be in charge.

That was the year when both Alabama and Missouri applied for statehood, the year James Tallmadge went for the jugular. At first Tallmadge didn't speak in behalf of his amendment to prohibit the further introduction of slavery into Missouri and to free slave children born in Missouri after it became a state. He was too sick and too distraught from his son's death. He allowed his friend John W. Taylor to carry the argument.

38. *Constitution of the State of Illinois* (1818), art. 6.
39. *Annals of Congress*, 15th Congress, 2d session, 1818–19, pp. 305–11.
40. Moore, *The Missouri Controversy*, 54.

Finally, just before the vote, Tallmadge took the floor. When he spoke, he seemed to be free of all pretense. He frankly admitted that the idea of extending the three-fifths rule to yet another state rankled him; the area west of the Mississippi had "no claim to such an unequal representation, unjust in its result upon the other States." And as he explained it, "with the courtesy of a gentleman" and "the authority and dignity of a presiding officer," his proposal was in the best republican tradition. He did not wish to interfere with slavery in the older states, or even in the Alabama Territory, which was surrounded by slave states. That would be playing with fire: it might set off a slave insurrection. But beyond the Mississippi, in new territory paid for by the entire nation, slavery was justly subject to national legislation. His amendment merely applied to Missouri the same pattern of race relations that existed in neighboring states. It merely extended to Missouri the same program of gradual emancipation that the revolutionary generation had enacted in New York, New Jersey, and other northern states. Even the great Jefferson, in words that were frequently quoted, advocated that slavery be abolished gradually by "imperceptible degrees." Here, then, was the opportunity: the proportion of slaves in Missouri was no greater than it had once been in New York. Why let slavery, "with its baleful consequences," inherit the entire West? Why disgrace the republican heritage by letting the "original sin" engulf Missouri?[41]

On the day after the Tallmadge amendment passed the House, John W. Taylor tried to extend it to the Arkansas Territory, a new territory to be created out of the southern portion of the old Missouri Territory. Missouri's leaders had sought statehood only for people living in the northern portion of the Missouri Territory, people living above the latitude line of 36° 30′. That meant that if Congress approved statehood for Missouri, the 14,000 people who lived below the line would be without civil government. Their leaders organized and applied for territorial status.

To the bill which would establish the Arkansas Territory, Taylor proposed an amendment similar to the Tallmadge amendment. If Taylor could maintain the northern majority that supported the Tallmadge amendment, the House would have barred slavery from

41. Hammond, *Political Parties in New York*, 2: 228; *Annals of Congress*, 15th Congress, 2d session, 1818–19, pp. 1203–14.

the entire nation west of the Mississippi, except for Louisiana, which had already entered the Union as a slave state.[42]

The House, sitting as a committee of the whole, rejected by a sixty-eight to eighty vote the first clause of the Taylor amendment prohibiting the further introduction of slavery into Arkansas, but approved by acclamation the second clause, which gradually freed all slave children born within the territory. The next day, in a formal session of the House, Taylor reintroduced his amendment. The first part was again rejected by a close vote of seventy-one to seventy-two, and the second part was again approved by a close vote of seventy-five to seventy-three. After a number of parliamentary maneuvers, the House agreed to consider the matter again the following day. This time, with both sides in full force, Speaker Clay broke an eighty-eight to eighty-eight tie, and after still another vote, Arkansas was opened to slavery.[43]

The Senate, as predicted, endorsed the proslavery Arkansas bill and rejected the Missouri bill with the Tallmadge amendment. Thus, after Tallmadge left Washington permanently in the spring of 1819, the Missouri question was still a matter of hot debate.

Pundits now talked freely of disunion and civil war. State legislators debated and formulated resolutions to send to Washington. Congress, when it convened again in December, went over the same ground again, but at much greater length. Everyone, it seemed, had to make a speech on the Missouri question. "So eager has been the competition to obtain the floor," wrote a New Hampshire congressman, "that a modest man would hardly dare to rise among such a mob."[44]

Throughout the two-year battle Tallmadge and Taylor, along with their fellow restrictionists, put Jeffersonian liberals on the defensive. Defenders of slavery like South Carolina's William Loughton Smith

42. White, *Politics on the Southwestern Frontier,* 5–8; William R. Johnson, "Prelude to the Missouri Compromise: A New York Congressman's Effort to Exclude Slavery from Arkansas Territory," *The New-York Historical Society Quarterly* 48 (January 1964): 31–50; *Annals of Congress,* 15th Congress, 2d session, 1818–19, p. 1235.

43. *Annals of Congress,* 15th Congress, 2d session, 1818–19, pp. 1235, 1237–39, 1272–74; *National Intelligencer,* 20 February 1819.

44. Everett S. Brown, ed., *The Missouri Compromise and Presidential Politics, 1820–1825, from the Letters of William Plumer, Junior, Representative of New Hampshire* (St. Louis, 1926), 7.

could simply dismiss their appeal as nonsense, but men like Kentucky's Henry Clay and Virginia's Philip Barbour were being asked to live up to their word. For years they had denounced slavery in the abstract. Why, then, did they want to fasten the same evil system on Missouri? To meet the challenge, the two men spoke for "the cause of humanity" and argued that the condition of the slaves would improve immensely if they were spread over a large area. Indeed, everyone would benefit. The fertile West would provide slaves with cheaper and more abundant food, and they would be happier and healthier than if they were cooped up in the Old South. At the same time, the scattering of the slave population would reduce the danger of insurrection.[45]

Jeffersonian liberals also harped on the theme that Tallmadge, Taylor, and the other restrictionists were not true humanitarians. The two New Yorkers, so the argument went, had no interest in the plight of the slave. They were motivated strictly by the desire for political power. Jefferson himself saw a Federalist plot at work, but others realized that both the Tallmadge and Taylor amendments originated with northern Republicans and that most of the amendments' supporters were northern Republicans.[46]

Were these men politically motivated? Undoubtedly, they were. Nearly every northern Republican, in the two-year battle over Missouri, spoke about the unfairness of the three-fifths rule. And nearly every northern state legislature, most of which were dominated by Republicans, sent a resolution to Congress complaining about the three-fifths rule. But, at the same time, northern Republicans presented a humanitarian argument. In so doing, they appealed to the Declaration of Independence, to the Bible, to "the opinion of the world," and to God. Their speeches and resolutions were some-

45. *Annals of Congress*, 15th Congress, 2d session, 1818–19, pp. 1174–75, 1184–93.

46. Ford, *Works of Thomas Jefferson*, 12: 180, 186–9; Lipscomb and Bergh, eds., *Writings of Thomas Jefferson*, 15: 280–1, 300–1, 491–3; Gaillard Hunt, ed., *The Writings of James Madison*, 9 vols. (New York, 1910), 9: 22; Stanislaus Murray Hamilton, ed., *The Writings of James Monroe*, 7 vols. (New York, 1902), 6: 114; *Annals of Congress*, 16th Congress, 1st session, 1819–20, p. 1436; *St. Louis Enquirer*, 10 November 1819; *Autobiography of Martin Van Buren*, 2 vols., ed. John C. Fitzpatrick (Washington, D.C., 1920), 1: 136–8; Thomas Hart Benton, *Thirty Years' View*, 2 vols. (New York, 1854–57), 1: 10.

times short on consistency, sometimes short on clarity, but rarely short in length. Most attacked the slavery question from every possible angle.[47]

In the end, it took all of Henry Clay's manipulative genius to bring the two-year battle over Missouri to a close. First, by using his full power as Speaker, Clay tried to ram Missouri down northern throats by making "the admission of Missouri the condition of that of Maine," which was also applying for statehood. That strategy failed. Finally, Senator Jesse Thomas of Illinois added a proviso to Clay's proposal that "forever prohibited" slavery in all parts of the Louisiana Purchase north of 36° 30´ with the single exception of Missouri. Clay then split the bill into two parts, so that southerners who opposed the Thomas Proviso could not join forces with northerners who opposed Missouri, and on the crucial vote to admit Missouri as a slave state he got a ninety to eighty-seven majority.

There were two more crucial battles after the two-year Missouri donnybrook. One was over the Missouri Constitution, which contained a

47. In *Space, Time, and Freedom: The Quest for Nationality and the Irrepressible Conflict, 1815–1861* (Westport, Conn., 1974), 22–48, 244 n. 4, Major L. Wilson detects a "significant difference" between the way northern members of the two national parties handled the Tallmadge amendments. The Federalists, he argues, were "keenly aware of the distinction between the political and moral argument" and preferred to place primary emphasis on the political argument, while northern Jeffersonians "mingled the two far more fully." At first glance Wilson seems to have a valid point. The Boston Federalist Harrison Gray Otis, who initially voted against the Tallmadge amendments and then regretted it, made a concerted effort to tone down the moral argument in Massachusetts. He also had help from John Lowell and several other prominent Federalists. But Otis, it turns out, was just being devious. Convinced that the Tallmadge amendments would go down to defeat if they were identified with Federalism, Otis wanted the northern Jeffersonians to take the lead. So in the second battle over the Tallmadge amendments, he worked behind the scenes to quiet the Federalists in New England. That was no easy task. Massachusetts Federalists had already taken a public stand against the Missouri bill, and some Massachusetts Federalists refused to abide by Otis's wishes. (Cf. *Boston Centinel*, 4 December 1819; "Memorial to Congress on Restraining the Increase in Slavery, December 15, 1819," in *The Writings and Speeches of Daniel Webster*, national ed., 18 vols. [Boston, 1903], 15: 55–73; Harrison Gray Otis to William Sullivan, 9, 13 February 1820, *Life and Letters of Harrison Gray Otis, Federalist*, 2 vols., ed. Samuel Eliot Morison [Boston, 1913], 2: 225–8; and Christopher Gore to Rufus King, 28, 29 January 1820, William Tudor to Rufus King, 12 February 1820, *Life and Correspondence*, 6: 259–61, 271–4.)

provision requiring the state legislature to pass laws to exclude free blacks and mulattoes from coming into the state, or settling in the state, "under any pretext whatsoever." The restrictionists immediately jumped on this clause, claiming that it represented an act of defiance on the part of Missouri, and that it violated the privileges and immunities of United States citizens. After a three-month stalemate, Clay worked out a second Missouri compromise, whereby Missouri should not gain admission to the Union until the legislature pledged that the controversial clause would never be construed as sanctioning the passage of any law abridging the privileges and immunities of United States citizens. The Missouri legislature never fully accepted this condition, but President Monroe pretended that it did and in August 1821 proclaimed the admission of Missouri as the twenty-fourth state.

The other battle was over who would be Clay's successor as Speaker of the House. Northern Republicans, who now had eighteen more seats in the House than their southern colleagues, put forth Tallmadge's close friend John W. Taylor as the Republican candidate. Southern Republicans refused to support him, and to them it mattered not in the least if he had the backing of the caucus or not. But instead of agreeing on an alternative candidate, some supported William Lowndes of South Carolina, some Samuel Smith of Maryland. As a result, instead of running one man for Speaker in 1820 and winning on the first ballot, the party had three men, all calling themselves loyal Republicans, running against the Federalist John Sergeant of Pennsylvania. None of the four obtained a majority on the first ballot, nor the tenth, nor the twentieth. Finally, with the help of Sergeant's supporters, Taylor prevailed on the twenty-third ballot. Never before had a Speaker's election gone to more than three ballots. King Caucus was clearly on its last legs.[48]

The success of Taylor and the restrictionists was again fleeting. In 1821, after twelve ballots, Taylor lost the Speakership to a Virginian. In 1825 he tasted victory again on the second ballot, this time over four rivals. But in 1827 he lost on the first ballot to another Virginian. In each case, his role in the Missouri question was central. Southern Republicans never forgave him, and they ex-

48. Lientz, "House Speaker Elections," 70–1; *Annals of Congress,* 16th Congress, 2d session, 1820–21, pp. 434–8; Alexander, "John W. Taylor," 28–31; Adams, *Memoirs,* 5: 202–3.

ploited every division among his northern colleagues to finally drive him permanently out of the Speaker's chair.[49]

The failure of Taylor and the other restrictionists was largely due to the three-fifths rule. It dictated the impact of every vote that was cast.

That first became clear in the battle over the Arkansas bill. In defeating the Taylor amendment, a solid South had the help of fifteen northern representatives. Four of these northerners had supported the Tallmadge amendment to the Missouri bill only a few days earlier. One, Ezekiel Williams of Massachusetts, explained his position. Both the North and the South, he argued, should have access to land west of the Mississippi, and thus slaveholders should be kept out of Missouri but not out of Arkansas, since the "settled part of Arkansas will be south of the southerly line of Kentucky."[50]

Much was made out of Williams's defection. But what made his vote critical? Without the South's seventeen slave representatives, his vote would have carried little importance, and Henry Clay would never have been in a position to cast the decisive vote that broke an eighty-eight to eighty-eight tie. John Taylor, for one, was well aware of that fact.

The ultimate defeat of the Tallmadge amendment in 1820 was much like the defeat of Taylor amendment the previous year. In one sense, it resulted from the action of fourteen northern representatives who joined a solid South in voting to admit Missouri as a slave state. Yet, without the South's seventeen slave seats, the likelihood of Clay putting together a three-vote majority would have been slim at best. Historians later forgot this fact; the restrictionists who fought the battle never did. It thus became one of the crucial ingredients in the development of the Slave Power thesis.

Similar dynamics were at work in Taylor's effort to become the kingpin of the House, a powerful Speaker who, like Henry Clay,

49. John W. Taylor to E. Cowen, 21 February 1821, JWT to Richard Taylor, 12 December 1821, JWT to William D. Ford, 18 January 1822, JWT to R. M. Livingston, 3 May 1826, Taylor Papers; Adams, *Memoirs*, 5: 428–32, 434–46, 450–2, 524; 7: 68–72, 363, 368–9; Edward K. Spann, "The Souring of Good Feelings: John W. Taylor and the Speakership Election of 1821," *New York History* 41 (October 1960): 379–99; *Dictionary of American Biography* (New York, 1936), 18: 336.

50. *Annals of Congress*, 15th Congress, 2d session, 1818–19, pp. 1276–79.

controlled the gavel year after year. Taylor had serious trouble with some northern Republicans who branded him a Clintonian and refused to support him.[51] But his main problem was the South's slave seats. Without them, he would have had an easier time getting elected in the first place—and a much easier time whipping party members into line and holding onto the Speakership. Again, he was keenly aware of that disadvantage.

Not only did the three-fifths rule make a difference in the political lives of Taylor and Tallmadge, but it continued to make a difference in the years to come. In 1830, for example, Andrew Jackson rammed through Congress the Indian Removal Act to acquire the lands of great southern tribes living east of the Mississippi. The bill was never as popular as historians later made out in textbooks, nor was it merely a triumph for Georgia and the West as scholars have often assumed. The bill sparked a furious debate and barely got through Congress, failing to clear the House on several test votes, and passing by a margin of 102 to 97 on the final vote. The vote was largely sectional, with two out of three northerners voting against the bill and four out of five southerners voting in favor.[52] Without the South's twenty-three slave seats, Andrew Jackson would have had to twist the arms of ten to fifteen more Pennsylvania and Ohio Democrats to get the needed majority. Could he have done so? At what cost?

Similarly, ten years later, southern hotspurs wanted a tougher gag rule to stifle the antislavery movement. The previous gag, first passed in 1836, called for the automatic tabling of any petition dealing in any way with the subject of slavery. It was a temporary House rule, one that had to be renewed at each session of Congress, and thus there were a few weeks at the beginning of each session when it was not in effect. That irritated some southerners. They wanted a permanent rule so that John Quincy Adams and other northern congressmen would never have the opportunity to legally present antislavery petitions. They also wanted a "more decided seal of reprobation" on such petitions. In keeping with these desires, in 1840 William Cost

---

51. Spann, "Souring of Good Feelings," 379–99.

52. *Register of Debates,* 21st Congress, 1st session, 1829–30, pp. 383, 456, 1132–33; Dale Van Every, *Disinherited: The Lost Birthright of the American Indian* (New York, 1966), 117, 120; Anthony F. C. Wallace, *The Long, Bitter Trail: Andrew Jackson and the Indians* (New York, 1993), 65–70.

Johnson of Maryland pushed for a more drastic gag rule, one that entailed the outright rejection of antislavery petitions and also made this measure a standing House rule. In the eyes of most northerners, the Johnson gag went too far, violating among other things the "sacred right to petition." It passed by just six votes, 114 to 108.[53] Without the South's twenty-five slave seats, southern Democrats would have had to win the support of ten more northern Democrats on this vote. Could they have done so? Again, at what cost?

When Stephen A. Douglas orchestrated the repeal of the Thomas Proviso in 1854, he too was dependent on the South's twenty-two slave seats. Without them, he would have had to persuade five more northern Democrats to vote against the ban on slavery north of the 36° 30′ line. As it was, he had to fight an uphill battle of nearly three months to whip the northern wing of his party into line.[54]

Lincoln and Seward, of course, were well aware of this fact. They had come of age hearing complaints about the impact of the three-fifths rule. And in their eyes, it was one of dynamic ingredients that made the Slave Power a reality. But there was another dynamic ingredient, one that irritated them even more—northerners who sided with the South, northerners who had come to be known as "dough-faces."

53. *Congressional Globe*, 26th Congress, 1st session, 1839–40, pp. 121, 150–1; William Cost Johnson, *Speech . . . on the Subject of . . . Petitions for the Abolition of Slavery* (Washington, D.C., 1840); Leonard L. Richards, *The Life and Times of Congressman John Quincy Adams* (New York, 1986), 115–28, 176–7.

54. *Congressional Globe*, 33d Congress, 1st Session (1853–54), 532; Appendix, 325–38; David Potter, *The Impending Crisis, 1848–1861* (New York, 1976), 165–67; Roy F. Nichols, *Blueprints for Leviathan: American Style* (New York, 1963), 104–20.

4 | Randolph's Pejorative

To the disgust of Rufus King, not every New York congressman supported the Tallmadge amendment.[1] On the crucial vote in 1820 to admit Missouri as a slave state, two New Yorkers "fought under the black flag" and two others "fled the field on the day of battle."[2]

The two blackguards who voted with the South were Henry Meigs of New York City and Henry Storrs of Whitestown. Meigs, a Connecticut Yankee by birth and a Yale graduate, was a Tammany Hall chieftain and the nephew of the postmaster general. Serving in his first and only Congress, Meigs's chief concern was federal patronage. He was a conduit between state politicians who sought federal patronage and those in Washington who had it to dispense.[3] His

1. King himself had voted against one half of the Tallmadge amendment in 1819, the part that would have freed the unborn children of Missouri slaves, but by 1820 he had conveniently forgotten that fact.

2. Charles R. King, ed., *The Life and Correspondence of Rufus King*, 6 vols. (New York, 1894–1900), 6: 291.

3. Henry Meigs to Josiah Meigs, 20 November 1818, Henry Meigs Papers, New-York Historical Society; Martin Van Buren to Henry Meigs, 4 April 1820, Henry Meigs to Van Buren, 10 April, 26 November 1820, Martin Van Buren Papers, Library of Congress (microfilm). See also Solomon Nadler, "Federal Patronage and New York Politics, 1801–1830" (Ph.D. dissertation, New York University, 1973).

vote was taken for granted by his New York colleagues. Storrs was also a Connecticut Yankee by birth and a Yale graduate, but he had no ties with the Monroe administration. On the contrary, he was a Federalist, a member of King's own party. Serving in his second term, he voted against the Tallmadge amendment in 1819, against the Taylor amendment to the Arkansas bill, and in favor of admitting Missouri as a slave state in 1820. King was totally disgusted with Storrs's behavior, and so were the Federalists in Storrs's district. They refused to nominate him for a third term in 1820. Yet, he would return to Congress three years later and serve until 1831.

Of the two New Yorkers who "fled the field on the day of battle," the one who most concerned King was Caleb Tompkins of White Plains. Tompkins's younger brother was the vice president, a schemer in King's eyes, who had long been dependent on the Virginians, first for patronage when he was governor of New York and now for his present position. Yet, despite his younger brother's political obligations, Caleb Tompkins had sided with the restrictionists in the early rounds of the Missouri controversy. He had supported both the Tallmadge and Taylor amendments in 1819. But in 1820, when the Missouri statehood bill came up for a final vote, he was conspicuously absent. King wondered how his absence would be construed. William W. Van Ness, one of King's allies, left no doubt. "That miserable sycophant" of a vice president, thundered Van Ness, "betrayed us to the lords of the South, to enable him to subserve his own interests."[4] Shortly thereafter, Caleb Tompkins dropped out of congressional politics and became a county judge.

Altogether, there were fourteen northerners who voted with South on the Missouri bill, and at least three others who purposely missed the crucial vote. King listed all of them in his correspondence and denounced them in the harshest terms.[5] Particularly ap-

4. King, *Life and Correspondence,* 6: 291; DeAlva S. Alexander, "John W. Taylor: New York's Speaker of the House of Representatives," *Quarterly Journal of the New York State Historical Association* 1 (January 1920): 28; Catharina V. R. Bonney, comp., *A Legacy of Historical Gleanings,* 2 vols. (Albany, N.Y., 1875), 1: 360–5.

5. A fourth northern congressman, Henry W. Edwards of Connecticut, also missed the vote. In a public apology to his constituents, he said that he had left the House chamber to get a bite to eat, assuming that the debate would continue for another hour or two, but because the Virginia congressman who had the floor fainted, the vote was taken earlier than anticipated. King apparently accepted this explanation. The *Hartford Courant* (28 March 1820) did not.

palling to King was the number of Yankees on the list. Not only did the two New Yorkers, Meigs and Storrs, hail from New England, but so did Henry Baldwin of Pittsburgh. And in addition to these men were two representatives from Maine, two from the "old state" of Massachusetts, two from Connecticut, one from Rhode Island, and one from Vermont. Thus, to King's disgust, eleven of the seventeen miscreants were fellow Yankees. Even more dismaying was the behavior of King's own half brother William, the kingpin of Maine politics, who at first sided with King and the restrictionists but ended up supporting the two Maine congressmen who voted with the South.[6]

King never found words to adequately describe his distaste for these men. Nor did any other northerner who railed against the outcome of the Missouri battle. The man who provided the words was John Randolph of Roanoke, who had represented Virginia in the House for seventeen years. Undoubtedly one of the weirdest men to ever serve in Congress, Randolph horrified northerners and fascinated them at the same time. They marveled at his high soprano voice, his boyish features, his hunting dogs, his whips, and his addiction to alcohol and opium. They knew that he was half crazy most of the time and completely mad on occasion. But they realized that even when he was in a towering rage, tilting at windmills, seemingly completely out of his mind, he had a gift that they lacked. In an age of oratory, he was a star performer, and one who spoke best in moments of doubtable sanity. He came to Congress dressed for a hunt, dogs at his side, whip in hand, and flayed his opponents with words. His invective, in particular, was always memorable.

Like King, Randolph had no use for northerners who voted with the South. Hence, once the South acquired their votes, he declared that he knew all along that these men would give way. They were weak men, timid men, half-baked men. "They were scared at their own dough faces—yes, *they were scared at their own dough faces!*—We had *them*, and if we wanted *three* more, we could have had them: yes, and if *these* had failed, we could have three more of

6. King, *Life and Correspondence*, 6: 291; Ronald F. Banks, *Maine Becomes a State: The Movement to Separate Maine from Massachusetts, 1785–1820* (Middletown, Conn., 1970), 191–7.

these men, *whose conscience, and morality, and religion, extend to 'thirty-six degrees and thirty minutes north latitude.'*"[7]

Not everyone understood Randolph's reference, and no one dared to ask for an explanation. A few apparently thought the sardonic Virginia aristocrat had a female deer in mind and the word he used was *doe*. Others thought he was referring to a child's game where children put dough on their faces, worked it up into strange configurations, and then looked at their reflections.[8]

Whatever Randolph had in mind, his words stuck. *Doughface* quickly became a synonym for "northern men with southern principles." It was applied indiscriminately to any northern man who voted with the South, regardless of his reasons. And in some circles it was also applied to any northern congressman who missed a crucial vote, to any northern newspaper that truckled to the South, to any northern clergyman who placated the South. Subserviency and servility were always connoted by the word, and in 1847 Webster's dictionary defined doughfacism as the "willingness to be led about by one of stronger mind and will."

The seventeen or eighteen doughfaces whom Randolph belittled made sectional peace possible in 1820. Along with the additional votes the South had because of three-fifths rule, they provided Henry Clay with his ninety to eighty-seven majority in the House of Representatives. Other doughfaces would play the same crucial role, time and again, of voting solidly with southern Republicans on slavery issues in the years to come. In 1836, when southern leaders demanded a gag rule to stop antislavery petitions from being read in the House, mentioned in the House, or printed in the official record, sixty northern congressmen went along with the South. Eleven years later, in the battle over the Wilmot Proviso to bar slavery in lands taken from Mexico, twenty-seven northerners sided with the South. In the 1850 showdown over the southern demand for a tougher fugitive slave law, one that gave the pursuers of runaway slaves more legal rights at the expense of northern whites and alleged runaways, thirty-five northerners yielded to the South. And in 1854, when the Kansas-Nebraska Act repealed the Missouri Com-

7. Quoted in Glover Moore, *The Missouri Controversy, 1819–1821* (Lexington, Ky., 1953), 104.
8. F. H. Hodder, "Doughfaces," *Nation* 100 (4 March 1915): 245.

promise's ban on slavery in the northern part of the Louisiana Purchase, fifty-eight northerners followed the dictates of their party leaders and voted with the South.[9]

The slave states, in contrast, had complete unity, not only in the battle over Missouri in 1820, but also over the Fugitive Slave Act of 1850. Occasionally a few southern congressmen took an essentially northern position: eight refused to support the gag in 1836; two supported the Wilmot Proviso in 1847; and eleven opposed the Kansas-Nebraska Act in 1854. Such men were labeled traitors in the southern press,[10] but their votes were not decisive, and they never had the impact on national politics that doughfaces did. The latter, in voting with the South on crucial measures, turned a southern minority position in the House, and the nation at large, into a majority political position.

There had been such men, of course, before the Missouri crisis. Indeed, there had been such men at the Constitutional Convention, and one could argue that Rufus King was one of them. But until Randolph gave them a name in 1820, they had never stood out in the public eye. They voted with the South and then disappeared among the great mass of northern politicians. With Randolph's epithet, they no longer had that luxury. John Holmes of Maine, for example, worked closely with southern leaders on both the Arkansas bill and the Missouri bills, and in so doing probably gained statehood for Maine. Many in Maine celebrated his leadership, and a grateful state legislature sent him to the United States Senate in 1820 and 1829. But Holmes never escaped the label Randolph pinned on him. He was forever remembered in the Portland press as

9. *House Journal*, 24th Congress, 1st session, 1835–36, p. 884; *Congressional Globe*, 29th Congress, 2d session, 1846–47, pp. 555, 573; Holman Hamilton, *Prologue to Conflict: The Crisis and Compromise of 1850* (Lexington, Ky., 1964), 190–1, 195–200; *Congressional Globe*, 31st Congress, 1st session, 1849–50, p. 1807; David M. Potter, *The Impending Crisis, 1848–1861* (New York, 1976), 165, 167; *Congressional Globe*, 33d Congress, 1st session, 1853–54, pp. 532, 1254.

10. J. M. Garnett, *Life of Charles Fenton Mercer* (Richmond, Va., 1911); Douglas R. Egerton, *Charles Fenton Mercer and the Trial of National Conservatism* (Jackson, Miss., 1989), especially chap. 2; John Howard Parks, *John Bell of Tennessee* (Baton Rouge, 1950), 294–301; Benjamin C. Merkel, "The Slavery Issue and the Political Decline of Thomas Hart Benton, 1846–1856," *Missouri Historical Review* 38 (July 1944): 388–407.

the "unblushing advocate of domestic slavery" and the "doughface of doughfaces."[11]

The men whom Randolph belittled in 1820 were all House members. In showering contempt on those northerners who provided Speaker Clay with a ninety to eighty-seven majority in the House on the vote to admit Missouri as a slave state, the acerbic Virginian ignored what had happened in the Senate. Yet during his lifetime and afterwards, the Senate was where doughfaces had the greatest impact.

It was largely a matter of numbers. As long as there was an equal number of slave and free states, the South needed just one northern vote to be an effective majority in the Senate. Usually Randolph and his southern colleagues could count on a half-dozen northern senators. At the time of the Missouri crisis, for example, they had the solid support of Illinois's first two senators, Ninian Edwards and Jesse Thomas. Thirty years later, they had the solid support of Iowa's first two senators, Augustus Caesar Dodge and George Wallace Jones. In North-South contests, these men might as well have been representing Alabama or Mississippi.

Controlling the Senate, therefore, was child's play for southern leaders. Time and again a bill threatening to the South made its way through the House only to be blocked in the Senate. In 1819, for example, after the House endorsed the Tallmadge amendments, the Senate rejected them. Five northern senators voted against Tallmadge's proposal to stop slaveholders from bringing additional slaves into Missouri, and twelve voted against his proposal to eventually free the unborn children of Missouri slaves. The same five northern senators voted with the South on both measures: Edwards and Thomas of Illinois, Harrison Gray Otis of Massachusetts, Abner Lacock of Pennsylvania, and William Palmer of Vermont. Included in the group that voted for the first measure but against the second was Rufus King, who had yet to launch his full-scale attack against the Slave Power.[12] That would come the following December.

Virtually the same scenario was repeated a quarter of the century

11. *Portland Gazette,* 14 March–30 May 1820; *Boston Columbian Centinel,* 19 July 1820; *Niles' Weekly Register* 31 (9 September 1826), 23; William Willis, *A History of the Law, the Courts, and Lawyers of Maine* (Portland, Maine, 1863), 275–89, 307–8.

12. *Annals of Congress,* 15th Congress, 2d session, 1818–19, p. 273.

later during the Mexican War. In 1846, in the closing hours of the congressional session, the House passed the Wilmot Proviso to bar slavery from any land taken from Mexico. In that session, the Senate adjourned without voting on the measure, but in the next session, when the House added the proviso to another appropriation bill, the Senate voted the proviso down, twenty-one to thirty-one. Among the naysayers were twenty-six slave-state senators and five free-state senators, two from Indiana, one from Illinois, one from Michigan, and one from New York.[13] The proviso never became law, and eventually the northern third of Mexico was added to the United States with no strings attached.

There were other occasions, as well, when southern leaders had to make herculean efforts to get their way in the House but had an easy time of it in the Senate. That, for example, was the case with the Arkansas bill of 1819. It took all of Henry Clay's skill to get that bill through the House, but in the Senate it passed with ease. James Burrill of Rhode Island tried to add the same restrictions that Tallmadge and Taylor had fought for in the House, but four northern senators voted against these restraints. Along with Edwards and Thomas (the two Illinois senators who always voted with the South) were Waller Taylor of Indiana and Jeremiah Morrow of Ohio. Burrill thus had only fourteen votes, his opponents had nineteen, and Arkansas became a territory fully open to slavery.[14]

A variant of this story was repeated again a decade later with Andrew Jackson's proposal to move the great tribes of the South to land west of the Mississippi. Jackson's Indian Removal Act of 1830, as we will see in more detail in the next chapter, was a difficult bill for northerners to support. And the most formidable spokesman against Indian Removal, Theodore Frelinghuysen of New Jersey, was a senator. Hence, unlike the Arkansas bill of 1819, the Indian Removal Act did not sail through the Senate in 1830. Jackson had to twist arms to get the bill passed. But, in the end, he found it much easier to get the bill through the Senate than the House. Indian

13. *Congressional Globe*, 29th Congress, 2d session, 1846–47, p. 555. For the ideological context of the Wilmot Proviso battle, see Eric Foner, "The Wilmot Proviso Revisited," *Journal of American History* 61 (September 1969): 262–79. Also illuminating is Major L. Wilson, *Space, Time, and Freedom: The Quest for Nationality and the Irrepressible Conflict, 1815–1861* (Westport, Conn., 1974), 22–48, 244 n. 4, chap. 6.

14. *Annals of Congress*, 15th Congress, 2d session, 1818–19, p. 274.

Removal barely squeaked through the House, 102 to 97, while it passed the Senate with votes to spare, 28 to 19. Voting for removal were nine northern senators, including both Illinois senators, both Indiana senators, and both New York senators.[15]

Getting the Fugitive Slave Act of 1850 passed was hardly a cakewalk, either. The seventy-three-year-old Henry Clay addressed the Senate seventy times in defense of his omnibus bill in which the Fugitive Slave Act was a key part. Finally, emotionally and physically exhausted, Clay left for Newport to recover, and Stephen A. Douglas stepped into the breach, split the omnibus bill into its separate parts, and ushered each part through Congress. The Senate was again less troublesome than the House. In the end, the Senate passed the measure first, and overwhelmingly, by a twenty-seven to twelve vote. Along with the two Iowans, Dodge and Jones, who were conspicuously proslavery, Daniel Sturgeon of Pennsylvania voted with the South. Fifteen other northern senators, including Douglas himself, missed the vote.[16] Three weeks later the House passed the measure, and it was quickly signed into law.

Four years later, in what became this nation's fiercest congressional battle, Douglas spent three and a half months fighting to get the Kansas-Nebraska Act through Congress. Bitterly attacked in and out of Congress, he could have traveled home to Chicago, as he said, by the light of his own burning effigies. For five weeks he totally dominated the Senate before bringing the bill up for a vote. The Senate passed the bill by an overwhelming margin, thirty-seven to fourteen. Voting to repeal the "sacred" Missouri Compromise were fourteen free-state senators, including both California senators, both Iowa senators, both Illinois senators, both Michigan senators, and both New Hampshire senators.[17] In the House the revolt of free-soilers was far more extensive. As a result, the bill was sent to the committee of the whole, where it was buried beneath fifty other bills. It took lavish grants of presidential patronage, along with threats to cut the bill's foes off from all federal spoils, to get the House to table the other bills and bring Kansas-Nebraska up for consideration. Finally, amid threats of bloodshed and the brandishing of weapons, the House passed the measure, 113 to 100.

15. *Register of Debates,* 21st Congress, 1st session, 1829–30, p. 383.
16. Hamilton, *Prologue to Conflict,* appendix A, 190–1.
17. *Congressional Globe,* 33d Congress, 1st session, 1853–54, p. 532.

In 1858 the House could not be won over, although the Senate still could. This time the issue was President Buchanan's attempt to get Congress to endorse the notoriously unrepresentative Lecompton constitution and admit Kansas into the Union as a slave state. At this point Douglas, fighting for survival at home and long the champion of "popular sovereignty," broke with the president and fought against the Slave Power. Buchanan, however, knew that he had the votes he needed in the Senate. After a spirited battle with Douglas, the president easily carried the Senate, thirty-three to twenty-five.[18] Buchanan's problem was the House, and even though he used the full power of the presidency to win over the disaffected—patronage, government contracts, commissions of various kinds, wine and women, even cash—he ultimately failed there.

Control of the Senate, along with control of the dominant party and of the White House, also meant that the South had a large voice in presidential appointments. Heads of departments, territorial governors, foreign ministers and consuls, chief accounting officers, judges of the federal courts, postmasters in the larger cities, collectors of custom, land agents, and district attorneys all needed Senate confirmation. Some appointments had required confirmation since Washington's day, others since the Tenure of Office Act of 1820. As the population grew and the country expanded, so too did the number of officers needing the Senate's blessing. By the 1850s there were over nine hundred such officers.

Since the days of Washington, every president had attended personally to these high-level appointments. Many presidents spent an inordinate amount of time dealing with them. Indeed, even lesser appointments often demanded many hours of the chief executive's time. Thanks to the diaries of John Quincy Adams and James K. Polk, we know that the process was an ordeal, a major presidential headache as well as a major presidential chore. Some sort of geo-

18. *Congressional Globe,* 35th Congress, 1st session, 1857–58, pp. 1264–65. Of the many excellent full-scale accounts of the Kansas crisis, the most recent is Kenneth M. Stampp, *1857: A Nation on the Brink* (New York, 1990), chaps. 10–12. Of the many books that emphasize Douglas's spirited battle in behalf of popular sovereignty, see Robert W. Johannsen, *Stephen A. Douglas* (New York, 1973), chap. 23, and Michael A. Morrison, *Slavery and the American West: The Eclipse of Manifest Destiny and the Coming of the Civil War* (Chapel Hill, 1997), chap. 7.

graphical balance always had to be found, and usually some sort of balance also had to be found between various factions within the party. According to Adams, half of the senators and representatives wanted offices for themselves, and another quarter sought offices for their relatives. According to Polk, senators like Sidney Breese of Illinois gave him no rest, always seeking major offices for their friends, complaining about appointments that went to others, and causing the White House to make some very bad decisions.[19]

Not every president, moreover, always got his way. Andrew Jackson in particular had a number of appointments rejected. In his first two years, he ran afoul of the Senate in appointing New England loyalists to customs houses in New Bedford and Portsmouth, to the district attorney's office in New Hampshire, and to the controller's office in Washington. Subsequently, his appointment of Martin Van Buren as minister to England was rejected, as was his repeated attempt to appoint Samuel Gwin as registrar of a Mississippi land office. The latter incident eventually led to a celebrated duel in which one man was killed and Gwin severely wounded.[20]

Yet, despite the presidential woes and the occasional rejections, the president was ultimately in control. And southerners, more often than not, controlled both the White House and the Senate. So it is not surprising that southern men came to occupy more than their fair share of important government posts. From 1789 to 1861, according to one study, half of all the cabinet and diplomatic appointments went to men from the slave states. According to another study, southerners held 51 percent of the top government posts under John Adams, 56 percent under Jefferson, and 57 percent under Jackson.[21]

But that was not the most telling fact. What is more striking is that the bias in favor of the South was so well entrenched that even southern extremists were given key government posts. By 1844, for

19. *Memoirs of John Quincy Adams, Comprising Portions of His Diary from 1795 to 1848,* 12 vols., ed. Charles Francis Adams (Philadelphia, 1974–77) 5: 238; Milo M. Quaife, ed., *Diary of James K. Polk during His Presidency,* 4 vols. (Chicago, 1910), 2: 426.

20. Leonard D. White, *The Jacksonians: A Study in Administrative History, 1829–1861* (New York, 1954), 106–11; *Niles' Weekly Register* 49 (6 February 1836): 389.

21. Philip H. Burch, Jr., *Elites in American History: The Federalist Years to the Civil War* (New York, 1981), 236–7; Sidney H. Aronson, *Status and Kinship in the Higher Civil Service* (Cambridge, Mass., 1964), 115.

example, John C. Calhoun of South Carolina was as extreme in his proslavery views as William Lloyd Garrison was in his antislavery views. Yet, while no president ever appointed an outspoken abolitionist to high office,[22] much less a man of Garrison's views, in 1844 President Tyler nominated Calhoun to be secretary of state, and the Senate confirmed the nomination without bothering to hold a hearing and without giving the matter a second thought.[23]

Calhoun, one might object, was by then a distinguished elder statesman who had given the best years of his life to federal service, and thus rejecting him was next to impossible. But that argument hardly applies to others who received top federal appointments. Consider, for example, the appointment of Nicholas P. Trist to the state department shortly after Calhoun left office. Trist lacked Calhoun's long and distinguished record. He was also less doctrinaire. He was just a well-connected Virginian with, to put it mildly, a checkered career. He had married Jefferson's granddaughter, studied law in Jefferson's law office, and served briefly as Jackson's private secretary. But after he was appointed consul to Cuba in 1833, he had become notorious for aiding and abetting American citizens engaged in the illegal African slave trade. Indeed, official Washington had been deluged with documents indicating that he was conniving with slave-trading "pirates."[24] Nonetheless, in 1845 Polk appointed him chief

22. By the mid-1840s even mild critics of slavery like Democrat Marcus Morton of Massachusetts had trouble getting federal appointments. Nominated to head the Boston customs office, he had to squirm for months and repeatedly deny any association with abolitionists to get Senate confirmation. See his letterbook, December 1845–April 1846, Marcus Morton Papers, Massachusetts Historical Society.

23. Charles M. Wiltse, *John C. Calhoun: Sectionalist, 1840–1850* (Indianapolis, 1951), 161. One much-disputed story has it that the nomination was forced on Tyler by Henry Wise of Virginia. Fearing the nomination wouldn't be made because Calhoun had twice refused the office, Wise allegedly took matters into his own hands, tendered the offer to Calhoun without Tyler's consent, and the outraged president went along with it. Cf. Henry A. Wise, *Seven Decades of the Union* (Philadelphia, 1876), 220–5; Wiltse, *Calhoun: Sectionalist*, 161–5, 508–9; and Craig M. Simpson, *A Good Southerner: The Life of Henry A. Wise of Virginia* (Chapel Hill, 1985), 57–8, 332 n. 42.

24. *House Reports*, 26th Congress, 1st session, 1839–40, no. 707; *House Documents*, 26th Congress, 2d session, 1840–41, no. 115; *Senate Documents*, 26th Congress, 2d session, 1840–41, no. 125; David Turnbull, *Travels in the West: Cuba; with Notices of Porto Rico, and the Slave Trade* (London, 1840), 435–59; William L. Mathieson, *Great Britain and the Slave Trade, 1839–1865* (London, 1929), 27.

clerk of the state department, and as such he served as acting secretary of state on several occasions, eventually going to Mexico to negotiate the treaty ending the Mexican War. Trist was subsequently fired, not for proslavery activity, but for disobeying the president.[25]

Consider the appointment of William Henry Trescot on the eve of the Civil War. Trescot also lacked Calhoun's long and distinguished record. He was just one of many South Carolina extremists who had made a name for himself defending the South and slavery. He was also an outspoken secessionist.[26] Yet in June 1860, at a time when the secretary of state was too infirm to carry out his duties, and talk of disunion and civil war was commonplace, Trescot was made assistant secretary of state. Months later, when the Union began to fall apart, Trescot stayed on the job and helped South Carolina secede. Indeed, he acted openly as a secessionist and as an agent of the secessionist governor of South Carolina. But he wasn't the only high official running errands for a secessionist governor. So too was Jacob Thompson of Mississippi, who had been appointed secretary of the interior.[27]

The same dynamics also assured the South of the dominant voice on the Supreme Court. Between Washington's election and Lincoln's, nineteen of the thirty-four Supreme Court appointees were slaveholders. Thus, while John Marshall's court and Roger Taney's court differed in their attitudes toward the burgeoning capitalism of the North, neither was a threat to slavery.

Many of Jefferson's followers, needless to say, never saw it that way. John Marshall, in their eyes, was a loose cannon who, in enhancing the power of northern capitalists, striking down acts of state legislatures, and aggrandizing the powers of the central government, had

25. Trist also had a falling out with the Democratic Party. Years later, he became a Lincoln Republican and after the Civil War obtained a postmastership from the Grant administration.

26. William Henry Trescot, *The Position and Course of the South* (Charleston, S.C., 1850); idem, "Oration before the South Carolina Historical Society," *Russell's Magazine* 3 (July 1859): 289–307.

27. Gaillard Hunt, ed., "Narrative and Letter of William Henry Trescot, Concerning the Negotiations between South Carolina and President Buchanan in December, 1860," *American Historical Review* 13 (April 1908): 528–56; Philip S. Klein, *President James Buchanan* (University Park, Pa., 1962), 353–4, 368–9, 378–9, 389–90; Roy F. Nichols, *Disruption of American Democracy* (New York, 1948), 406.

endangered the South. John Taylor and other Virginia Republicans contended that Marshall had virtually given Congress the right to free every slave in the Union. He thus had to be stopped before it was too late, and states' rights had to be restored as the first line of defense against the federal government tampering with slavery. Jefferson was generally in agreement with this sentiment, more so as time passed.

What Taylor and Jefferson overlooked, of course, was that the South's predicament might have been much worse if northerners had their fair share of seats on the Court, or if a northern justice like Joseph Story of Massachusetts sat in Marshall's chair. Marshall, a Virginia slaveholder, was no threat to slavery. He was much like Jefferson, critical of slavery in his youth, but no longer likely to do anything about it.[28] Like Jefferson, he clearly believed that the federal government had no right to meddle with slavery in states where it was established by law, and with some misgivings he defended slave representation and the planters' inordinate power in Virginia politics.[29] His associate Joseph Story, however, might have posed a real threat. On several occasions Story instructed jurors that slavery was "so repugnant to the natural rights of man and the dictates of justice" that it was difficult to find "any adequate justification" for it. At one point he declared the slave trade contrary to international law. Marshall and the southern majority on the Court overruled him.[30]

If Marshall was the wrong kind of slaveholder (a man who infuriated his fellow Virginians for some thirty years), the Jacksonian appointees who followed him were not. With the death of Marshall in 1835, as well as other deaths and resignations, Jackson and Van Buren had the opportunity to reshape the Court. They hardly filled it with the likes of Joseph Story. Of the eight men they appointed, six were slaveholders, and not one was suspect on the slavery question. That

28. Marshall's views on slavery were both more hardheaded and more softheaded than Jefferson's. On the one hand, Marshall rejected as wishful thinking the common Jeffersonian notion that science and progress would somehow eradicate slavery. On the other hand, he became a luminary in the American Colonization Society, which hoped to stimulate emancipation by sending free blacks "back to Africa," a project that Jefferson dismissed as a pipe dream.

29. *Proceedings and Debates of the Virginia Convention of 1829–1830* (Richmond, Va., 1830), especially 561f.

30. James McClellan, *Joseph Story and the American Constitution* (Norman, Okla., 1971), 297–9; Gerald T. Dunne, *Justice Joseph Story and the Rise of the Supreme Court* (New York, 1970), 241–6.

of course was not the only reason these men were selected. Jackson's choice for chief justice, Roger B. Taney of Maryland, undoubtedly was selected because he had been a loyal supporter since 1824, and as acting secretary of the treasury had done the president's bidding in removing federal deposits from the Bank of the United States. But he had also shown his true colors as Jackson's attorney general when he supported North Carolina's policy of jailing free black and mulatto sailors whenever their ships were in port.[31] True to form, in the Dred Scott case of 1857, he denied Congress's authority to prevent the spread of slavery in the territories. The five justices who joined him in that decision were cut from roughly the same cloth. All were good Jackson men, nominated to the Court by Jacksonian presidents and confirmed by Jacksonian senates. And all but one owned slaves.

Of the slaveholders on the Taney court, it was possible to argue that at least three of the associate justices—James M. Wayne of Georgia, John Catron of Tennessee, and John A. Campbell of Alabama—were reasonable and judicious men. All three, to be sure, were southern proslavery Democrats and firm defenders of slaveholding rights in the territories. But extremists? That was arguable. In the case of the fourth associate, Peter V. Daniel of Virginia, there was little room for argument. An aristocrat who had studied law under Washington's attorney general and married his mentor's daughter, Daniel was a proslavery fanatic, a fire-eater who likened abolitionists to monsters and refused to tread on northern soil, a brooding zealot who hoped that his fellow southerners would go to "any extremity" to ensure that slave property received greater protection than any other form of property. Appointed to the Court by Van Buren in 1841, he was proof that no southerner was so extreme in his proslavery views as to be ineligible for a lifetime appointment on the nation's highest court.[32]

If the Senate was such a bastion of southern strength, then how does one account for the furor over admitting California as a free state in

---

31. Carl B. Swisher, *Roger B. Taney* (New York, 1935), 146–7, 151–8.

32. John P. Frank, *Justice Daniel Dissenting: A Biography of Peter V. Daniel, 1784–1860* (Cambridge, Mass., 1964), 154–67, 243–6. For the intensity of Daniel's feeling against the Missouri Compromise's restrictions on slavery, see *Dred Scott v. John F. A. Sandford*, 19 Howard 393 (1857), 488–90.

1849 and 1850? The story is a familiar one, repeated in every American history textbook.

In 1848, thanks to the Mexican War, the United States forced Mexico to sell California to the United States. Nine days before the treaty was signed, a carpenter from New Jersey found several pieces of gold on the land of a Swiss immigrant, now a Mexican citizen, who had hoped to build an agricultural empire in the Sacramento valley. Within a year the discovery attracted hundreds of thousands of unruly immigrants and created a desperate need for some sort of government. In this crisis, President Zachary Taylor, to the horror of those southerners who supported him because he was a slaveholder, told the Californians to bypass the territorial stage, draw up a state constitution without bothering to get congressional authorization, and apply directly for admission as a free state when Congress convened in December 1849.

The Californians followed the president's direction and pasted together a constitution. In so doing, the statemakers outlawed slavery by unanimous vote. Not only did those who disliked slavery in principle vote for the ban, so too did men from the Deep South who still had slaves back in their native states. Many delegates contended that allowing slaves to work in the mines undermined the dignity of the white miners and hard manual labor; many also discussed the possibility of barring from California all blacks, free or slave, a step that had recently been taken in the Oregon Territory. The voters then ratified the constitution and simultaneously elected two congressmen. A few weeks later the new state legislature elected two United States senators. All four were sent straightway to Washington, even though there was as yet no assurance that California would be admitted to the Union as a free state.[33]

News of California's stand on slavery, along with Taylor's actions, infuriated southern congressmen. Passions flared, and the Congress that met in December 1849 was quickly out of control. With legislators screaming and shouting at one another, carrying Bowie knives and revolvers, the House took three weeks and sixty-

33. For details in this and the following paragraphs, I have relied on William H. Ellison, *A Self-Governing Dominion: California, 1849–1860* (Berkeley, 1950), chaps. 1–4; Cardinal Goodwin, *The Establishment of State Government in California, 1846–50* (New York, 1914); and Woodrow Hansen, *The Search for Authority in California* (Oakland, Calif., 1960).

three ballots to elect a Speaker, twenty-one ballots to elect a clerk, three ballots to elect a chaplain, and eight ballots to elect a sergeant at arms. In the Senate, the aged Henry Clay tried to rally the forces of moderation and compromise by presenting an omnibus bill covering all the disputed questions arising from the slavery issue. That hardly ended the turmoil. Southerners complained bitterly that the admission of California as a free state would cost the South its equal strength in the Senate. And what about New Mexico? Would it follow California's example and ask for admission as a free state? That, clearly, was what Zachary Taylor wanted. And that, said one southern spokesman after another, would make a bad situation even worse.[34] With California, the fifteen slave states would be outnumbered by sixteen free states, with New Mexico, by seventeen. The followers of Calhoun angrily threatened disunion. Mississippi's Jefferson Davis demanded that all the West lying below the Missouri Compromise line of 36° 30′ be open to slavery.

In the end, California was admitted as a free state, and New Mexico was given territorial status with the right to vote slavery up or down. The outcome created storms of protest across the Deep South. Opponents of a free California clamored for secession, and southern Whigs and moderate southern Democrats had their hands full keeping the secessionists at bay. But did a free California really matter? Were the two California senators sitting on the doorstep really a threat to southern dominance in the Senate? One potential senator, John C. Frémont, definitely was. Although born and raised in the Deep South, and the son-in-law of a Missouri slaveholder, Frémont was a free-soiler. But Frémont had drawn the lot for the short Senate term which ended in March 1851, and the man entitled to the full six-year term, Dr. William McKendree Gwin, was no threat whatsoever. Indeed, he was a protégé of the great Calhoun.

A Mississippi slaveholder who had served one term in the House, Gwin had set off for California in 1849 in search of a Senate seat. He had never achieved great political success back east, and he was determined to change his political fortune out west in the gold country, in a place where most men were in the hot pursuit of great wealth, not political office. Hence the competition for a Senate seat

34. For an annotated bibliography of congressional speeches, see Robert G. Cowan, *The Admission of the 31st State by the 31st Congress* (Los Angeles, 1962).

would be light. As soon as he stepped off the boat in San Francisco, he traveled north to the gold fields to take the political pulse of the region. His trained eye noted that the gold diggings could be worked efficiently by slave labor. But he learned quickly that the miners would have none of it. That summer, miners along the Yuba River had forcibly ordered a Texas slaveholder and his slaves out of the region. Shortly thereafter, that same group hanged a major-domo who refused to remove his Chilean peons, and they cut off the ears off another man who ignored their warnings.[35]

After just two months in California, Gwin managed to get himself elected to the state constitutional convention. Backing him was a coalition of southern-born politicians who came to be known as the Chivalry faction in the California Democratic Party. A handful of Chivs had tried to bring slaves into California; others like Gwin still owned slaves back in their home states. Undoubtedly some hoped that California—or at least the southern half of California—would someday be open to slavery. But that was not their pitch at the state constitutional convention. Not only did Gwin verbally endorse a proposal to outlaw slavery in California, he got all the Chiv delegates to vote for the ban.

As soon as the convention adjourned, Gwin campaigned hard for a Senate seat, got elected, and drew the six-year term. Upon arriving in Washington, he shepherded California's two aspiring House members around the city and systematically courted his old southern friends. His mentor Calhoun, sick and dying, mildly reproached him for his role in the California constitutional convention and told him that the admission of California as a free state would destroy the equilibrium between the North and the South in the Senate. Gwin responded that he had done what was necessary to gain a Senate seat.

Gwin's political shrewdness and opportunism continued to pay off. In 1851 he and his Chiv colleagues maneuvered the state legisla-

35. For the details of Gwin's political career, see Arthur Quinn, *The Rivals: William Gwin, David Broderick, and the Birth of California* (New York, 1994) and James O'Meara, *Broderick and Gwin* (San Francisco, 1881). Less satisfactory overall, but occasionally revealing, are Gwin's memoirs, which were published in four installments in 1940 in the *California Historical Society Quarterly*, vol. 21. Helpful because it provides the perspective of Gwin's chief rival in California politics is David A. Williams, *David C. Broderick: A Political Portrait* (San Marino, Calif., 1969), chaps. 5–14.

ture into replacing Frémont with a dependable ally, a mere errand boy really, in John B. Weller, a onetime congressman from Ohio with avowed prosouthern, proslavery leanings. With Weller under his thumb, and the election of a Democratic president in 1852, Gwin gained control of all federal patronage in California. In time, however, he and the Chivs had to battle another politician on the make, a young Tammany Hall veteran and staunch free-soiler, for control of the state Democratic Party. That battle resulted in a deadlock, so that for two years the California legislature failed to fill a Senate seat. But in 1857 Gwin managed to get himself elected to second term.

In a nutshell, then, the two men who represented California for most of the 1850s were doughfaces. In the case of Gwin, many of the southern spokesmen who ranted and raved about the danger of a free California undoubtedly knew all along that they could count on his vote. He told them as much when he arrived in Washington bearing California's request for statehood. In any event, they got his vote time and again. Both Gwin and Weller voted for the repeal of the Missouri Compromise in 1854. And Gwin backed to the hilt the attempt to admit Kansas to the Union as a slave state under the Lecompton constitution in 1858. Indeed, he led Lecompton Democrats in California in calling for the total proscription of all anti-Lecompton Democrats.

In 1861, with the onset of the Civil War, Gwin demonstrated his loyalty to the South once again. He and most of his Chiv followers supported the Confederacy. His teenage son enlisted in the Confederate army, his eldest daughter moved to Richmond and became a Confederate belle, and his wife was accused at one point of being a Confederate spy. Gwin himself was briefly arrested, and after being released by Lincoln, retired to his Mississippi plantation. He remained there until the Battle of Vicksburg, when his plantation was burnt to the ground. After that, he worked for the Confederacy in France and Mexico and upon return to the United States was imprisoned. In short, while Gwin may have been more opportunistic than his mentor Calhoun would have liked, he was never a threat to the Deep South.

Men like Gwin, then, made the Senate a bastion of southern strength throughout the antebellum period. To dominate the Senate, southern leaders needed only one or two such men. As we have seen, they could usually count on a handful at any given time. In the House, however, the South's position was becoming more and more precarious.

That was largely because the assumptions made by James Madison and other southern delegates to the Constitutional Convention—that the South's population would grow at a faster rate than the North's—turned out to be a pipe dream. For a decade or so after the convention, it seemed that the South might at least keep up with the North. Immigration from Europe was down, and the importation of slaves from Africa was higher than in any previous period. But once the legal importation of slaves came to an end in 1807, the old slave states along the Atlantic seaboard became almost totally dependent on their own birthrates while the North benefited from European immigration, which picked up after the War of 1812.

Each year, Virginia and the Carolinas witnessed thousands of wagon trains leaving for the new country to the west and south. In this respect they were no different from most of the New England states. But unlike the New England states, they never received much in the way of foreign or outside replacements. In the three decades following the War of 1812, about 850,000 desperate Irish set off for the New World. Then came the potato famine, a disaster so complete than in only eight years 1,250,000 Irish rushed to the United States. Outnumbering them by about three to two were the hundreds of thousands who came out of the poor and overpopulated valleys in Norway, from the Black Forest district of Württemberg, from Bavaria and Baden and Prussia, and from England. Thousands upon thousands landed at New Orleans and fanned out through the Mississippi Valley. But for every immigrant who landed in New Orleans, six or seven landed in New York and another one or two landed in Boston and Philadelphia. They crowded the meanest streets of urban America, worked for the meanest wages, dug canals and built railroads, and spread out through the countryside. But only a precious few ended up in the old slave states. By 1850 only 1 percent of South Carolina's population was foreign born and only 2 percent of Virginia's was. In contrast, 16 percent of Massachusetts residents and 21 percent of New York's had been born overseas. Thus, while losing hundreds of thousands of residents to the West, Massachusetts and New York enjoyed a net gain from migration while South Carolina and Virginia witnessed huge losses.[36]

With every census the changes became official, and within a year or two were translated into seats in Congress and votes in the electoral college. The Constitutional Convention had given the slave states 46 percent of the seats in Congress.[37] The first census in 1790 created no change, nor did the second census of 1800. After that, the slave states steadily lost ground, falling to 43 percent after the 1810 census, then to 42 percent, then 41, 40, 38, and finally 35 on the eve of the Civil War. Mighty Virginia, which once had over 18 percent of the seats in the House, saw its proportional power fall to about 4.5 percent. South Carolina saw its share fall from 5.7 percent to 1.7 percent.[38]

For a while Congress hid the full impact of these changes by expanding the size of the House with each census, so it was not until 1822 that Virginia actually lost a seat in Congress. Even then optimists could take comfort in the fact that Kentucky, which had originally been Virginia's Second District, gained two seats. Or they could point to Tennessee, which had once been North Carolina's Fifth District, and note that it had gained three seats. But after the 1840 census, Congress decided to reduce the total size of the House, and this action acutely emphasized the political decline of the Old South. Virginia lost six seats and Kentucky three, while North Carolina lost four seats and Tennessee two.[39] Even the western offshoots of the Old South were declining in congressional importance.

Much of this decline, moreover, was due to the declining role of

36. J. Potter, "The Growth of Population in America, 1700–1860," in *Population in History: Essays in Historical Demography*, ed. D. V. Glass and D. E. C. Eversley (London, 1965), 631–88; Phillip Taylor, *The Distant Magnet* (New York, 1971); Marcus Lee Hansen, *The Atlantic Migration, 1607–1860* (Cambridge, Mass., 1940), chaps. 7–13; Robert Greenhalgh Albion, *The Rise of New York Port* (Devon, England, 1970), appendixes 27 and 28.

37. At the Constitutional Convention there were two slave states—New York and New Jersey—that eventually became free states. I have excluded them from the list of slave states (which is also what James Madison did at the time), including only those states that remained slave states after the first decade of the nineteenth century.

38. Kenneth C. Martis and Gregory A. Elmes, *The Historical Atlas of State Power in Congress, 1790–1990* (Washington, D.C., 1993), especially 6–7.

39. Ibid., 150.

slave representation. At the time of Jefferson's victory in 1800, Virginia had six of the South's fourteen slave seats, and slave representation had made Jefferson president. By the 1840s, when Virginia's John Tyler became president, the importance of slave representation had fallen, not only in Virginia, but throughout the South. Whereas in Jefferson's day slave seats had accounted for 13 percent of all the seats in the House, by the time of Tyler's presidency they accounted for only 9 percent.[40]

Southern leaders, needless to say, were well aware of these trends. When the French pundit Alexis de Tocqueville visited the country in the early 1830s, he found them noticeably "irritated and alarmed" by their declining influence in the House.[41] Twenty years later, the situation had gone from bad to worse. Speaking on a bill to amend the naturalization laws, Senator Stephen Adams of Mississippi blamed the South's plight on foreign immigration. In the House, he contended, the slave states had been the equal of the free states in Jefferson's time but now trailed by fifty-four seats. In just the last decade, the North had gained seven seats "not from natural causes, but from foreign immigration." Indeed, twenty-four members of the "present House" represented "the foreign population—20 from the North, and 4 from the South." If this trend continued, the North would in fifteen years have a two to one majority in the House and probably a similar majority in the Senate.

What would happen then? While some northern politicians claimed that many of the "foreign" representatives in fact sided with the South in sectional showdowns, the Mississippi senator

40. Figuring out the impact of the three-fifths ratio is not a straightforward mathematical procedure. The basic information on the slave population and seats in Congress is easy enough to compile from the census returns and from Kenneth C. Martis, *Historical Atlas of United States Congressional Districts, 1789–1983* (New York, 1982). The problem is that Congress, in apportioning seats, varied the way it handled population figures. In 1792, 1802, 1811, 1822, and 1832, the method was to find a common divisor (usually after long and contentious debate), divide the divisor into the state's population under the three-fifths rule, and then reject the remaining fraction. In 1842 Congress opted to count the major fractions, and in 1850 Congress adopted a new method—the so-called Vinton method. For details on how Congress juggled the numbers, see Michael L. Balinski and H. Peyton Young, *Fair Representation: Meeting the Ideal of One Man, One Vote* (New Haven, 1982), 16ff., and Martis, *Congressional Districts*, 2–3.

41. Alexis de Tocqueville, *Democracy in America*, ed. Phillips Bradley, 2 vols. (New York, 1958), 1: 418.

would have none of it. "The whole education of the foreigners, and their prejudices when they come to this country, are against the institution of slavery; and every thing they hear at the North but confirms that prejudice, and establishes them in their opposition to the South." The outcome, as he saw it, was thus clear. "Does any one doubt, if such political power existed, that the North would not at once change the Constitution so as to abolish the three-fifths representation for our blacks in the House?"[42]

To some proslavery zealots, the impact of foreign immigration was just half the story. To them even more troubling was the declining importance of slavery in some parts of the Old South. At the time of the Constitution, three out of five slaves had toiled in the Chesapeake region. But in the early nineteenth century those numbers changed dramatically. With Congress's abolition of the African slave trade in 1807, along with the decline of the old tobacco and wheat belts in the upper South and the rise of the King Cotton in the Deep South, struggling Chesapeake planters had slaves to sell and ready buyers in the rapidly expanding cotton kingdom. In addition, many masters decided to move their entire plantations south and west. As a result, some 750,000 slaves were relocated or sold down river, and three out of five slaves ended up working in the Deep South by the time of the Civil War. Maryland's and Virginia's shares of the nation's slaves declined from 60 percent in 1790 to 18 percent in 1860, while the lower South's share rose from 21 percent to 59 percent. Simultaneously, the proportion of slaveholding families declined in the old tobacco kingdom and rose in the new cotton kingdom.[43]

Were slaveholders, then, gradually losing control of the land of Jefferson and Madison? The historical record does not support this conclusion, but proslavery zealots worried about the possibility. Especially worrisome to them were southerners like Charles Faulkner and Samuel Garland, who in the great Virginia slavery debate of 1832 likened slavery to a cancer, a national calamity, and a

42. Quotes in this and the preceding paragraph from the *Congressional Globe*, 34th Congress, 1st session, 1855–56, p. 1413.

43. Robert William Fogel and Stanley L. Engerman, *Time on the Cross: The Economics of American Negro Slavery* (Boston, 1974), 44–58; Paul A. David et al., *Reckoning with Slavery: A Critical Study in the Quantitative History of American Negro Slavery* (New York, 1976), 99–129.

pestilence that endangered the safety of poor whites, destroyed "at the fountain, the streams of vigorous and healthful existence," and thus brought on the "premature decay" of old Virginia.[44] More threatening still was Cassius Marcellus Clay, a Kentucky Whig who blamed slavery for the severe depression that border state farmers faced in the early 1840s. Slavery, argued Clay, "impoverished the soil" and was the "source of indolence, and destructive of all industry." It caused the poor to despise labor by degrading it, while it simultaneously turned the mass of slaveholders into idlers. Slaves themselves, because they had no incentives to work hard, performed only about one-half the work of free laborers of the North. The sooner that the border South got rid of the slave system, therefore, the better off it would be.[45]

Might such thinking gain the upper hand in the border South? South Carolina's Waddy Thompson had no doubt that it would. By the 1840s he envisioned slavery very soon disappearing in Maryland, Virginia, North Carolina, Tennessee, and Kentucky, and imagined those states very soon embracing the "fanatical spirit" that was "now pervading the whole world." Thus the Deep South would lose its most important allies at the ballot box and be driven to the cartridge box as its "last defence." In his eyes, the addition of Texas as a slave state in 1845 hardly compensated for this gigantic loss.[46] Virginia's Abel Upshur, who as Tyler's secretary of state negotiated the annexation of Texas, secretly shared the same fear. As he saw it, there were already too many white Virginians who no longer had a stake in the old system and too many parts of Virginia and Maryland where slavery was all but dead. The expansion of slavery westward, and the scattering of slaves over a vast land, had not been the blessing that so many Virginians believed. It had provided them with thousands of dollars from the interstate slave trade, but it also had weakened white Virginia's allegiance to slavery, and further expansion westward would weaken that allegiance even more.[47]

44. Alison Goodyear Freehling, *Drift toward Dissolution: The Virginia Slavery Debate of 1831–1832* (Baton Rouge, 1982), 144–7, 156–7; Joseph Clarke Robert, *The Road from Monticello: A Study of the Virginia Debate of 1832* (Durham, N.C., 1941), 77–8, 92, 99.

45. Cassius Marcellus Clay, *Writings* (1848; reprint, New York, 1969), 204–5, 224.

46. *Niles' Weekly Register* 66 (13 July 1844): 318.

What all these changes meant, of course, was that, as time passed, southerners became more dependent on northern dough-faces. To men like Thompson and Upshur this was a horrible thought. Doughfaces, in their eyes, were exactly as John Randolph had pictured them—weak men with no firm moral convictions, certain to sell out to the highest bidder for the spoils of office.

47. Abel Upshur to Nathaniel Beverly Tucker, 13 March 1843, as reprinted in William H. Freehling, *The Reintegration of American History: Slavery and the Civil War* (New York, 1994), 125–9. See also Claude H. Hall, *Abel Parker Upshur: Conservative Virginian, 1790–1844* (Madison, Wisc., 1964), especially 69–80.

5 | Bucktails into Doughfaces

Of the men belittled by Randolph and deemed untrustworthy by Thompson and Upshur, only a handful have made it into history books. The vast majority of doughfaces remain virtually unknown. Yet it was largely these unknowns who made the Senate into a bastion of southern strength and repeatedly turned a southern minority position in the House into a majority political position. What manner of men were they?

At first glance they seem to have been a motley assortment of individuals with disparate reasons for voting with the South. During the Missouri crisis, for example, Henry Meigs's decision to support the admission of Missouri as a slave state was easy to explain. Meigs was part of the Monroe administration's patronage machine and wanted to remain in the good graces of the president. John Holmes's vote was also easy to understand. Holmes voted consistently against the proposals of Tallmadge and the other restrictionists and worked hand in hand with southern leaders to add slave states to the Union in exchange for statehood for Maine. But Henry Storrs also voted with the South, and he had no chance whatsoever of getting patronage from the White House. He was a Federalist. Moreover, he was at odds with Meigs and Holmes on virtually every issue except slavery in the West. And then there was Caleb Tompkins, the vice president's older brother. The elder Tompkins obviously agreed with Taylor, Tallmadge, and the other restriction-ists. He voted with them several times in 1819. But in 1820, he took a walk. At his brother's urging? In all likelihood, yes.

If we jump ahead twenty or thirty years, to another generation of doughfaces, we encounter another variegated group who seemingly had dissimilar reasons for siding with the South. In the 1850s, for example, two of the staunchest northern supporters of the South were Augustus Caesar Dodge and George Wallace Jones, Iowa's first two senators. They were the only northern senators to vote both for the Fugitive Slave Act in 1850 and for the repeal of the Missouri Compromise in 1854. Both men had southern roots and once owned slaves. Both cherished southern ways. Their votes were thus easy to comprehend. But other than being dependable doughfaces, what did they have in common with Mike Walsh of New York? Walsh was an Irish immigrant who glorified John C. Calhoun and his proslavery doctrines, yet he hardly marched to the same drummer as the two Iowans. He had nothing but contempt for southern no-tions of chivalry.

To be sure, if one tries hard enough and twists the evidence a bit, one can find additional common ground between Walsh and the two Iowans. Walsh portrayed himself as a spokesman for downtrodden Irish immigrants; the two Iowans portrayed themselves as spokes-men for transplanted southerners. In so doing, all three made it clear that their constituents' hostility to Yankee moralists outweighed any concern that their constituents had about slavery or the South.[1]

Was doughfacism, then, a hostile reaction to overbearing Yankees? Some historians have suggested as much.[2] But that explanation, at

1. Louis Pelzer, *Augustus Caesar Dodge* (Iowa City, 1908); John C. Parish, *George Wallace Jones* (Iowa City, 1912); Robert Ernst, "The One and Only Mike Walsh," *New-York Historical Society Quarterly* 36 (January 1952): 43–65.

2. For what historians have said about northerners who sided with the South, see Henry Clyde Hubbart, "'Pro-Southern' Influence in the Free West, 1840–1865," *Mississippi Valley Historical Review* 20 (June 1933): 45–62; Philip S. Foner, *Business and Slavery* (Chapel Hill, 1940); Howard C. Perkins, "The Defense of Slavery in the Northern Press on the Eve of the Civil War," *Journal of Southern History* 9

best, has only limited scope. Many Yankees also carried the dough-face banner. And these were men whose Yankee credentials were beyond dispute, men who served New England in Congress, men who had been born and raised in New England, men whose Yankee heritage went back to Puritan days, men such as Harry Hibbard of New Hampshire, Thomas Fuller of Maine, and Colin Ingersoll of Connecticut. And let us not forget the man whom Lincoln declared to be the worst doughface of them all, Stephen A. Douglas. Born in Brandon, Vermont, Douglas was a sixth-generation Yankee, the descendent of an old and distinguished Puritan family who had been farming, fighting, and procreating in New England since 1640. He spent the first seventeen years of his life in the "green hills and green valleys of Vermont," and it was there, he later proclaimed, that he "first learned to love liberty." He had moved west as a young man, like thousands of his fellow Vermonters, but never completely lost his Yankee twang.[3]

One fact is certain. Doughfaces were more likely to be Jeffersonian Republicans than Federalists, and they were far more likely to be Jacksonian Democrats than Whigs. Between 1820 and 1860, of the 320 congressmen who clearly earned the label *doughface*, all but ten were either Jeffersonian Republicans or Jacksonian Demo-

---

(November 1943): 501–31; Madeleine Hook Rice, *American Catholic Opinion in the Slavery Controversy* (New York, 1944); Russel B. Nye, *Fettered Freedom* (East Lansing, Mich., 1963); Joel H. Silbey, "Pro-Slavery Sentiment in Iowa, 1838–1861," *Iowa Journal of History* 55 (October 1957) 289–318; William Dusinberre, *Civil War Issues in Philadelphia, 1856–1865* (Philadelphia, 1965); Thomas B. Alexander, *Sectional Stress and Party Strength* (Nashville, 1967); Lorman A. Ratner, *Powder Keg: Northern Opposition to the Anti-Slavery Movement, 1831–1840* (New York, 1968); Morton M. Rosenberg and Dennis V. McClurg, *The Politics of Pro-Slavery Sentiment in Indiana, 1816–1861* (Muncie, Ind., 1968); Gerald S. Henig, "The Jacksonian Attitude toward Abolitionism in the 1830's," *Tennessee Historical Quarterly* 28 (Spring 1969): 42–56; Donald B. Cole, *Jacksonian Democracy in New Hampshire, 1800–1851* (Cambridge, Mass., 1970), 175–82; Leonard L. Richards, *"Gentlemen of Property and Standing": Anti-Abolition Mobs in Jacksonian America* (New York, 1970); Murray E. Heimbinder, "Northern Men with Southern Principles: A Study of the Doughfaces of New York and New England" (Ph.D. diss., New York University, 1971); Jean H. Baker, *Affairs of Party: The Political Culture of Northern Democrats in the Mid–Nineteenth Century* (Ithaca, N.Y., 1983); and Larry E. Tise, *Proslavery: A History of the Defense of Slavery in America, 1701–1840* (Athens, Ga., 1987).

3. Robert W. Johannsen, *Stephen A. Douglas* (New York, 1973), 3–15.

crats.[4] Of the fourteen representatives who voted with the South on the Missouri bill, only Henry Storrs was a die-hard Federalist. Two others were suspect. The rest were staunch members of Jefferson's Republican Party. But the Federalists held so few seats in Congress at the time of the Missouri crisis that this comparison is hardly significant. Ten years later, after the Jeffersonian party collapsed and new parties formed in response to Andrew Jackson and his policies, the numbers are far more striking. Indeed, the different reactions of the Jackson men and their opponents in sectional conflicts jump out from the congressional record and demand notice.

As many historians have long known, anti-Jackson doughfaces were clearly an anomaly. Daniel Webster, to be sure, supported the Fugitive Slave Act in his famous Seventh of March speech, "not as a Massachusetts man, nor as a northern man, but as an American."

4. This generalization is based on career-line studies of northern congressmen who voted on the Missouri bill of 1820, the Indian Removal Act of 1830, the Pinckney gag of 1836, the Johnson gag of 1840, the Texas annexation bill of 1845, the Three Million bill of 1847, the Fugitive Slave Act of 1850, the Kansas-Nebraska Act of 1854, and the Montgomery-Crittenden amendment of 1858.

These were not ordinary, everyday roll calls. They all sparked heated sectional debate, intense pressure from the party leadership, and the applause and condemnation of the press. The selection process is therefore simpler and more old-fashioned than, say, the selection process for the construction of a Guttman scalogram.

It is also less likely to produce the bizarre results often associated with random sampling. The problem with random sampling, at least for the antebellum period, is that a congressman's vote on secondary matters often did not reflect his position on the larger issues of the day. John Quincy Adams and other antislavery Whigs, for example, frequently voted with the South on procedural matters, not out of conviction, but just to cause trouble, to keep debate alive. On one occasion Adams and his allies even voted with congressmen who were trying to censure him. (See *Congressional Globe*, 27th Congress, 2d session, 1841–42, pp. 200–1.)

Scaling such legislators is delicate work under any circumstances, and with back-benchers whose views are unknown, it is even more difficult, if not risky and conjectural. Some scholars have simply ignored the inconsistencies; others have "corrected" the votes; and still others have set inconsistent legislators aside as unscalable. All this has generated some weird tables, including one that "proves" that Stephen A. Douglas was more proslavery than Jefferson Davis.

The sample I used includes some thirteen hundred men. Political affiliation as well as other biographical information was compiled from many sources, but mainly from the U.S. Congress, *Biographical Directory of the American Congress, 1774–1971* (Washington, D.C., 1971), the *Congressional Quarterly's Guide to U.S. Elections* (Washington, D.C., 1975), and Kenneth C. Martis, *The Historical Atlas of Political Parties in the United States Congress, 1789–1989* (New York, 1989).

But his behavior in 1850 hardly typified the northern wing of his party, and historians who have portrayed him as a typical northern Whig or a typical New England Whig clearly missed the mark. Northern Whigs as a group were either less fearful of a breakup of the Union or just less willing to compromise with the South. In Congress only one New England Whig and three other northern Whigs followed Webster's lead; sixty-five others voted "no." More than half of the northern Democrats, on the other hand, sided with Webster and the South.

Such behavior was typical throughout the Jackson era. In the two decades between the Pinckney gag of 1836 and the Kansas-Nebraska Act of 1854, members of the two national parties were remarkably consistent in sectional showdowns. The northern opponents of Andrew Jackson rarely voted with their southern colleagues, although on occasion a number of them made themselves scarce when it came time to vote. Here, for example, is how they voted on six of the most divisive bills that came before the House of Representatives in the Jackson era:

	Voting with South	Against	Not Voting
Pinckney Gag (1836)	1	45	4
Johnson Gag (1840)	1	60	1
Texas (1845)	0	51	1
Wilmot Proviso (1847)	0	52	7
Fug. Slave Act (1850)	4	49	21
Kans.-Nebr. (1854)	0	39	6

In contrast, the northern Jacksonians provided their southern colleagues with scores of votes and turned a southern minority position in the House into a majority political position. Here is how they voted on the six bills that their Whig rivals overwhelmingly opposed:

	Voting with South	Against	Not Voting
Pinckney Gag (1836)	59	16	15
Johnson Gag (1840)	27	39	4
Texas (1845)	54	28	1
Wilmot Proviso (1847)	22	41	13
Fug. Slave Act (1850)	28	16	9
Kans.-Nebr. (1854)	44	43	6

Northern voters who cared about the North-South struggle, in turn, knew what they were getting. If a man was elected as a Whig, the chances that he would vote with the South in the next sectional crisis were at best one in twenty. If he was elected as a Democrat, the odds were one in two. Antislavery historians have frequently noted that abolitionists invariably supported the Whig Party as the lesser of two evils. The English traveler Edward S. Abdy, after touring northern slums in the 1830s, reported that he never met a black person who was not "an anti-Jackson man."[5] It is easy to understand why.

All this does not mean, however, that doughfaces represented the mainstream of the northern Democracy.[6] The only time southern Democrats found it easy to get northern support was in the early years of the gag rule. At other times, they had to work weeks, sometimes months, to marshal enough votes to get their measures passed. Often they took a beating in a series of preliminary votes before they prevailed. But they did get northern support, and that was something southern Whigs never accomplished. The high point for southern Whigs was in 1850, when four northern Whigs sided with Webster and the South and twenty-six others missed the crucial vote. Even in that year, southern pleading, southern threats, and southern bullying had less effect on northern Whigs than it had on northern Democrats.

Why was this the case? Why were northern Democrats so much more receptive to southern demands than their Whig rivals? One reason is that the two major parties were not mirror images of one another. Structurally, they differed in several major respects.

The Jacksonian coalition, in contrast to the Whig, was like the Jeffersonian coalition had been—initially southern based, proslavery at heart,[7] with a growing but largely subservient northern wing.

5. E. S. Abdy, *Journal of a Residence and Tour in the United States*, 3 vols. (London, 1835).

6. For the "mainstream" theme, see Joel H. Silbey, "'There Are Other Questions Beside That of Slavery Merely': The Democratic Party and Antislavery Politics," in *Crusaders and Compromisers: Essays on the Relationship of the Antislavery Struggle to the Antebellum Party System*, ed. Alan M. Kraut (Westport, Conn., 1983), 143–75.

7. Some historians have quarreled with the notion that Jackson and his followers were "proslavery at heart." See, for example, Robert V. Remini, *Andrew Jackson and the Course of American Democracy, 1833–1845* (New York, 1984), 343, and *The*

In 1828 Jackson triumphed with 92 percent of the electoral vote in the slave states, 49 percent in the free states. His party, while not as overpowering as Jefferson's, won six of nine presidential elections between 1828 and 1860, controlled the House for twenty-four of those thirty-two years and the Senate for twenty-eight. Southerners, moreover, were not just minority or equal partners in the Jackson caucus. They were invariably the majority in the Senate and often the majority in the House.

In Jackson's heyday, to be sure, the congressional caucus no longer nominated men for president. The Jeffersonian caucus had lost that power in the 1824 presidential election, when it tried to convince the nation to vote for William Crawford, who had just suffered a debilitating stroke. Instead of accepting the caucus's decision, Jackson and two other Jeffersonian Republicans continued to run for president, and two of the three outpolled the choice of King Caucus in the electoral college. All three, moreover, denounced the caucus as an undemocratic, aristocratic cabal.

After the death of King Caucus, national parties scrambled to find another way of choosing national candidates and making binding nominations. After toying with various alternatives, the followers of Jackson turned to a national nominating convention, a procedure which had been pioneered by the Antimasons, to choose

---

Legacy of Andrew Jackson: Essay on Democracy, Indian Removal, and Slavery (Baton Rouge, 1988), 83. Usually they point to the early writings of the Jacksonians, contending that in the early days of the Jackson era only a few worried much about slavery and only a few were explicitly and unequivocally proslavery like John C. Calhoun and James Henry Hammond. That indeed may have been the case when slaveholding wasn't under attack, but to go a step further and imply that Jackson and his followers were neutral on the slavery question is far-fetched. In a society in which slavery was a well-established institution and in which slaveholders clearly had a privileged position, one did not have to be a blatant apologist for slavery to be a defender of slavery. All one had to do was support the established slaveholding order, and that the Jacksonians clearly did. (See, for example, *Register of Debates*, 24th Congress, 1st session, 1835–36, passim.) As for Jackson himself, he may not have said much about slavery, but he conspicuously exercised his property rights, buying and selling slaves regularly, offering rewards with harsh punishments for runaway slaves, even wagering slaves on horse races. (See Chase C. Mooney, *Slavery in Tennessee* [Bloomington, Ind., 1957], 52, 91; Michael Paul Rogin, *Fathers and Children: Andrew Jackson and the Subjugation of the American Indian* [New York, 1975], 57; and James C. Curtis, *Andrew Jackson and the Search for Vindication* [Boston, 1976], 135–7.)

a vice presidential candidate to run with Jackson in the 1832 presidential election. Under this system, each state had the right to send delegates, even the states that Jackson had no chance of winning. Also, potential power was based on the number of electoral votes a state had, rather than how many party members it elected to Congress. Thus the three-fifths rule and Senate parity still had a role, but at first it seemed to be a less decisive role than under King Caucus.

The delegates at the first Jacksonian convention, however, made a decision that enhanced the value of the South's "rotten boroughs" and gave the South a veto over whomever the northern majority might want for president or vice president. The delegates agreed that Jackson's running mate had to have a two-thirds majority, purportedly to reduce the weight of delegations from New England, where the party was weak. That decision set them apart from the convention system adopted by the Whigs and other parties, which held that a simple majority vote was all that was necessary for nomination.

The impact of the two-thirds rule was minimal in 1832, when the party nominated Martin Van Buren of New York for the vice presidency. Nor was it much of a problem in 1836, when the party gave Van Buren its presidential nomination. In 1840, when the party renominated Van Buren by acclamation, it was of no consequence whatsoever. But in 1844, when Van Buren failed to endorse the annexation of Texas, the impact of the rule became clear to all: a well-organized minority could derail the candidate of the majority and dictate terms. The convention began with a majority of the delegates pledged to Van Buren. But that proved to be meaningless as the pro-Texas men insisted on a two-thirds majority, succeeded in blocking his nomination, and after a long deadlock made a zealous expansionist, James K. Polk of Tennessee, the party's nominee.[8]

Once firmly established, the two-thirds rule was hard to dislodge, lasting until 1936. It was a mighty weapon—one that southern Whigs never had—which forced northern Democratic presidential hopefuls

8. Richard C. Bain, *Convention Decisions and Voting Records* (Washington, D.C., 1960), 17ff., appendix; James S. Chase, *Emergence of the Presidential Nominating Convention, 1789–1832* (Urbana, Ill., 1973), 264–6; and David M. Potter, *The South and the Concurrent Majority* (Baton Rouge, 1972).

to pay heed to their southern compatriots, prove that they were indeed "northern men with southern principles," or suffer the fate of Van Buren. Only northern Democrats like Lewis Cass, Franklin Pierce, and James Buchanan had any chance of winning their party's nomination. Even so, it took forty-nine ballots for Pierce to win the nomination in 1852 and seventeen ballots for Buchanan to win in 1856.[9]

The South also continued to exercise disproportionate power in the Jacksonian caucus. Although the legislative caucus lost control of presidential nominations, it became gradually stronger in organizing Congress and shaping the political agenda. In 1837 the old system of electing the Speaker by secret ballot was discarded in favor of voice voting so that dissenters could be readily identified. Discipline became tighter.

Also, like its Jeffersonian predecessor, the Jacksonian caucus represented some sections of the country far more than others. The party was initially weak in New England, strong in the slave states, and the early caucus reflected this imbalance. In 1830, for example, Jacksonians from the slave states outnumbered their northern allies by seventy-two to sixty-four in the House, nineteen to six in the Senate. Gradually the party became more national in makeup, competitive in every state except Massachusetts and Vermont. By 1840 the free-state men were the majority in the House, seventy-one to forty-eight, and a sizable minority in the Senate, fourteen to sixteen.[10] Still, the northern wing had the Speaker's chair for only two of the twenty-four years the Democrats were the majority, and the chair of Ways and Means for just seven years.

The subordinate position of northern Democrats undoubtedly influenced their behavior. All those with national aspirations knew that they had an advantage over their Whig rivals in being members of the nation's dominant party. But they also knew that they had to pay more heed to their southern colleagues to have any chance of being nominated for the presidency or Speaker of the House or chair of House Ways and Means. Some, like Franklin Pierce and James Buchanan, accepted this reality and catered to their southern col-

9. Congressional Quarterly, *National Party Conventions, 1831–1872* (Washington, D.C., 1976).

10. Computed from data in Martis, *Historical Atlas of Political Parties.*

leagues for their entire political careers. Others, like Martin Van Buren and Stephen A. Douglas, spent the better part of their political lives catering to the South but eventually found southern demands intolerable.

The internal structure of the two national parties, however, only partly explains why northern Democrats were more likely than northern Whigs to side with the South. Some weight also has to be given to the fact that the Jackson party from the outset attracted men who favored harsher forms of white supremacy.

Historians have shown repeatedly that in the 1820s race-baiting politicians and newsmen gravitated to the Jacksonian camp, and by the 1830s the two major parties could be distinguished on the issue of race.[11] Not every Whig, to be sure, shunned race baiting. One of the worst race-baiting editors in the North, James Watson Webb of the *New York Courier and Enquirer*, was a Whig. But some northern Whigs clearly sympathized with the plight of blacks, and others were too busy denouncing the Irish and the Catholic Church to have any time for "nigger-knocking." The Jacksonians took the opposite tack, eventually defending the Irish on the one hand, while appealing to the worst strains in white racism and Anglophobia on the other.

Terrorizing blacks came first. Historians have sometimes implied that the Irish turned the Democracy into a hard-line racist party. In fact, the Democracy already had more than its share of race-baiting leaders and racist thugs in the 1820s and 1830s, long before the British government and the Irish potato famine drove millions of Catholic Irish across the Atlantic, and long before boatloads

11. For the race question and party behavior in various northern states, see James T. Adams, "Disfranchisement of Negroes in New England," *American Historical Review* 30 (December 1925): 543–7; Dixon Ryan Fox, "The Negro Vote in Old New York," *Political Science Quarterly* 32 (June 1917): 252–75; John L. Stanley, "Majority Tyranny in Tocqueville's America: The Failure of Negro Suffrage in 1846," *Political Science Quarterly* 84 (September 1969): 412–35; Phyllis F. Field, *The Politics of Race in New York* (Ithaca, N.Y., 1982); Marion T. Wright, "Negro Suffrage in New Jersey, 1776–1875," *Journal of Negro History* 32 (April 1948): 168–224; Edward R. Turner, *The Negro in Pennsylvania* (Washington, D.C., 1911); and Ronald P. Formisano, "The Edge of Caste: Colored Suffrage in Michigan, 1827–1861," *Michigan History* 56 (Spring 1972): 19–41.

of half-starved Irish tenant farmers descended upon Boston, New York, Philadelphia, and other port cities in the 1840s and 1850s. The newcomers added to the animosity but clearly didn't instigate it.[12]

In New York, the most populous northern state and the port of entry for most Irish, the men who led the Jackson party had a long history of playing the race card. At the state's constitutional convention in 1821, against conservative opposition, they pushed through a provision that disfranchised most of the state's 30,000 free blacks. Previously, black men had voted on equal terms with white; they too had to possess $50 worth of property or pay $5 yearly rent to vote for assemblyman. Now, under the new constitution, they had to possess a freehold estate worth at least $250.[13]

Similarly, in Pennsylvania, the second most populous northern state, Buck County Democrats in 1838 campaigned for a revision to the state constitution that stripped 40,000 blacks of the right to vote. At the time, black men had the same voting rights as white men, although in some counties they never had been allowed to vote. Of the seventy-seven convention delegates voting to disfranchise all black Pennsylvanians, at least fifty-seven were Jacksonian Democrats.[14]

New York and Pennsylvania were hardly unique. Across the North, racism had become more virulent long before the coming of the famine Irish. Connecticut and New Jersey also disfranchised black voters shortly after the War of 1812, and none of the new states admitted to the Union after 1819 allowed blacks to vote. Black men had the legal right to vote in nine northern states in

12. Cf. Noel Ignatiev, *How the Irish Became White* (New York, 1995), especially chap. 3; David Roediger, *The Wages of Whiteness* (New York, 1991), chap. 7; Alexander Saxton, *The Rise and Fall of the White Republic: Class Politics and Mass Culture in Nineteenth Century America* (New York, 1990), pts. 1 and 2; and Ronald Takaki, *A Different Mirror: A History of Multicultural America* (Boston, 1993), chap. 6.

13. John Anthony Casais, "The New York State Constitutional Convention of 1821 and Its Aftermath" (Ph.D. dissertation, Columbia University, 1967), 185–6. For the depth and breadth of antiblack sentiment, see Nathaniel H. Carter and William L. Stone, *Reports of the Proceedings and Debates of the Convention of 1821* (Albany, 1821), 180ff.

14. Turner, *Negro in Pennsylvania*, 190. For the depth and breadth of antiblack sentiment, see *Pennsylvania Constitutional Debates of 1837–38*, 9 vols. (Philadelphia, 1839), 9: passim.

1815, but only five by 1840. In most northern states, moreover, blacks were denied access to public schools, prohibited from serving on juries or in the militia, excluded from many trades, and barred from scores of public places. Across the north, blacks also suffered at the hands of white rioters, not only in big cities like Providence and Cincinnati in 1829 and New York and Philadelphia in 1834, but also in small rural towns like Canterbury, Connecticut, in 1833.

Occasionally a few Whig politicians tried to make amends. In 1838, for example, the Whig candidate for lieutenant governor of New York denounced the state's black voting restrictions as a gross violation of democratic principles. He lost the election, while his noncommittal running mate for governor, William H. Seward, won by 10,000 votes.[15] Eight years later, Seward and several other Whig leaders showed more gumption and backed unrestricted black male suffrage at the state constitutional convention. They lost decisively. After a long and heated debate, half the Whig delegates supported the pro-black position on every vote, but the Democrats were in the majority and 80 percent of them opposed equal suffrage. Over half, in fact, wanted to disfranchise the thousand or so blacks who had met the stiff property qualifications and had registered to vote.[16]

In this battle, as well as in others, Democratic politicians relentlessly held blacks up to ridicule, denounced them for the urban crime rate, and accused them of lusting after white women. That, indeed, was the stock-in-trade of one Jacksonian politician after another. Leading the pack were doughface Democrats, who invariably portrayed themselves as patriots trying to save the country and the white race from Federalist traitors, British conspirators, and "nigger-loving" Yankee agitators who promoted abolitionism, racial amalgamation, slave insurrections, and sectional conflict.

Not only did northern Democrats have a long history of tormenting blacks before the coming of the famine Irish, they initially paid scant attention to the Irish. Few realized that the first boatloads of Irish immigrants marked the beginning of a major population movement and that the nation's cities would soon be inundated with hundreds of thousands of Irish Catholics. Like their Whig rivals, Democratic leaders initially courted the Irish vote but hardly wel-

15. *Niles' Weekly Register* 55 (3, 24 November 1838): 155–8, 206.
16. Stanley, "Majority Tyranny," 414–7; Field, *Politics of Race in New York*, 54–5.

comed the Catholic Irish into the party apparatus.[17] To win elections, they had to have the support of native-born Protestants, many of whom were vehemently anti-Catholic. A few ardent Jacksonians, like the famous inventor Samuel F. B. Morse, even led full-scale assaults against the Catholic Church.[18] But like their Whig counterparts, these anti-Catholic Democrats acted largely on their own.

A change came in the early 1840s when adamant nativists formed independent parties and won control of several northern cities. The Whigs generally backed the nativists, while the Jacksonians tried to appease both sides, holding meetings to denounce nativism but waffling on some issues and keeping Irishmen off their tickets. The Whig-nativist alliance, however, proved decisive. It drove the Irish into the Democratic Party, and, reluctantly, by the late 1840s or early 1850s Democratic politicians became the voice of the Irish and "the party of the immigrant."[19]

Once the Catholic Irish joined the northern Democracy, urban racism became even more acrimonious. Starting at the bottom of the labor market and harassed constantly by white Protestant workers, unskilled Irishmen fought with blacks for jobs and living space. Through sheer numbers and terrorism, they drove blacks off the docks, took away their jobs as hackney coachmen and draymen, and stripped them of their livelihoods as domestic servants and ditchdiggers. In 1830 most of New York City's servants were black; twenty years later, Irish servants outnumbered the city's entire

17. Jackson himself was Irish and was referred to as such, but he was Protestant Irish. People of his ethnic background, who later came to be known as Scotch-Irish, generally had little use for the Catholic Irish and often led nativist attacks against them.

18. Leo Hershkovitz, "The Native American Democratic Association in New York City, 1835–36," *New-York Historical Society Quarterly* 46 (January 1962): 41–60; Bruce Laurie, *Working People of Philadelphia, 1800–1850* (Philadelphia, 1980), 169–71.

19. Amy Bridges, *A City in the Republic: Antebellum New York and the Origins of Machine Politics* (New York, 1984), 83–4, 99–100, 148; Kerby A. Miller, *Emigrants and Exiles: Ireland and the Irish Exodus to America* (New York, 1985), 295–300, 328–31; Dale T. Knobel, *Paddy and the Republic: Ethnicity and Nationality in Antebellum America* (Middletown, Conn., 1986); Michael Feldberg, *The Philadelphia Riots of 1844: A Study of Ethnic Conflict* (Westport, Conn., 1975); Ray A. Billington, *The Protestant Crusade, 1800–1860: A Study of the Origins of American Nativism* (New York, 1938), 151–5, 193–211; Oscar Handlin, *Boston's Immigrants, 1790–1865: A Study in Acculturation* (Cambridge, Mass., 1941), 197–204.

black population by ten to one. Meanwhile, scores of would-be politicians, men like Mike Walsh and David Broderick, became leaders of volunteer fire companies, formed local constituencies, gained prominence in bare-knuckled ward politics, stormed Tammany Hall and other Democratic organizations, and eventually forced the Democracy to run Irishmen for public office. Invariably, these men outdid their rivals in race baiting.[20]

At best, however, racism only partly explains northern Democrats' voting patterns on slavery issues. Northern Whigs also had racists in their ranks, but as a rule none of them voted with the South. Historians, moreover, have unearthed scores of northern politicians who opposed the South for largely racist reasons.[21] Many northern Negrophobes clearly hated blacks, slavery, and southern planters with almost equal vehemence. Many blamed the "black menace" on slaveholders. Many more supported the free-soil movement. To them, free soil meant not only keeping slavery out of the West but keeping blacks out as well.

Even Irish politicians, men who came off the mean streets of New York, moved in different directions. Mike Walsh, who fought his way up the party ladder to become an assemblyman and then a United States congressman, was an ardent supporter of John C. Calhoun. His onetime associate David Broderick moved to San Francisco and became the leader of the free-soil faction of the California Democratic Party, the man who tried to drive William Gwin and his doughface followers out of politics. Negrophobia, in short, affected different northern whites in strikingly different ways.

So why did racist northern Democrats, rather that racist northern Whigs, provide the South with an edge in one congressional battle

20. Ernst, "The One and Only Mike Walsh"; David A. Williams, *David C. Broderick: A Political Portrait* (San Marino, Calif., 1969), chaps. 1 and 2. For a sense of the world in which these men thrived, see George Wilkes, *The Mysteries of the Tombs: A Journal of Thirty Days Imprisonment in the New York City Prison for Libel* (New York, 1844).

21. See, for example, Eugene H. Berwanger, *The Frontier against Slavery: Western Anti-Negro Prejudice and the Slavery Extension Controversy* (Urbana, Ill., 1967); James A. Rawley, *Race and Politics: "Bleeding Kansas" and the Coming of the Civil War* (Philadelphia, 1969); and Eric Foner, "Racial Attitudes of the New York Free Soilers," *New York History* 46 (October 1965): 311–29, and "Politics and Prejudice: The Free Soil Party and the Negro, 1849–1852," *Journal of Negro History* 50 (October 1965): 239–56.

after another? And why did they do this from the outset of the Jackson era, even before the two-thirds rule for Democratic nomination and the dictates of the party caucus limited the choices of ambitious northern Democrats? These are tough questions to answer, but one line of argument points to Martin Van Buren of New York, the political magician of the age. Many scholars have long suspected that Van Buren and his colleagues purposely fashioned the Jackson coalition so that it protected slavery and southern interests.[22]

Van Buren's skills as a political manipulator are legendary. The son of a Dutch tavern keeper of the tiny village of Kinderhook, he first gained attention as an accomplished lawyer. In this respect he was no different from many politicians of his day, except that his legal prowess was so widely respected that John Quincy Adams (hardly a political ally) later urged his appointment to the Supreme Court.[23] But it was not in court that Van Buren made his mark. Nor was it in the numerous political offices he held. Even though he progressed up the political ladder, from state senator, to state attorney general, and later to United States senator, governor of New York, secretary of state, minister to England, vice president, and finally, president of the United States, his fame rested largely on his talent as a behind the scenes political operator.

To the public, observing him from a distance, Van Buren was anything but a charismatic leader. He lacked the command presence, the overbearing personality, the colossal ego of DeWitt Clinton, once his chief rival in New York politics. His forte was political organization and political manipulation, and for that his opponents derisively labeled him a magician and a schemer, the American Talleyrand, and the Red Fox of Kinderhook. Behind him stood the Albany Regency, a group of like-minded men who for nearly thirty years sought to control political office in New York, rule the state party with an iron hand, and provide the Empire State with scrupulously honest government. Behind the Regency stood the "Bucktails," a well-disciplined political machine that sought to control the vote in every nook and cranny in the Northeast.

22. Probably the best known rendition of this argument is Richard H. Brown, "The Missouri Crisis, Slavery, and the Politics of Jacksonianism," *South Atlantic Quarterly* 61 (Winter 1966): 55–72.

23. Charles Warren, *The Supreme Court in United States History*, 2 vols. (Boston, 1926), 1, 591–4.

Van Buren and his followers, so the argument goes, became alarmed after the War of 1812 when the old Republican Party of Jefferson's heyday gradually fell apart. Especially divisive, as they saw it, was the debate over admitting Missouri as a slave state in 1819, and the attendant attacks against slavery, the three-fifths clause of the Constitution, and southern domination of the national government. These attacks, which were provoked mainly by James Tallmadge, John Taylor, and other New York politicians, convinced Van Buren that the collapse of Jeffersonian Republicanism might lead to antislavery political parties. Such a development would not only send shock waves through the nation, it would also destroy the working arrangement between the Van Burenites and the Virginia elite and rend New York's political fabric. To avoid such a possibility, Van Buren and his Virginia allies allegedly constructed a party that would fight the old battles of Jefferson's heyday once again, quiet the slavery issue, and protect the South's dominant position within the Union. Later, when the Little Magician became a presidential contender, he took further steps to placate the slave states to win southern votes.[24]

Whether or not Van Buren acted as this argument claims, he and his Bucktail followers capitalized on the political fallout of the Missouri crisis. The Monroe administration, like previous Virginia-dominated administrations, used patronage to keep New York Republicans divided. In 1817, when Monroe took over the presidency, DeWitt Clinton was riding high in New York politics. Clinton had won the governorship with almost unanimous support, got his Erie Canal proposal through the legislature, and the first year of digging "Clinton's ditch" was well under way. Out of fear of Clinton's political ambitions, and probably in revenge for his previous attempts to unseat a Virginia president, Monroe immediately shifted patronage away from Clinton and toward Clinton's New York rivals. In 1818 the Monroe administration sent a clear message to New York politicians by firing a strong Clinton ally as postmas-

24. Cf. Brown, "Missouri Crisis"; John M. McFaul, "Expediency vs. Morality: Jacksonian Politics and Slavery," *Journal of American History* 62 (June 1975): 24–39; George C. Rable, "Slavery, Politics, and the South: The Gag Rule As a Case Study," *Capitol Studies* 3 (Fall 1975): 69–87; and Howard Alexander Morrison, "Gentlemen of Proper Understanding: A Closer Look at Utica's Anti-Abolition Mob," *New York History* 61 (January 1981): 61–82.

ter of Niagara Falls and appointing two of Clinton's best-known enemies to the U.S. Customs House in New York City.[25]

When the Missouri controversy broke out in 1819, Monroe envisioned the evil hand of Clinton at work. Like his fellow Virginians, he laid much of the blame on disgruntled Federalists, but he also assumed that his old Federalist enemy Rufus King was working in concert with the New York governor. Hence a full-scale battle ensued. When the Clinton administration purged anti-Clintonians from state jobs, the Monroe administration found places for these men on the federal payroll. When federal judges resigned, the Monroe administration replaced them with men who were fiercely anti-Clintonian. The word quickly spread, and soon office-seeking politicians throughout New York knew that allegiance to Clinton, or even a rumor of such allegiance, would disqualify them for federal office.

The Bucktails by this time were the major out-faction in the contentious New York Jeffersonian party. Many of them, including their leader Van Buren, had once supported Clinton's presidential ambitions. But Clinton's egotism, disregard of party discipline, and cavalier treatment of his own followers had driven many into opposition. Monroe's appointment policies caused others to join their ranks. Thus the Bucktails would have benefited even if they had idly sat on their hands. But they weren't idle. They played to Monroe's fears. Without taking a clear-cut position in favor of slavery and southern power, they made it clear to the Monroe administration that they were much safer on these issues than the Clintonians. They also gave credence to Monroe's fear that the Missouri crisis was a Clintonian attempt to topple twenty years of Virginia rule. In turn, Monroe agreed to Van Buren's request that several upstate Clintonian post-

25. For much of the information in this and the following paragraphs, I am indebted to Solomon Nadler, "Federal Patronage and New York Politics, 1801–1830" (Ph.D. dissertation, New York University, 1973), 193–207 and idem, "The Green Bag: James Monroe and the Fall of DeWitt Clinton," *New-York Historical Society Quarterly*, 59 (July 1975), 204–14. See also James Tallmadge to Clinton, 11 February 1818; John Savage to Clinton, 8 March 1818; Elijah Hayward to Clinton, 4 July 1818; Matthew Tallmadge to Clinton, 7 January 1819, Clinton Papers, Columbia University Library; and Henry Meigs to Josiah Meigs, 20 November 1818, Henry Meigs Papers, New-York Historical Society.

masters be replaced by "loyal" Bucktails. The president also endorsed a Bucktail plan whereby his postmaster general would use federal patronage to defeat Clinton's reelection bid in 1820.[26]

Clinton won reelection in 1820, but his victory margin fell far short of his previous triumph. Furious over the outcome, especially given the budding success of the Erie Canal, he began collecting affidavits, certificates, and letters proving that the Monroe administration, in conjunction with the Bucktails, had systematically interfered in New York politics. In 1821 he transmitted this evidence to the New York Assembly in a large green bag, and in what came to be known as the "Green Bag Message," denounced the Monroe administration for completely ignoring the principle of states' rights and actively using federal patronage to destroy party unity in the Empire State. His evidence took up twenty-five pages of the assembly journal. The Bucktails, who now controlled the state legislature, responded with a forty-four-page report that exonerated the Monroe administration.[27]

By this time, the Bucktails were in the saddle, controlling virtually all the federal jobs that had once been in the hands of the Clintonians. For the next ten years they fought desperately to maintain control of the spoils of office, winning some battles, losing others. Overall, the mid-1820s were rocky years for them, thanks mainly to their decision to buck popular opinion in New York and support Georgia's William H. Crawford in the 1824 presidential race, although the reemergence of Clinton as a force in New York politics and the presence of John Quincy Adams in the White House were also factors. But with Clinton's death in 1828 and the emergence of Andrew Jackson as the towering figure in national politics, they solidified their position and retained the upper hand for the next fifteen to twenty years. They were so dominant that a political

26. In addition to Nadler's work cited in the preceding note, see Van Buren to Henry Meigs, 4 April 1820, and Meigs to Van Buren, 10 April, 26 November 1820, Martin Van Buren Papers, Library of Congress; Catharina V. R. Bonney, comp., *A Legacy of Historical Gleanings*, 2 vols. (Albany, N.Y., 1875), 1: 349–50, 357–9; *National Advocate*, 9 March, 29 May 1820; and the steady barrage of articles in the *New York Columbian*, April–December 1820.

27. *Journal of the New York Assembly*, 44th session, 1820, pp. 114–46, 930–9, appendix: 1–35.

historian of New York later wrote: "I do not believe that a stronger political organization ever existed."[28]

The Bucktails thus profited while more outspoken critics of slavery and southern power suffered. But did they vote with the South? At the time of the Missouri crisis, most did not. Henry Meigs, their key contact with the Monroe patronage machine, was the exception that proved the rule. He voted to admit Missouri as a slave state, but the others kept their distance. That pattern changed, however, after Andrew Jackson became president. In the 1830s, Van Buren's followers provided the lion's share of doughface votes.

Consider, for example, the vote on the one bill that Jackson put the full weight of his office behind—the Indian Removal Act of 1830. For northeastern congressmen, this was a tough bill to support. For one thing, the bill benefited only a handful of their own constituents. The chief beneficiaries were white southerners who clamored for the twenty-five million acres still in the hands of the Cherokees, Creeks, Choctaws, Chickasaws, and Seminoles. Indeed, in Georgia, Alabama, and Mississippi there was no issue more central than getting the lands of the great tribes of the South. The dreams of town promoters and speculators, the dreams of planters and farmers, all depended on getting the red man's land. Some northeastern wheelers and dealers were certain to benefit from these schemes, but overall their numbers were relatively small.[29]

The bill also obliged northeastern congressmen to renege on a host of federal laws and treaties in which the federal government had promised to protect the great tribes of the South from white in-

28. DeAlva S. Alexander, *A Political History of the State of New York,* 4 vols. (New York, 1906), 2: 1–2.

29. Of the literature on Indian removal, I have relied heavily on several excellent studies: Ronald N. Satz, *American Indian Policy in the Jacksonian Era* (Lincoln, Nebr., 1975); Dale Van Every, *Disinherited: The Lost Birthright of the American Indian* (New York, 1966); Grant Foreman, *Indian Removal: The Emigration of the Five Civilized Tribes of Indians* (Norman, Okla., 1932); Angie Debo, *And Still the Waters Run: The Betrayal of the Five Civilized Tribes* (Princeton, 1940); Anthony F. C. Wallace, *The Long, Bitter Trail: Andrew Jackson and the Indians* (New York, 1993); and Mary Hershberger, "Mobilizing Women, Anticipating Abolition: The Struggle against Indian Removal in the 1830s," *Journal of American History* 86 (June 1999): 15–40.

vasion. Upon taking office, Jackson made it clear that he would not honor these obligations, nor would he stop Georgia and the other southern states from running roughshod over tribes within their borders. This led to howls of protest. In turn, many southerners pointed out that the "eastern" people had no grounds for such moralizing. Hadn't they repeatedly broken promises to the tribes of the Northeast? Hadn't they used the foulest methods in killing off King Philip and his followers? That of course was true, but it did not stop northeastern congressmen from being deluged with petitions and memorials from churches, benevolent societies, and town meetings demanding justice for the Native Americans.

Time and again northeastern congressmen were told to act honorably and follow the lead of "the Christian statesman" Theodore Frelinghuysen of New Jersey, who in a three-day speech accused the Jackson administration of violating sacred treaties, dishonoring the nation's good name, and acting in a manner that no true Christian could condone. Challenging Frelinghuysen was not easy. He was a distinguished lawyer who had the respect of colleagues in both parties. At one time or another, moreover, he had been president of the American Board of Commissioners for Foreign Missions, president of the American Bible Society, president of the American Tract Society, vice president of the American Sunday School Union, and an officer of the American Temperance Union. His opinion thus carried much weight in religious circles throughout the Northeast.

Could a northeastern congressman simply ignore this sentiment and vote for a bill that did nothing for his own constituents? For a bill that benefited southern slaveholders? Van Buren himself labeled Indian Removal a "southern measure." He also had no doubt that it was unpopular with the voters back home. And he hardly wanted to be closely identified with a process that stirred up humanitarian opposition in New York, one that would cause even his own niece to rebuke him and wish for his defeat. He hoped that somehow Georgia would find an amicable resolution to its conflict with the Cherokees and that Mississippi would deal honorably with the Choctaws.[30]

30. *Autobiography of Martin Van Buren*, 2 vols., ed. John C. Fitzpatrick (Washington, D.C., 1920), 2: 289–95; Van Buren to John Forsyth, 18 December 1832, VB to Francis P. Blair, 12 September 1842, VB to James R. Rey, 24 October 1848, Martin Van Buren Papers.

But Andrew Jackson needed every vote he could get. Three times, amendments were added in the Senate to weaken the bill, and each time the amendment came within one vote of passing. Twice the bill failed to clear the House. Finally, after much arm twisting, Jackson got the votes he needed. The bill passed the Senate by a comfortable margin, 28 to 19, and squeaked through the House, 102 to 97.

Where did Van Buren's followers stand in all this? They went the extra mile in behalf of Andrew Jackson and their southern colleagues. Indeed, they provided far more support than Democrats from the Old Northwest, where Indian Removal had much stronger voter support. Of northeastern Democrats, three out of four backed Indian Removal and only one out of thirty voted against it. Elsewhere, most northern Democrats defected and voted with Frelinghuysen and the opposition party. Here is a breakdown of the northern Democratic vote in the House:

	New England	New York	Other Free States[a]
Dems. for removal	8	16	10
Against	0	1	20
Not voting	2	3	4

[a] New Jersey, Pennsylvania, Ohio, Indiana, Illinois

Was the vote as costly as some feared? Van Buren certainly thought so. He estimated that support for Indian Removal cost him and his followers "not less than eight or ten thousand voters" in New York alone. And he never forgot his niece's scathing rebuke: "Uncle! I must say to you that it is my earnest wish that you may lose the election, as I believe that such a result ought to follow such acts!"[31]

The Van Buren forces also played a decisive role a few years later in stopping antislavery petitions from being heard in Congress. In 1835 the American Anti-Slavery Society became the hottest issue in national politics. That summer, the society bombarded the country with free pamphlets portraying the slavemaster as a brute who lusted after black women, mutilated his slaves, and even sold his own mulatto children "down river." When the pamphlets reached Charleston and other southern ports, the South exploded. Fiery speeches calling

31. Van Buren, *Autobiography*, 2, 293–4.

for the blood of the abolitionists became everyday news; strangers were stopped and questioned; vigilance committees searched post offices, ships, and stages for antislavery literature. Several southern communities went even further, posting $50,000 for the delivery of Arthur Tappan, president of the society, dead or alive.[32]

Simultaneously, Tappan and his associates began a massive campaign to bombard Congress with thousands of petitions calling for the end of slavery in the nation's capital. Following the example of the leading evangelists of the day, the society relied heavily on church women, especially in New England, upstate New York, and northern Ohio, to go door to door gathering signatures and to keep attention focused on the "SIN" of slavery. After the names were gathered, they were usually pasted onto a standardized form addressed to the "Fathers and Rulers of the Country" and forwarded to Washington. Once in Washington, the plan was to have individual congressmen present the petitions and thus get the slavery question on the House agenda.

The approach, in one sense, was an old one. Since Washington's administration, congressmen had been receiving petitions framed by ordinary citizens, and thus presenting them was just one of the perfunctory duties of every congressman. The practice in the House was to routinely call for petitions, beginning with Maine and moving southward. Congressmen were expected to be brief, to state only the subject of the petition, note the number of signatures and the place from which it came, and move that the petition be referred to committee. Antislavery petitions were also a commonplace. They too had been received since Washington's day. Generally, they had been few in number, treated as insignificant, and quietly buried in committee.[33]

That was not the case in 1835. The American Anti-Slavery Society did not just send a handful of petitions. The society sent thousands—indeed, hundreds of thousands. And, as a horrified John Tyler told a Virginia audience, these petitions were not signed by

32. Richards, *"Gentlemen of Property and Standing,"* 50–2.

33. Initially, during Washington's administration, antislavery petitions had provoked howls of protest from Deep South congressmen. See Stuart Knee, "The Quaker Petitions of 1790: A Challenge to the Democracy of Early America," *Slavery and Abolition* 6 (May 1985): 151–9; and Richard S. Newman, "Prelude to the Gag Rule: Southern Reaction to Antislavery Petitions in the First Federal Congress," *Journal of the Early Republic* 16 (Winter 1996): 571–99.

just a few men; his Committee on the District of Columbia had received one signed by fifteen hundred women. And these women, argued the future president, were not doing the bidding of "a mere handful of obscure persons." They were the "instruments" of "a powerful combination" of "vicious" propagandists, who were also bombarding the South with "incendiary pamphlets" filled with "inflammatory pictures" that were certain to arouse slaves to rebellion and carnage and sharpen "the dagger for midnight assassination." These incendiaries, moreover, were not just making women "the instrument of destroying our political paradise." They were also publishing "horn-books and primers" to corrupt young minds "in the nursery." Thus they had to be stopped—and stopped quickly.[34]

Tyler's refrain was standard throughout the South. The American Anti-Slavery Society, thanks largely to its pamphlet campaign, sent chills of terror through the white South in the summer and fall of 1835. Hence, when Congress met in December 1835, the American Anti-Slavery Society was the hottest issue on the political agenda. Andrew Jackson wanted severe penalties invoked to suppress the antislavery movement's "unconstitutional and wicked" activities. Charging northern abolitionists with making "inflammatory appeals," aimed at "the passions of the slaves" and intended "to stimulate them to insurrection, and to produce all the horrors of servile war," he also praised northern mobs that had broken up antislavery meetings and destroyed abolitionist property.[35]

In Congress the battle over petitions began immediately. On December 16, a Maine congressman presented a petition calling for the abolition of slavery in the nation's capital. A Virginia congressman quickly moved that it be tabled, and by an overwhelming vote the House endorsed his motion. Two days later, a Massachusetts congressman presented a similar petition. This time, James Henry Hammond of South Carolina called for "a more decided seal of reprobation." He wanted the House to reject such petitions peremptorily. Hotspurs from across the South backed him. Indeed, memorials from one slave state after another not only backed his demand to the hilt but also called on

34. The speech, which appeared in the *Richmond Whig* and was reprinted by many other newspapers in September and October 1835, also appears in Lyon Gardiner Tyler, *Letters and Times of the Tylers*, 3 vols. (Richmond, Va., 1884–94), 1: 573–81.

35. Richards, *"Gentlemen of Property and Standing,"* 50–3.

northern states to pass penal laws that would silence forever any "incendiary" who dared to hurl "firebrands" at the South.[36]

Northern congressmen, by and large, had no sympathy for the abolitionists. The stepped-up pamphlet campaign against southern slavery had little support in their home districts. Throughout the summer and fall of 1835, northern anti-abolition rallies had drawn record-breaking crowds. Such prominent politicians as the governor of New York, the attorney general of Massachusetts, and the speaker of the Pennsylvania state senate had taken the podium to denounce the abolitionists. And many northerners had taken to the streets to mob abolitionists. A Boston crowd had terrorized the antislavery agitator William Lloyd Garrison, and on the same day a Utica mob had broken up a convention of the New York State Anti-Slavery Society. The leader of that mob, Samuel Beardsley, was a sitting member of Congress.[37]

Beardsley, moreover, was a Van Buren Democrat. Accordingly, many thought he was doing the Little Magician's bidding, trying to prove to the South that the Bucktails were safe on the slavery issue, and thus that their leader was a safe presidential candidate. Providing such proof was a constant problem for Van Buren. Although he was Jackson's handpicked successor, he had to fend off all sorts of accusations from southerners who dreaded the thought of a northerner in the White House. Some accused him of Catholicism, others of Mormonism. But above all, they accused him of being a closet abolitionist. Wasn't he once a close friend of Rufus King, the fiery opponent of the Missouri bill? Weren't the abolitionist "fanatics" headquartered in his home state? Wasn't their president a New York merchant? Van Buren, for his part, found all this exasperating. To the wife of a Virginia senator, he wrote: "God knows I have suffered enough for my Southern partialities. Since I was a boy I have been stigmatized as the apologist of Southern institutions, & now forsooth you good people will have it . . . that I am an abolitionist."[38]

36. *Congressional Globe*, 24th Congress, 1st session, 1835–36, pp. 24–35; *Register of Debates*, 24th Congress, 1st session, 1835–36, pp. 1966ff. For concise summaries of the debates, see Robert P. Ludlum, "The Antislavery 'Gag Rule': History and Argument," *Journal of Negro History* 26 (April 1941): 203–43; and George C. Rable, "Slavery, Politics, and the South," 69–87.

37. Richards, *"Gentlemen of Property and Standing,"* passim.

38. Morrison, "Gentlemen of Proper Understanding," 61–82; Donald B. Cole,

Yet, despite northern hostility to the abolitionists and Van Buren's need to placate the South, Hammond and his backers were clearly demanding too much. In the eyes of most northern congressmen, the constitutional right of petition included the right to be heard. Even Samuel Beardsley, the congressman who led a mob against Utica abolitionists, would not yield on this point. The House, as he understood constitutional law, could table a petition or reject a petitioner's prayer. But if the petition "was respectful in its language," the House had no constitutional right to reject it outright, to reject it peremptorily without a hearing. To do so would be tantamount to denying the sacred right of petition.[39]

Such objections led to one legal argument after another, but southern diehards were in no mood for constitutional objections. One after another made it clear that, regardless of the law, the abolitionists had to be stopped. The only way to deal with "fanaticism," said one South Carolinian, was "to strangle it in its infancy." Northern congressmen made it clear that there was no way they could ignore the Constitution and allow one of the "pillars of freedom" to be trampled underfoot.[40]

And so it went, back and forth, for nearly six weeks. Meanwhile, nothing had been done to stop the flood of antislavery petitions; they came by the thousands, and a few even made it to the House floor. This added to the chaos; confusion reigned. Finally, in February 1836, Henry Pinckney of South Carolina proposed that all such petitions be referred to a select committee, with the understanding

---

Martin Van Buren and the American Political System (Princeton, 1984), 261; Van Buren to Mrs. (Judith) Rives, 1, 25 April 1835, William C. Rives Papers, Library of Congress; William C. Rives to Van Buren, 10 April 1835, Martin Van Buren Papers, Library of Congress. For a recent account of Van Buren's troubles in the 1836 election, see also William G. Shade, "'The Most Delicate and Exciting Topics': Martin Van Buren, Slavery, and the Election of 1836," *Journal of the Early Republic* 18 (Fall 1998): 459–84.

39. *Register of Debates,* 24th Congress, 1st session, 1835–36, especially 1971, 1975, 1979–80.

40. *Speech of Mr. [Francis] Pickens, of South Carolina . . . January 21, 1836 . . .* (Washington, D.C., 1836). For the vehemence of the southern response and the debates in general, see *Niles' Weekly Register* 49 (December 1835–January 1836): passim, as well as *Register of Debates,* 24th Congress, 1st session, 1835–36, passim. At this session, debate over antislavery and antislavery petitions consumed by far the greatest amount of time.

that the committee would devise an alternative to Hammond's demand for total rejection. Pinckney's proposal enraged other South Carolinians, who denounced him as a traitor to the South and claimed that he had sold out to the Jacksonian presidential hopeful, Martin Van Buren, who clearly wanted to bury the constitutional issue. Whatever Pinckney's motives, his proposal was hardly the compromise that some historians later maintained. From the standpoint of the abolitionists, it was far more dangerous than Hammond's proposal, which in 1836 had little chance of passing.

Once Pinckney had proposed an alternative, the situation changed dramatically. Within a week Pinckney had the votes he needed to get a select committee established. Three months later the committee came back with a new rule for the House. Known from the beginning as the "gag rule," it prohibited the House from printing, discussing, or even mentioning the contents of any petitions related in any way to the subject of slavery. Such petitions were to be "laid on the table" with "no further action whatever." Any congressman who tried to present such petitions would be out of order and subject to the discipline of the House. The main purpose of this rule, said Pinckney, was "to arrest discussion of the subject of slavery within these walls." The measure passed by an overwhelming margin, 117 to 68.[41]

Where did Van Buren's men stand in this conflict? Their stance was virtually the exact opposite of northern Whigs. Of the fifty-five northern Whigs in the House, only one voted for the Pinckney gag, while forty-six voted against it. In contrast, fifty-nine northern Democrats voted for the gag, only fifteen against it. The New York delegation, as in the case of Indian Removal, led the way. Only one of the thirty-one New York Democrats voted against the gag, while twenty-five voted for it:

	New England	New York	Other Free States[a]
Dems. for the gag	12	25	22
Against	4	1	10
Not voting	3	5	7

[a] New Jersey, Pennsylvania, Ohio, Indiana, Illinois

41. *Congressional Globe*, 24th Congress, 1st session, 1835–36, pp. 402–6; Leonard L. Richards, *Life and Times of Congressman John Quincy Adams* (New York, 1986), 119–21.

This remained the pattern for the next three years. Since the Pinckney gag was a resolution, not a standing House rule, it expired at the end of the session.[42] At the beginning of the next session, John Quincy Adams and other northern Whigs had a free rein to present antislavery petitions until another gag rule was passed. That took a month to accomplish. The Van Buren men again went the extra mile to get the gag reestablished, but the pro-gag forces knew that they had to move more quickly in subsequent years, before Adams and others had a chance to present stacks of antislavery petitions. By 1838 they succeeded in imposing a new gag on the first petition day. Maine was called first, according to custom, and two antislavery memorials were presented. But next was New Hampshire, a Jacksonian stronghold, and a staunch New Hampshire Democrat, Charles G. Atherton, presented a gag and forced its immediate passage.

According to the Washington correspondent of the *Connecticut Courant,* Atherton's action resulted from a horse trade between Van Buren and John C. Calhoun. To get southern votes for his subtreasury proposal, Van Buren allegedly agreed to have Atherton introduce a gag written by Robert Barnwell Rhett of South Carolina. Whether this was true or not is uncertain.[43] But, as before, the Van Burenites led the way in providing northern support for the Atherton gag. In disgust, the American Anti-Slavery Society listed in their almanac the fifty-three "northern serviles" who voted with the Slave Power. That, however, turned out to be the last time the Van Burenites earned the top spot on the Society's "Roll of Infamy."[44]

42. The gag's expiration infuriated Jackson. He apparently expected Speaker James K. Polk, a fellow Tennessee slaveholder, to declare the gag a standing House rule at the beginning of the next session. Whether Jackson was unaware of the House rule governing House resolutions, was confused about it, or simply expected the Speaker to ignore the rule is not clear. See Remini, *Andrew Jackson and the Course of American Democracy,* 406.

43. *Connecticut Courant,* 15, 22 December 1838. I have found no compelling evidence to prove or disprove this assertion.

44. *Emancipator,* 20 December 1838; *American Anti-Slavery Almanac* (Boston, 1840), 32–4.

6 | Bucktails into Rebels

By the late 1830s the overwhelming support Van Buren and the Bucktails provided the South was hard to sustain. Not only did northern Whigs take a staunch northern position, but they were also fierce competitors on Election Day. With dozens of strident newspapers and scores of spellbinding orators trying to get out the vote and woo away their supporters, landslide victories increasingly were the exception, close contests the rule.

Jackson's Indian Removal Act, in Van Buren's estimate, had cost the New York party "not less than eight to ten thousand voters" in the 1832 election. It had brought the Bucktails next to "death's door." By the late 1830s such losses could no longer be absorbed. In many districts the loss of just one vote in every one hundred meant defeat. In the Empire State the number of congressional elections decided by less than 250 votes increased from three in 1834 to ten in 1838. The Van Burenites in 1838 carried one New York district by only 43 votes, another by 44, and statewide the loss of just 155 votes would have cost them four congressional seats.[1]

1. *Autobiography of Martin Van Buren,* 2 vols., ed. John C. Fitzpatrick (Washington, D.C., 1920), 1: 294; Martin Van Buren to Francis P. Blair, 12 September 1842, as quoted

Picking up an additional hundred votes here, another hundred there, thus became a major consideration for Van Buren and his followers. That was no easy task, since many voters blamed the Little Magician for the hard times following the Panic of 1837. Democrats were swept out of office in one Jacksonian stronghold after another— in Tennessee, in Mississippi, in North Carolina, in Maine, and most important to the Bucktails, in New York.[2] Partial economic recovery in 1838 briefly slowed the Whig surge, enabling the Jacksonians to retain a majority in the 1838 congressional elections, but a second and deeper economic tailspin in 1839 gave their opponents new life.

To the Van Burenites, the real issues of the day were economic issues, especially those involving currency and banking. They had joined forces with Jackson in the early 1830s to destroy the Second Bank of the United States. In doing so, they had fought with Bank Democrats in Tammany Hall and elsewhere, coming to terms with some, driving others into the opposition party. Now, on the independent treasury bill, which came up for a vote time and again, they could count on 97 percent of the Jackson men, north and south, to support it and 99 percent of the Whigs, north and south, to oppose it. Similarly, on the Whig proposal to establish a third national bank, they knew that 99 percent of their Jacksonian colleagues, north and south, would oppose it and 95 percent of the Whigs would support it. These issues, in their minds, were the issues that truly counted. These were the issues that bound them to southern Democrats. These were the issues that polarized the two national parties. And these were the issues that elections should be about.[3]

---

in William Ernest Smith, *The Francis Preston Blair Family in Politics*, 2 vols. (New York, 1933), 1: 157; *Congressional Quarterly's Guide to U.S. Elections* (Washington, D.C., 1975), 562–3, 570–1.

2. In New York, the Bucktails lost both the governorship and the legislature to William Henry Seward and his Whig followers during the hard times following the Panic of 1837. Out of power for the first time since the mid-1820s, some Bucktails blamed the leadership's banking and fiscal policies, while others called for the purging of all those who were Democrats "by profession" rather than Democrats "by principle." (See, for example, Silas Wright to Azariah C. Flagg, 23 March 1839, Azariah C. Flagg Papers, New York Public Library.) These rifts would split the party in the 1840s into warring factions, Barnburners versus Hunkers.

3. The literature on what the parties stood for, as well as what the Van Burenites thought the parties stood for, is vast. For brief summaries, along with party voting patterns, see Frank Otto Gatell, "Sober Second Thoughts on Van Buren, the Albany

Unfortunately, there were hundreds of voters who strongly disagreed. Not everyone in their home districts accepted the notion that currency and banking were the central issues of the day. Nor did all their constituents regard the gag rule and similar matters as just peripheral issues. That was especially true throughout much of New England, upstate New York, and northern Ohio, where antislavery and antisouthern sentiment was on the rise. In the years preceding the Panic and during the ensuing economic tailspin, the American Anti-Slavery Society had sent antislavery preachers from town to town, organizing men, women, and children into antislavery societies, expanding the antislavery network nationwide from forty-seven locals in 1833 to some thirteen hundred by 1839.[4] Intensive organizing had led to mob violence, which scared off the fainthearted but radicalized others and left the antislavery movement with a hard core of committed members. These women and men, in turn, circulated petitions by the thousands. In 1837–38 alone, they bombarded Congress with over 130,000 petitions calling for the abolition of slavery and the slave trade in the nation's capital, and with over 180,000 petitions opposing the annexation of slaveholding Texas.[5]

Regency, and the Wall Street Conspiracy," *Journal of American History* 53 (June 1966): 19–40; Jean Alexander Wilburn, *Biddle's Bank: The Crucial Years* (New York, 1964); John M. McFaul, *The Politics of Jacksonian Finance* (Ithaca, N.Y., 1972); John Ashworth, *'Agrarians and Aristocrats': Party Political Ideology in the United States, 1837–1846* (Cambridge, England, 1983), 47–51, 272–8; Thomas B. Alexander, *Sectional Stress and Party Strength* (Nashville, 1967), 24–36, 137–52; 272–8; and Michael F. Holt, "The Election of 1840, Voter Mobilization, and the Emergence of Jacksonian Voting Behavior," in *A Master's Due: Essays in Honor of David Herbert Donald,* ed. William J. Cooper, Jr., Michael F. Holt, and John McCardell (Baton Rouge, 1985), 16–58.

On the state level, "bank wars" were also a commonplace, with "radical" hard-money Democrats battling Whigs and "conservative" Democrats over currency and banking policy. See especially James R. Sharp, *The Jacksonians versus the Banks: Politics in the States after the Panic of 1837* (New York, 1970); William G. Shade, *Banks or No Banks: The Money Issue in Western Politics, 1832–1865* (Detroit, 1972); Herbert Ershkowitz and William G. Shade, "Consensus or Conflict? Political Behavior in the State Legislatures during the Jacksonian Era," *Journal of American History* 58 (December 1971): 591–621.

4. Computed from data from the New England Anti-Slavery Society, *First Annual Report* (Boston, 1833); idem, *Second Annual Report* (Boston, 1834); and American Anti-Slavery Society, *Second Annual Report* (New York, 1835) through *Fifth Annual Report* (New York, 1838).

5. Leonard L. Richards, *"Gentlemen of Property and Standing": Anti-Abolition*

The abolitionists, moreover, were relentless. Denying them a voice in Congress hardly sapped their energy. They turned the gag into an asset and portrayed themselves as the defenders of white liberties as well as the champions of hapless slaves. The movement steadily grew. The first gag "was passed in response to . . . 34,000 signatures; the next 110,000; the next 300,000; and the last nearly 500,000."[6] In 1836, the year of the first gag, the American Anti-Slavery Society had 88 local affiliates in Van Buren's home state. By the time of the Atherton gag, the number had expanded to 369.[7]

Not every northern congressman, to be sure, had such zealous constituents to worry about. Despite the abolitionists' pledge to organize societies throughout the country, they tended to concentrate on certain districts more than others, so that by 1839 many counties in Massachusetts and several in New York and Ohio had more antislavery societies than the entire states of Rhode Island, New Jersey, Illinois, Indiana, and Michigan. The result was that some congressmen had to be more alert to antislavery agitation than others. Only at their peril, for instance, could representatives from Oneida County, New York, or Trumbull County, Ohio, ignore the abolitionists. Those representing Long Island or southern Indiana, on the other hand, had little reason to be concerned.[8]

For the most part, the abolitionists made their heaviest inroads in districts represented by Whigs. As a result, even though northern Whigs were anything but doughfaces, they were in danger of losing antislavery votes to the new Liberty Party, an avowed abolitionist party that was active mainly in their districts. In response, northern Democrats preyed on these divisions, accentuated them, and benefited at the polls from the Whigs' predicament. At the same time, however, the Whigs claimed to be the true defenders of northern in-

---

Mobs in Jacksonian America (New York, 1970); American Anti-Slavery Society, *Fifth Annual Report*, 48.

6. Philip G. Wright and Elizabeth Q. Wright, *Elizur Wright: The Father of Life Insurance* (Chicago, 1937), 110, 112; American Anti-Slavery Society, *Fifth Annual Report*, 48. For a full appreciation of the magnitude of the petition campaign, see Legislative Records, RG 233, National Archives.

7. Calculated from data from the American Anti-Slavery Society, *Second Annual Report* through *Fifth Annual Report*.

8. Computed from data from the American Anti-Slavery Society, *Fifth Annual Report*, and Kenneth C. Martis, *The Historical Atlas of United States Congressional Districts, 1789–1983* (New York, 1982).

terests, denouncing the Liberty men as irresponsible agitators and roasting the Democrats as a proslavery, prosouthern party. Would Whigs ever be able to make the charge stick? That possibility worried many Democrats.

Simultaneously, the Van Burenites found southern Democrats unrelenting in their demands. Even the Pinckney gag, which called for the automatic tabling of antislavery petitions, had failed to satisfy southern hotspurs. The followers of John C. Calhoun had demanded more—the outright rejection of antislavery petitions. In 1840 William Cost Johnson, a Maryland Whig, recast this old demand, and, as usual, northern Whigs would have none of it. Southern Democrats jumped into the fray and pressed their northern brethren for support. That was asking too much, in the eyes of many Van Burenites. In essence, they agreed with Samuel Beardsley, now a former congressman and the former attorney general of New York, that outright rejection was unconstitutional. Yet, even though a majority of the Van Buren men balked at supporting the Johnson gag, enough yielded to get it passed and to keep it from being repealed.[9]

The 1840 gag foreshadowed two notable changes in the voting behavior of northern Democrats. For the first time, more northern Democrats voted against the gag than for it, with twenty-seven casting "aye" votes and thirty-nine voting "nay." In comparison, only one of the sixty northern Whigs voted for the gag. Also for the first time, the Van Burenites failed to provide their southern colleagues with the most help. Only seven New York Democrats out of a nineteen-man delegation voted for the Johnson gag; the other twelve voted "nay," and not one man missed the roll call:

	New England	New York	Other Free States[a]
Dems. for the gag	6	7	14
Against	9	12	18
Not voting	0	0	4

[a] New Jersey, Pennsylvania, Ohio, Indiana, Illinois, Michigan

9. *Register of Debates,* 24th Congress, 1st session, 1835–36, pp. 1971, 1975, 1979–80; *Congressional Globe,* 26th Congress, 1st session, 1839–40, pp. 143–51; *Congressional Globe,* 28th Congress, 1st session, 1843–44, pp. 317, appendix: 28–32; Leonard L. Richards, *The Life and Times of Congressman John Quincy Adams* (New York, 1986), 115–21, 175–79.

By this time the Van Burenites had concluded that supporting the gag would cost them votes on Election Day. But did it? Did the election of 1840 bear out their fears? In 1840 the Whigs carried both houses of Congress and the presidency for the first time. But the election campaign, in the eyes of most observers, was anything but a referendum on the serious issues of the day. Instead it became a mighty outpouring of songs, torchlight parades, monster rallies, and log cabin symbolism.

Nationally, a whopping 78 percent of the eligible males went to the polls, and one-third of these men were casting their first ballot. No election before or since brought out so great a portion of new voters. What brought these men to the polls? Sober argument and self-interest? Or three-mile-long Whig parades, political jingles like "Tippecanoe and Tyler Too," and the marketing of the Whig presidential candidate (who was something of a Virginia-born aristocrat) as a cider-drinking man of the people? Many commentators at the time, and most historians over the years, claimed the latter. Humbug, as they saw it, determined the outcome of the presidential election and scores of congressional contests.

In the Bucktails' home state, the situation was somewhat different. Voter turnout in New York had been high for years, and although it peaked in 1840, the surge was less impressive than in other states. Two years earlier, with both parties working diligently to get out the vote, some 375,000 New Yorkers had gone to the polls; in 1840 the number rose to 438,000. Also, unlike Democrats elsewhere, the Bucktails did not lose congressional seats in 1840. They gained one.

But how did they fare in districts where their man had supported the Johnson gag? As one might expect, they held onto the seats which they had won previously by whopping margins. But in the tight races, in districts where the incumbent had won the prior election with less than 51 percent of the total vote, they lost all three in which the incumbent had voted for the Johnson gag. They lost two of the four in which the incumbent voted against the gag. They also had trouble in the heart of antislavery country, in districts where the abolitionists had established fifteen or more locals. They held only two of eight seats before the election, and in both cases their men had voted against the Johnson gag. One of the seats had been won two years before by just forty-four votes; the other they had won handily by over a thousand. This time, they lost the first seat by eight hundred votes and won the second by five hundred. Elsewhere the election news was better. In New York City they ousted four Whigs who voted against the gag.[10]

Although it would be foolhardy for a statistician to make much of these returns, Van Buren and his followers concluded that, except in the major cities, supporting the South would be costly on Election Day. The problem, as Benjamin Bidlack of Pennsylvania later explained, had little to do with the abolitionists' crusade for the immediate abolition of slavery. The people of Wilkes-Barre, his hometown, treated the abolitionists as crackpots, taunted and jeered them, even rode one agitator out of town on a rail. Denouncing the abolitionists, which he did constantly, was thus good politics. And so was belittling the Whigs as the abolition and racial amalgamation party. The problem, said Bidlack, was the South's insistence on the gag rule. It allowed abolitionists to speak out as defenders of white liberties and to portray the national government and the Democratic Party as being totally dominated by slaveholders. And that had hit a responsive chord.[11]

William McCauslen of Ohio agreed. Not only the Whigs, he said, but "every political aspirant of easy political virtue" in his district rode this "hobby-horse" to his party's detriment. In New York the party faithful had no doubt that "every limb" of the state party had been hurt often and severely by its constant support of "southern men" and "southern measures." Lemuel Stetson, a Van Buren loyalist from upstate New York, was more specific. The New York party, he predicted, would lose "1/4" of its "friends" if it did not shed its prosouthern image.[12]

In the early 1840s that was easier said than done. Van Buren, even though he lost the presidency in 1840, still had presidential ambitions. He thus needed southern support and worked diligently to get

10. Computed from data from the *Congressional Globe*, 26th Congress, 1st session, 1839–40, pp. 150–1; American Anti-Slavery Society, *Fifth Annual Report*, 138–44; *Congressional Quarterly's Guide to U.S. Elections*, 726–7, 729.

11. *Congressional Globe*, 28th Congress, 1st session, 1843–44, appendix: 113–4.

12. *Congressional Globe*, 28th Congress, 1st session, 1843–44, pp. 117, 317, appendix: 40–1; Van Buren to Francis P. Blair, 12 September 1842, as quoted in Smith, *Francis Preston Blair Family*, 1: 157; Lemuel Stetson to Azariah. C. Flagg, 31 December 1844, Azariah C. Flagg Papers.

it. The results, however, were disappointing. While he maintained the solid backing of his old Missouri allies, he fared poorly elsewhere in the South, obtaining a firm commitment from only 5 of some 90 delegates to the 1844 Democratic nominating convention. In contrast, in the North, where he also had plenty of critics, he obtained the backing of 134 out of 153 delegates.[13] That was enough to be nominated on the first ballot if only a simple majority was required. But, as it turned out, he needed more than a simple majority.

The main reason for his predicament was that, by the time the Democratic convention met in Baltimore, the annexation of Texas had become the central issue in national politics. For the Van Burenites, this issue had always meant trouble. In the mid-1830s when the Texans rebelled against Mexico, they had tried to portray their revolution as a battle for freedom, but John Quincy Adams and other northern Whigs had labeled it a Slave Power conspiracy. The Texans, Adams had argued, were not fighting for freedom, they were fighting to keep their slaves in bondage; and Andrew Jackson and other slavemasters were aiding them, not for the sake of human freedom, but to further southern interests and to add a covey of slave states to the Union. Since then, northern Whigs had been dead set against the expansion of slavery, and Whigs in general opposed expansion. And Van Buren, as Jackson's successor in 1837, had decided not to touch the Texas issue. It was too explosive, certain to disrupt the Democratic agenda.[14]

Not all Democrats were as cautious as Van Buren, and in the

13. In a recent article, "Martin Van Buren, the Democracy, and the Partisan Politics of Texas Annexation" (*Journal of Southern History* 61 [November 1995]: 695–724), Michael A. Morrison minimizes the difference in delegate count and emphasizes the general unhappiness with Van Buren in both the North and the South. In my judgment, ignoring the delegate count distorts the overall picture.

14. Of the vast literature on the acquisition of Texas, I have relied especially on Justin H. Smith, *The Annexation of Texas*, corrected ed. (New York, 1941); David M. Pletcher, *The Diplomacy of Annexation: Texas, Oregon, and the Mexican War* (Columbia, Mo., 1973); Charles G. Sellers, *James K. Polk: Continentalist, 1843–1846* (Princeton, 1966); Frederick Merk, *Slavery and the Annexation of Texas* (New York, 1972); Thomas R. Hietala, *Manifest Design: Anxious Aggrandizement in Late Jacksonian America* (Ithaca, N.Y., 1985), chaps. 2 and 3; and William W. Freehling, *The Road to Disunion: Secessionists at Bay, 1776–1854* (New York, 1990), chaps. 20–25. For Van Buren's views on the Texas question, see also James C. Curtis, *The Fox at Bay: Martin Van Buren and the Presidency, 1837–1841* (Lexington, Ky., 1970), chap. 8.

early 1840s the penny press and a new school of Democratic politicians calling themselves "Young America" preached the glories of expansionism. They wanted more land added to the United States. They claimed that a democracy of states' rights and limited federal powers could be extended indefinitely. They insisted that the young Republic's manifest destiny would not be fulfilled until "the whole boundless continent is ours."

Added to this mix was a propaganda campaign devised by the president of Texas, General Sam Houston. He had his ministers to the United States and England nourish the rumor that the British government wanted an independent Texas as a buffer against American expansion, as a source of cotton, and as a duty-free market for British industrial goods. He also had them feed the story that British officials would provide Texas with gold and military protection if the Texans gave up slavery.

At first the White House resisted such rumors and demands for American intervention. Van Buren wanted no part of them, and when he lost the presidency in 1840 the pro-Texas lobby's influence was nil. The victorious Whigs had no appetite whatsoever for acquiring huge chunks of additional land. But the new Whig president, William Henry Harrison, died one month after he took office, and his successor, John Tyler of Virginia, was hardly a Whig at all. He had been given second place on the Whig presidential ticket only because his presence might win the support of Virginians, states' rights advocates, and former Jackson men like himself. He had no use for the nationalistic and probusiness policies championed by Henry Clay and other congressional Whigs. True to his beliefs, he vetoed three different bank bills on constitutional grounds. In disgust, Whigs read him out of the party.

Deprived of party support, Tyler decided to push Texas to the fore. Hoping that it would enable him to run for president in 1844 as the candidate of a new pro-Texas third party, or better yet as the Democratic nominee, he launched a propaganda campaign in 1842 that harped on the dangers of a British takeover of Texas. British monarchists, so the argument went, hated and dreaded republicanism; their goal was to destroy the American Republic. Thus they had to be stopped before it was too late.[15] In Congress and in the

15. Whether the Tyler administration and other annexationists actually believed their anti-British rhetoric is open to debate. Years ago, Frederick Merk, after pointing

press, a small coterie of loyal followers, aided by some Democrats, sang the praises of immediate annexation, appealing mainly to the South, Young America, and the widespread hatred of the British. Meanwhile Secretary of State Abel Upshur, a proslavery zealot, negotiated a treaty of annexation with Texas authorities. The negotiations were all but over when Upshur was killed in a freak accident. To complete negotiations, Tyler turned to slavery's foremost spokesman, John C. Calhoun of South Carolina.

That sealed the link between slavery and Texas. After completing negotiations in April 1844, Calhoun sent the treaty to the Senate, along with a copy of a letter that he had written to Richard Pakenham, the British minister to Washington. The letter was a bombshell. Besides denouncing Pakenham's government for interfering in Texas and supporting abolition throughout the Atlantic world, Calhoun sang the praises of slavery and cited statistics to prove that blacks were better off as slaves than freedmen—and that southern slaves were better off than white workers in industrial England. More importantly, he justified annexation as a defense measure in behalf of slavery. The annexation treaty was thus officially labeled a proslavery measure.

No one knows for certain why Calhoun sent this indiscreet letter to the Senate, but according to one theory he wanted to undermine Van Buren's presidential aspirations.[16] If that was his intention, he succeeded. A senator quickly leaked the letter to the press, and suddenly cries of "Slave Power conspiracy" rang through the North. Within four days the frontrunning Whig presidential contender,

out that both sides in the Texas dispute relied on "a mixture of fact and fancy, of truth and falsehood, of humanitarianism and racism," insisted that the "propaganda of the Tyler circle" contained an "exceptionally high percentage of misconception, misrepresentation, and outright falsehood." More recently, Sam W. Haynes has argued that Anglophobia had deep roots in antebellum America and "pro-annexation Democrats viewed alleged British meddling with genuine alarm." Cf. Merk, *Slavery and the Annexation of Texas,* especially xii; and Sam W. Haynes, "Anglophobia and the Annexation of Texas: The Quest for National Security," in *Manifest Destiny and Empire: American Antebellum Expansionism,* ed. Sam W. Haynes and Christopher Morris (College Station, Tex., 1997), 115–45, quote p. 117. Blaming the British for antislavery agitation, it should be noted, was a commonplace by 1844–1845. For over a decade antiabolitionists had portrayed the American antislavery movement as part of a British conspiracy. See Richards, *"Gentlemen of Property and Standing,"* 65–71.

16. Sellers, *Polk: Continentalist,* 57–8.

Henry Clay, announced his opposition to annexation "at this time." The next day Van Buren followed suit. Clay's announcement created only a minor stir among his followers, who by and large opposed territorial expansion, and he won his party's nomination by acclamation. Van Buren's Texas letter, however, raised a storm of protest among Democrats, especially in the southern and western states. Even Jackson turned on his handpicked successor. And at the Democratic convention held in Baltimore, pro-Texas strategists rammed through a measure requiring a two-thirds majority for the presidential nomination.[17]

The two-thirds rule blocked Van Buren's presidential aspirations. Although he came to the convention with a majority of the delegates pledged to him, he could not get two-thirds. Nor could his archrival, Lewis Cass of Michigan. Finally, after a long deadlock, the party turned to James K. Polk, a Tennessee slaveholder whose hardmoney views satisfied the Van Burenites, and whose zeal for expansion satisfied the annexationists.

For the Bucktails the outcome was a bitter pill to swallow. Although Polk was technically a Van Buren loyalist, he was no Van Buren. Nor was he a charismatic leader like Jackson. A minor hero of the Bank War, he had served two terms as Speaker of the House and won the Tennessee governorship but had been defeated twice in subsequent gubernatorial races. Thus, in their eyes, Van Buren had been dumped for a lesser candidate. Moreover, at least thirty-four delegates pledged to vote for Van Buren had deserted the Bucktail leader in the battle over the two-thirds rule. Included among these "traitors" were three men from Massachusetts, three from Connecticut, and twelve from Pennsylvania.

In a strict mathematical sense, these men cost Van Buren the

---

17. For the controversial 1844 Democratic convention, see especially James C. N. Paul, *Rift in the Democracy* (Philadelphia, 1957); James P. Shenton, *Robert John Walker: A Politician from Jackson to Lincoln* (New York, 1961), chap. 4; and Sellers, *Polk: Continentalist*, 61–107. For a minority view, which minimizes the sectional nature of the controversy, see Morrison, "Van Buren, Democracy, and Partisan Politics." For more on how the delegates voted, see Richard C. Bain, *Convention Decisions and Voting Records* (Washington, D.C., 1960), 32–5, appendix; Congressional Quarterly, *National Party Conventions, 1831–1988* (Washington, D.C., 1991), 177; *Albany Argus*, 30, 31 May 1844; and *Northampton Democrat*, 4 June 1844.

nomination in 1844. Yet there was no doubt who orchestrated his defeat. The leading manipulator, the man most responsible for having the two-thirds rule adopted by the convention, was Robert Walker of Mississippi, and most of the Walker's coconspirators were from the slave states. On the critical vote to adopt the rule, 90 of the 104 slave-state delegates voted with Walker, as compared to 58 of the 160 free-state delegates.[18] Finally, after Polk won the presidency by a razor-thin margin, he made Walker his secretary of the treasury. That added insult to injury.

Polk's narrow victory in the general election also troubled Van Buren's followers. The outcome turned on a Democratic plurality of some 5,000 votes in New York, where an outburst of nativism brought thousands of Irish Democrats to the polls, while 16,000 voters supported the antislavery Liberty Party. According to pundits, the desertion of antislavery Whigs to the Liberty Party cost Clay the election. But to Van Buren's followers, Polk's success also hinged on the fact that they had talked a reluctant Silas Wright into running for governor. They believed that Wright's name on the ballot had increased the Democratic turnout and thus offset the impact that antislavery propaganda had against Polk in upstate New York.

What disturbed Bucktail leaders was the magnitude of antislavery and antisouthern sentiment in parts of New England, New York, and northern Ohio. In key districts, Polk trailed the Democratic ticket, running several thousand votes behind Wright in New York, and well behind Bucktail congressional candidates. The leadership concluded that the Texas controversy had given the balance of power to the abolitionists in dozens of communities, including ten upstate New York congressional districts, and hence the state was in danger of falling into Whig hands. They decided it was time to distance themselves from the South.[19]

18. Bain, *Convention Decisions*, appendix; Congressional Quarterly, *National Party Conventions*, 177; *Albany Argus*, 30, 31 May 1844; *Northampton Democrat*, 4 June 1844; Shenton, *Robert Walker*, 42–8.

19. John Arthur Garraty, *Silas Wright* (New York, 1949), 287–329; John M. Niles to Gideon Welles, 12, 24, 25, 31 January 1845, Gideon Welles Papers, Library of Congress. In "Van Buren, Democracy, and Partisan Politics," 721–4, Morrison points out correctly that Polk won more votes in the Northeast than Van Buren did four years earlier. The problem, in the eyes of the Bucktails at least, was that Polk's candidacy didn't provide coattails that helped other Democratic candidates; instead, it was a drag on the ticket.

The opportunity came quickly. In December 1844, a month after Polk's victory, Adams once again called for the repeal of the gag rule. He had done this before, and each time had been voted down. This time, without fanfare or debate, northern Democrats refused to come to the aid of their southern colleagues. Instead of providing the necessary votes to table his motion, they provided the votes to get it passed, 108 to 80. On Adams's side, as always, were all the northern Whigs and four southern Whigs. Also on his side were 78 percent of the northern Democrats, much more than the 59 percent of recent years, and more than enough to kill the gag forever. Portentous was the vote of New York Democrats: eighteen sided with Adams and only two supported their southern colleagues.[20]

Equally portentous was the vote a few months later on the annexation of Texas. The treaty of annexation, which had been formulated by Upshur and finalized by Calhoun, had been voted down by the Senate. But since Polk ran as a zealous expansionist, politicians of both parties had assumed that a vote for Polk was a vote for Texas. After Polk won by a whisker, Tyler and Calhoun claimed that his victory amounted to a popular endorsement of their defeated treaty. Tyler called on Congress to vindicate the treaty by passing a joint resolution that embodied the treaty's precise language. That was too much for most northern Democrats, who wanted no association with the renegade president or Calhoun's Pakenham letter, but many of them also interpreted the results as a mandate for immediate annexation. A host of counterproposals were soon in the making: nine in the House, six in the Senate. No two were alike, and for a time it appeared that Congress would get bogged down in endless squabbling.[21]

At this point, however, a few southern Whigs decided that this was an opportunity to reverse an election trend. In the fall elections southern Democrats had roasted them with the Texas issue, claiming that they were in league with British and northern abolitionists in opposing annexation, and these charges had resonated with many southern voters. To avoid further losses at home, Milton Brown of Tennessee, with the backing of a handful of southern Whigs, offered a

20. *Congressional Globe,* 28th Congress, 2d session, 1844–45, p. 7.
21. For a handy guide to the various Texas proposals, see Sarah Elizabeth Lewis, "Digest of Congressional Action on the Annexation of Texas, December 1844 to March 1845," *Southwestern Historical Quarterly* 50 (October 1946): 251–68.

resolution that would enable Texas, once admitted to the Union, to divide into five slave states.[22] As usual, northern Whigs would have none of it. But southern Democrats, eager to acquire the votes of Brown and his backers, embraced the proposal.

What would northern Democrats do? In some districts Young America and the penny press dominated debate. Together they sang the praises of westward expansion, harped on the dangers of British meddling, and drowned out the voices of the antislavery minority. Here the choice for northern Democrats was easy. If they supported the Texas bill, all would be well. But elsewhere, and especially in districts where antisouthern rhetoric was common, northern Democrats faced a dilemma. If they backed their southern colleagues, they were certain to be denounced as backing a Slave Power conspiracy. If they broke with the southern Democrats, they were equally certain to be denounced for betraying the party's campaign promises. Hadn't the party agreed to a platform calling for the annexation of Texas "at the earliest practicable moment"? Hadn't Polk run on a campaign slogan calling for "the reoccupation of Oregon and the reannexation of Texas"?[23] Given this predicament, most northern Democrats went along with the South, and the Texas bill passed the House, 120 to 98.

But the Van Buren Democrats refused to go along with the majority. During the debate leading up to the vote, several spoke openly against annexation. Lemuel Stetson from upstate New York hid his real objections and focused instead on the bill's constitutional shortcomings. But Jacob Brinkerhoff of Ohio lambasted the annexationists for hatching up a purely "sectional question . . . for the benefit of the South; for the strengthening of her institutions; for the promotion of her power; for her benefit, for the advancement of her influence." George Rathbun, also from upstate New York, not only opposed annexation on antislavery grounds but reminded his colleagues that northern doughfaces who sold their votes to the South

22. *Congressional Globe*, 28th Congress, 2d session, 1844–45, pp. 129–30. The final wording of the Brown amendment is reprinted in Merk, *Slavery and the Annexation of Texas*, 289–90.

23. The predicament of Van Buren and his followers was a constant source of anguish in 1844–45. See Martin Van Buren Papers, Library of Congress; Gideon Welles Papers; Wright-Butler Letters, New York Public Library; and the Azariah C. Flagg Papers. See also "Secret Circular" and "Joint Letter to the Democratic-Republican Electors of the State of New York, July 15, 1844," reprinted in Parke Godwin, *A Biography of William Cullen Bryant*, 2 vols. (New York, 1883), 1: 416–23.

during the Missouri crisis had paid dearly with the electorate.[24] Meanwhile, in the background, trying to organize the vote against Texas, was Preston King, one of the two Bucktails who voted to retain the gag rule.[25] When it came time to vote, he and twenty-six other Van Buren Democrats conspicuously voted against the annexation of Texas, even though they were accused of being defectors and violating the dictates of the party caucus. Below is a breakdown of northern Democratic vote:

	New England	New York	Other Free States[a]
Dems. for annexation	9	10	37
Against	8	13	7
Not voting	0	1	0

[a] New Jersey, Pennsylvania, Ohio, Indiana, Illinois, Michigan

For years Van Buren and his followers had made a fetish of obeying the dictates of the party caucus. They had opposed DeWitt Clinton because he was not a dependable party man. They had supported Indian Removal even though they knew it was unpopular back home. Year in and year out, they had championed party regularity. How, then, could they now break with the dictates of the party caucus? The answer was simple, contended a Connecticut Van Burenite: only men with "no sagacity" and "no instinct" could have failed "to discover public sentiment in their Districts."[26]

The pattern continued—then became even more pronounced—during the Mexican War. Although Polk ran for president as a zealous expansionist, a man who would expand the United States to include all of Oregon and all of Texas, he compromised on the Oregon question. In 1846 he agreed to split with Great Britain the vast Oregon country that stretched all the way from the northern California border to southern Alaska. The British got all the land above the forty-ninth parallel, along with Vancouver Island, and the United States

24. *Congressional Globe,* 28th Congress, 2d session, 1844–45, pp. 173, appendix: 58–61; Lemuel Stetson to Azariah C. Flagg, 31 December 1844, Azariah C. Flagg Papers.

25. Preston King to Azariah C. Flagg, 21 December 1844, 8, 11 January 1845, Azariah C. Flagg Papers.

26. John M. Niles to Gideon Welles, 31 January 1845, Gideon Welles Papers.

got the land to the south. But while Polk was willing to compromise on the Oregon question, he was not willing to compromise with Mexico on Texas. He wanted as much of northern Mexico as he could get, particularly California with its three magnificent harbors, and he deliberately courted war with Mexico to get it.

Mexico was an easy mark. No Mexican regime could survive and give in to the United States, especially to its bullying and bribery. The Polk administration not only demanded that Mexico give up vast chunks of land, but also dispatched troops onto soil that most observers, not just Mexicans, regarded as Mexican land. Then, when these troops were fired upon in April 1846, the Polk administration stampeded Congress into declaring war against Mexico.

The Van Burenites, like most congressmen, were dragooned into supporting the war effort. None sided with John Quincy Adams and the handful of Whig congressmen who voted against the war. But some privately agreed that the Polk administration and its southern supporters wanted to acquire territory in the southwest to expand the dominion of slavery. Van Buren himself never doubted that such suspicions would lead to political trouble. The previous spring he had warned the historian George Bancroft, Polk's secretary of the navy, that the utmost care had to be taken to avoid any war about "which the opposition shall be able to charge us with plausibility, if not truth, that it is waged for the extension of slavery." In any such war, he predicted, northern Democrats would "be driven to the sad alternative of turning their backs upon their friends, or of encountering political suicide with their eyes open."[27]

By the time the war broke out, moreover, Van Buren and his followers were furious at Polk for his handling of federal patronage. Hadn't the Bucktails made Polk president? Hadn't they delivered New York to Polk in the 1844 campaign? Wasn't one of their men entitled to a top cabinet post, either secretary of state or secretary of the treasury? Various major offices were dangled before their eyes, but in the end they got nothing. Instead, they saw the treasury go to Robert Walker, the Mississippi schemer who had blocked Van Buren's nomination, and the War Department go to William L.

27. Martin Van Buren to George Bancroft, 15 February 1845, "Van Buren–Bancroft Correspondence, 1830–1845," *Proceedings of the Massachusetts Historical Society* 42 (June 1909): 439–40. See also Gideon Welles to Van Buren, 28 July 1846, Martin Van Buren Papers.

Marcy, once a New York ally but now a conspicuous enemy. To make matters worse, scores of federal appointments had gone to "Hunkers," a rival faction who were trying to gain control of *their* New York party. And finally, Francis Blair's *Washington Globe*, long the symbol of their dominance nationally, had been replaced as the party's official newspaper by the *Washington Union*, edited by Thomas Ritchie of Virginia. The message, as they saw it, was clear: Polk was deliberately trying to weaken their position and strengthen rival factions not only in the nation at large but also in New York politics.[28]

Hence, while none of the Van Buren men were willing to openly oppose the administration's war efforts, many were angry at Polk and highly suspicious of his war aims. They wanted no part of any war that might lead to the expansion of slave territory. Still, they were slow to push the slavery issue. Not until the last days of the congressional session, in August 1846, did a small band of Van Burenites decide to take a stand. They had been in session for nine months, and were just about to go home, when Polk sprang on them a last minute request for two million dollars "to provide for any expenditure which it may be necessary to make in advance for the purpose of settling all our difficulties with Mexico." During a two-hour recess they decided to amend the bill to prohibit slavery in any land obtained by virtue of the appropriation. To present this amendment, they looked to David Wilmot, an obscure Pennsylvania Democrat who was friendly with the South and would have little trouble gaining the floor. If Wilmot had had any previous antislavery tendencies, he had kept them well hidden. The preceding December he had voted with the South to annex Texas and against an amendment prohibiting slavery in part of Texas.[29]

28. Joseph G. Rayback, "Martin Van Buren's Break with James K. Polk: The Record," *New York History* 31 (January 1955): 51–62; Ivor Debenhorn Spencer, *The Victor and the Spoils: A Life of William L. Marcy* (Providence, R.I., 1959), 133–4, 139–40; Garraty, *Wright*, 342–56.

29. *Congressional Globe*, 29th Congress, 1st session, 1846–47, pp. 64–5. Wilmot's motives—as well as his role in formulating the proviso—have long been a matter of dispute. Along with Wilmot, at least nine other Democrats had a role in formulating the proviso: Preston King, Martin Grover, Timothy Jenkins, and George Rathbun of New York, Hannibal Hamlin of Maine, Paul Dillingham of Vermont, James Thompson of Pennsylvania, and Jacob Brinkerhoff of Ohio. (Some accounts also list John Parker Hale of New Hampshire, but he was not a member of this particular Congress.) All ten men

When Wilmot presented this proviso, it created only a minor stir. Half the members clearly had their minds on getting out of Washington's unbearable heat and catching a train home, and some of the most outspoken antislavery Whigs were already on their way home. The first round of voting, however, proved that the proviso had bite, resonating well beyond the small antislavery faction in Congress. The ayes and nays were not generally recorded that hot August night, but in the one vote that was recorded, southerners were in opposition, sixty-seven to two, and northerners in favor, eighty-three to twelve. Eight northern Whigs put their antiexpansionist feelings first and voted against putting aside any money for the purchase of *any* land, slave or free. Only four northern Democrats and two southern Whigs truly crossed sectional lines and voted with the other side. The proviso passed the House by a four to three margin, but neither the proviso nor the Two Million Bill got through the Senate in the few hours before adjournment.[30]

That fall, relations between the White House and the Bucktails deteriorated even further. In a battle for control of the New York party, some of Polk's Hunker appointees sabotaged the reelection bid of Governor Silas Wright, the Bucktail candidate. Polk threatened to fire the miscreants, but his words proved to be only words and Hunker officials continued to work against Wright. When Wright lost the election by 5,000 votes, Preston King and many other Bucktails were livid. As they saw it, the treachery of the White House had cost them control of the state government. Why,

---

were Van Buren Democrats. And all came from districts where the antislavery vote was significant or Polk clearly had been a drag on the Democratic ticket. In Wilmot's district, for example, Polk had run roughly seven hundred votes behind Wilmot and two hundred behind the Democratic gubernatorial candidate. In Dillingham's district, the Liberty Party had captured 10 percent of the vote. In his fine dissertation, Jonathan Earle indicates that these men also represented constituents who had frequently petitioned Congress to set aside the public lands for white northern farmers and their children. See Jonathan Halperin Earle, "The Undaunted Democracy: Jacksonian Antislavery and Free Soil, 1828–1848" (Ph.D. dissertation, Princeton, 1996), 355.

Of the literature on the proviso, I have relied mainly on Charles Buxton Going, *David Wilmot: Free Soiler* (New York, 1924); Champlain W. Morrison, *Democratic Politics and Sectionalism: The Wilmot Proviso Controversy* (Chapel Hill, 1967); and Eric Foner, "The Wilmot Proviso Revisited," *Journal of American History* 61 (September 1969): 262–79.

30. *Congressional Globe*, 29th Congress, 1st session, 1845–46, pp. 1217–18.

then, should they back Polk and his southern supporters in the interest of party harmony? He wasn't loyal to them. Nor were his southern backers. Moreover, his identification with slaveholding interests was clearly a liability for them in New York politics. The Whigs had roasted them time and again for being the junior partners in a proslavery and prosouthern party.[31]

Thus when Congress resumed in December, King and his associates were anxious to reintroduce the Wilmot Proviso. "The time has come," announced King at the turn of the year, "when the Republic should declare that it will not be made an instrument to the extension of slavery on the continent of America."[32] But the White House played a waiting game. One month passed, then two, before Polk renewed his request for money. This time the request was for three million dollars to cover "extraordinary expenses" in making peace with Mexico. To this bill King and his cohorts prodded Wilmot to add a tougher version of his proviso, one that would bar slavery in "any territory on the continent of America which shall hereafter be acquired."[33]

On reintroducing his proviso, Wilmot appealed to northern racism. "I have no squeamish sensitiveness upon the subject of slavery, nor morbid sympathy for the slave," he declared. "I plead the cause of the rights of white freemen. I would preserve for free white labor a fair country, a rich inheritance, where the sons of toil, of my own race and own color, can live without the disgrace which association with negro slavery brings upon free labor."[34]

This fusion of antislavery with racism clearly had wide appeal, especially among northern Democrats. Hence, more than ever, the proviso was a threat to the South. This led to long and heated debates, along with a series of parliamentary roadblocks. Finally, in February 1847, King and his cohorts succeeded in bringing the pro-

31. Garraty, *Wright*, 362–88; Herbert D. A. Donovan, *The Barnburners* (New York, 1925), 74–83; Jabez D. Hammond, *History of Political Parties in the State of New York*, 2 vols. (Albany, 1842), 2: 677–90.

32. *Congressional Globe*, 29th Congress, 2d session, 1846–47, pp. 114–5.

33. Preston King to Azariah C. Flagg, 18 January–22 February 1847, Azariah C. Flagg Papers; Going, *Wilmot*, 161–3.

34. *Congressional Globe*, 29th Congress, 2d session, 1846–47, p. 317; Eugene H. Berwanger, *The Frontier against Slavery: Western Anti-Negro Prejudice and the Slavery Extension Controversy* (Urbana, Ill., 1967), 123–37.

viso up for a vote. The administration worked frantically to defeat the measure, and eighteen northern Democrats joined the South in opposition. But none of these votes came from the Van Burenites; the Bucktails and their allies voted overwhelmingly for the proviso, as did the northern Whigs. The proviso and the Three Million Bill thus passed the House, 115 to 106.

Four days later in the Senate, Calhoun lambasted the proviso. The passage of the proviso, he thundered, would give the North overwhelming power in the future, and such a destruction of sectional balance would mean "political revolution, anarchy, civil war, and widespread disaster." As a southern man, a cotton planter, a slaveholder, he would never acknowledge inferiority. "The surrender of life is nothing to sinking down into acknowledged inferiority."[35] Shortly thereafter, the Senate rejected the proviso and passed its own Three Million Bill without any mention of slavery.

The Senate bill gained the upper hand and came before the House on March 3, the last day of the session. If the bill passed as it was, Polk would have his three million dollars with no strings attached and the proviso would be dead. To prevent this, antislavery forces again tried to attach the proviso, but this time they were defeated, 97 to 102. The administration, stepping up its efforts to kill the proviso, got six northern Democrats to switch their votes and six more to absent themselves from the proceedings. As a result, while every northern Whig voted for the proviso, twenty-two northern Democrats now voted with the South:

	New England	New York	Other Free States[a]
Dems. for the proviso	9	16	17
Against	0	3	19
Not voting	1	2	10

[a] New Jersey, Pennsylvania, Ohio, Indiana, Illinois, Michigan, Iowa

Not one of the twenty-two men who voted with the South was a Van Buren loyalist—not even one of the three New Yorkers. Who, then, were they? Nearly all were backbenchers, obscure men whose lives never received much biographical attention. But one fact stands out: all but four were lame duck congressmen serving out the

35. *Congressional Globe*, 29th Congress, 2d session, 1846–47, pp. 453–5.

last day of their term. Two had been beaten by men who had run for Congress as Free-Soilers. Of the three New Yorkers, only William Woodworth, who represented Dutchess County, had even tried to get the Democratic nomination in 1846. He had failed, a casualty of the bitter infighting in the New York party. A speculator, he had interests in slaveholding Cuba and later made a small fortune in railroad building, real estate, and banking.[36]

All the big names in the Van Buren coalition voted against the South. Relations with Polk and southern Democrats thus deteriorated even further. During the next year some Bucktail elders tried to keep the younger generation in check, counseling them to proceed with caution rather than declare open war against the Polk administration. But both old and young were in constant battle with Polk's New York supporters. These men, who were generally Hunkers, used essentially the same strategy against the Bucktails as the Bucktails had used against the Clintonians some twenty years earlier. They portrayed themselves as dependable Democrats, men who were much more supportive of the South and slavery than their Bucktail rivals. And like the Bucktails in Clinton's day, they profited from it.

Finally, in 1848, the matter came to a head. Unable to settle their differences, the Hunkers and Bucktails sent rival delegations to the Democratic convention in Baltimore. The Van Burenites insisted on being seated as the only valid New York delegation, but they failed to gain the upper hand and saw their rivals treated as equals or as superiors. In the end the Van Burenites bolted, proclaiming that a Free-Soil Democratic convention would be held in Utica. At Utica, and then later at Buffalo, almost all the old Van Burenite leadership showed up. So did many younger followers, and together with defectionist Whigs and Liberty Party men they put together the Free-Soil Party. Van Buren himself was chosen to be the standard-bearer, Charles Francis Adams, John Quincy's youngest son, was chosen for the vice presidency, and the Liberty men got a chance to put their imprint on the platform. The chief goal was to stop the expansion of

36. Computed from data from the *Congressional Globe*, 29th Congress, 2d session, 1846–47, p. 573; *Congressional Quarterly's Guide to U.S. Elections*, 739–40; and U.S. Congress, *Biographical Directory of the American Congress, 1774–1971* (Washington, D.C., 1971).

slavery and the domination of southern power. The new party specifically attacked the "aggressions of the slave power."[37]

The old ties with the South were thus completely broken. But the election was a disaster for the New York party. In the previous election, they had lost the governorship by 5,000 votes; this time they lost by 95,000 votes. In the New York congressional races, they lost every seat except the one held by Preston King. Their Hunker rivals did no better, winning only one House seat and losing the gubernatorial election by even a bigger margin than the Bucktails. Against a divided Democracy, the Whigs had an easy time of it, winning virtually every office in the Empire State, including thirty-one of thirty-four congressional seats, most by huge margins.[38]

After the debacle, pragmatists in both camps tried to reach a truce. But hard-line Hunkers would have none of it and insisted on punishing Free-Soilers for desertion. Shortly thereafter, the two camps split into three factions: Hard Shell Democrats, Soft Shell Democrats, and Free-Soilers. Led by Senator Daniel S. Dickinson, the Hards called for the purging of all Free-Soilers, firmly backed the South, and chastised the Softs for trying to find middle ground. The Free-Soilers were isolated in most districts but willing to work with the Softs if they nominated suitable candidates. In 1850, enough of these warriors temporarily banded together to win half the state's

37. Of the literature on the Van Burenite decision to bolt the Democratic Party, I have relied mainly on Richard H. Sewell, *Ballots for Freedom: Antislavery Politics in the United States, 1837–1860* (New York, 1976), 142–56; Joseph G. Rayback, *Free Soil: The Election of 1848* (Lexington, Ky., 1970); Donovan, *Barnburners*, 90–7; and O. C. Gardiner, *The Great Issue* (New York, 1848), 45–176.

The sincerity of the Van Burenites in joining the antislavery cause has long been questioned. Much of the doubt centers on Van Buren's son John, who in 1847–48 vigorously campaigned against proslavery Democrats and helped bring old guard Bucktails—including his father—into the antislavery fold, then left the free-soil movement in 1849 and later supported the proslavery administrations of two doughface presidents, Franklin Pierce and James Buchanan. John Van Buren was neither typical nor atypical; some followed his twisted path, others did not. For a recent account, see Earle, "Undaunted Democracy," 128–66.

38. There was a third Democratic victor, Gideon Reynolds of Rensselaer County, a former Whig who broke with his party over the Anti-Rent War and ran as an Anti-Rent Democrat. Neither the Van Burenites nor the Hunkers ran candidates in his district. For the election returns, see *Congressional Quarterly's Guide to U.S. Elections*, 518, 739–40, 743–4.

congressional seats and to come within 250 votes of putting a Soft Shell Democrat into the governor's office. In 1852, the same coalition prevailed in the governor's race by some 25,000 votes and carried two-thirds of the House districts.[39]

But the discipline of the old Van Buren party was missing. No longer could the South count on the New York party to deliver the lion's share of the doughface vote. Senator Dickinson and his followers were dependable, but the rest were not. Only Hiram Walden, the one Hunker elected in 1848, supported the Fugitive Slave Act in 1850, and only nine New York Democrats supported the repeal of the Missouri Compromise in 1854. Gone were the days when the South could turn to the Bucktails for sixteen to twenty-five votes.

Gone too were the days that the South could count on New England Democrats for support. During the battle over Indian Removal, Jackson and his southern backers got far more help from New England Democrats than from Democrats representing Pennsylvania or the Old Northwest. Not one voted against the removal act, and eight voted for it. Five years later, at the time of the Pinckney gag, two-thirds of the New England Democrats voted with the South and only one-fifth against. In so doing, they provided their southern colleagues with as much help as Democrats from Pennsylvania and the Northwest.

Yankee Democrats who had moved west were just as helpful as those who represented New England. Indeed, in the 1830s Democrats who hailed from one of the six New England states were invariably more supportive of the South than other northern Democrats.[40] On

39. For details on the various attempts to reconstruct the New York Democratic Party, see Walter L. Ferree, "The New York Democracy: Division and Reunion, 1847–1852" (Ph.D. dissertation, University of Pennsylvania, 1953). For the 1850 and 1852 elections, see *Congressional Quarterly's Guide to U.S. Elections*, 518, 747, 751–2.

40. In Congress, Yankees were legion, representing the Berkshires as well as Boston, rural backwaters as well as burgeoning factory towns, many districts in New York and the Old Northwest as well as every district in New England. Outside New England, denouncing Yankees, poking fun at them, accusing them of being pious cheats and liars—all were commonplaces. Nonetheless, between the War of 1812 and the Civil War, over 40 percent of all northern congressmen hailed from one of the six New England states. Originally they tended to identify with one party more than the other. In the early Jacksonian period, two Yankees out of three were anti-Jackson men. By the mid-1830s, when the second two-party system became firmly established, half were in Van Buren's camp, half in opposition.

the Pinckney gag, for instance, 75 percent of the northern Democrats who were born and raised in New England voted with the South, as compared to 61 percent of the non-Yankees. Well aware of this tendency, antislavery newspapers frequently compiled long lists of Yankee doughfaces and repeatedly claimed that New Hampshire was the most doughface state in the Union.[41] Every member of the New Hampshire congressional delegation was a Democrat, all supported Indian Removal, all backed the gag rule. In 1838, the South used a New Hampshire man to get the gag reestablished for that session of Congress.

In the 1840s all this changed. Just as it had in New York, the American Anti-Slavery Society made a deep imprint on many a New Englander's district, and while few constituents cared much about black freedom, talk about northern subservience to an overbearing "slave oligarchy" became increasingly common. That troubled Yankee congressmen,[42] and soon Yankee Democrats were less likely than non-Yankees to yield to the South, especially to the South's expansionist demands. On the crucial bill to annex Texas, 50 percent of the Yankee Democrats voted with the South as compared to 75 percent of the non-Yankees, on the Wilmot Proviso, 17 percent to 34 percent, and on Kansas-Nebraska, 27 percent to 57 percent.

Particularly instructive is the case of New Hampshire. The state party was like New York's in that it was well organized, was run with a firm hand, and put a premium on party discipline. At the polls, it was even more successful, winning election after election by huge margins, making New Hampshire the Jacksonians' banner state. Until 1840 it also had a perfect doughface record. Then Jared Williams voted against the new, tougher gag rule. Three years later John Parker Hale followed suit. The following year came the Texas issue, and suddenly the state's doughface leadership had trouble keeping the party faithful in line.

Part of the problem lay with the leadership. For years Isaac Hill, who ran the state party with an iron hand, had opposed the annexation of Texas. His newspaper had even denounced it as a disgrace

41. See, for example, *Boston Liberator*, 6, 13 July, 21, 18 December 1838; 24 January 1845; *Emancipator*, 20 December 1838, 27 February 1840.

42. The growing anger and dismay of Van Buren's Yankee followers, especially in 1844 and 1845, is a recurring theme in the Martin Van Buren Papers, the Gideon Welles Papers, the Azariah C. Flagg Papers, and the Wright-Butler Letters.

that would bring "the just retribution of an angry God."[43] But his views on Texas never matched his fear of losing federal patronage. Hill and the other party chieftains wanted more patronage, not less, and in 1844 that seemingly meant backing the annexationists. So in 1844 Hill reversed himself, jumped on the Texas bandwagon, and called for the immediate annexation of Texas. Then, after Polk barely won the presidency on an expansionist platform, Hill got the state legislature to pass a series of resolutions instructing New Hampshire congressmen to push for annexation. Half of the congressional delegation went along. The other half, however, revolted and voted against annexation.

Especially irritating to the state's doughface leaders was the behavior of John Parker Hale. He not only voted against annexation and spoke in Congress against the Texas bill, but he also sent a letter to his constituents, telling them that the Texas bill was a proslavery measure and asking them to act decisively as "a committee of the whole people."[44] In short, he went over the heads of the party leadership to appeal for support. That was outright treason in the eyes of the party chieftains, and they gave Franklin Pierce the job of driving Hale out of politics. Pierce acted swiftly, ran another Democrat against Hale, and successfully blocked Hale's reelection.

That, however, failed to restore party discipline. Minirebellions repeatedly sprang up across the Granite State. In 1847 the entire House delegation voted for the Wilmot Proviso and against the expansion of slavery into the Mexican Cession. By 1854 even the charm and power of the gregarious Franklin Pierce was ineffective. Now president and in control of vast amounts of patronage, Pierce

43. For this paragraph and the preceding, I am dependent on the voting records of the pertinent congressmen, along with two reminiscences and several excellent secondary sources: John L. Hayes, *Reminiscences of the Free Soil Movement in New Hampshire, 1845* (Cambridge, Mass., 1885), 10–7, 32–42 ; Amos Tuck, *Autobiographical Memoir of Amos Tuck* (N.p., 1902), 70–81; Donald B. Cole, *Jacksonian Democracy in New Hampshire, 1800–1851* (Cambridge, Mass., 1970), 218–24; Lucy Lowden, "'Black As Ink—Bitter As Hell': John P. Hale's Mutiny in New Hampshire," *Historical New Hampshire* 27 (Spring 1972): 27–50; Roy F. Nichols, *Franklin Pierce: Young Hickory of the Granite Hills* (Philadelphia, 1958), 118–22, 133–7; and Richard H. Sewell, *John P. Hale and the Politics of Abolition* (Cambridge, Mass., 1965), 50–3.

44. John P. Hale, *Letter to His Constituents on the Proposed Annexation of Texas* (Washington, D.C., 1845). Also reprinted in the *New Hampshire Patriot and State Gazette,* 23 January 1845.

went to great lengths to rally House members from his home state for the Kansas-Nebraska Act. In the end, however, only Harry Hibbard sided with the South.

Overall, then, southern Democrats during the 1840s lost the hard core of their original doughface support. No longer could they count on New England and New York Democrats to provide them with winning margins in the House. Not only had many old allies turned their backs on the South, many had joined the opposition and added their voices to the growing crusade against the Slave Power.

The new voices, however, often jarred with the old. In lambasting the Slave Power, the Van Burenites generally had a much different story to tell than the men and women who had been carrying on the battle for years, especially those who came out of the New England Federalist tradition. Instead of blaming Thomas Jefferson and his Virginia associates, the Little Magician's followers celebrated the author of the Declaration of Independence and called their local organizations "Jefferson Committees."[45] And instead of tracing the Slave Power back to the days of Jefferson, they focused on the last years of the Jackson era.

To them the movement to acquire Texas, and the fight over the Wilmot Proviso, marked the turning point, the time when aggressive slavemasters stole the heart and soul of the Democratic Party and began dictating the course of the nation's destiny. Many argued that until then the nation's leaders had regarded slavery as a curse that in time would die out completely if confined to its existing limits. To prove their point, they often quoted Jefferson and cited the prohibition of slavery in the Old Northwest in 1787. Hadn't the noble Jefferson denounced slavery and the African slave trade in the original draft of the Declaration of Independence? Hadn't he called for barring slavery in the entire West in 1784 and successfully blocked its expansion north of the Ohio River in 1787?[46]

45. Donovan, *Barnburners,* 106.

46. See, for example, the speeches of Preston King, George Rathbun, Timothy Jenkins, John Dix (all of New York), Robert McClelland (Michigan), and James Dixon (Connecticut), in *Congressional Globe,* 29th Congress, 2d session, 1846–47, pp. 114, 365, 420, 523, appendix: 180, 335, 392; the speech of Martin Grover at the Barnburner convention at Utica, New York, June 1848, in Gardiner, *The Great Issue,* 108; *The Herkimer Convention: The Voice of New York!* (Albany, 1847); Theodore Sedgwick,

Just as Jefferson was often central to their story line, so too was the Jacksonian tradition. Rejecting the notion that they had broken with their Jacksonian past, they portrayed themselves as carrying on the sacred Jacksonian battle in behalf of producers' rights, widespread land ownership, economic equality, and "extending the area of freedom." In the past, so they argued, they had led the battle against banks and monopolies that had threatened the rights and liberties of the people. Now, just as they had overcome a "monstrous Money Power," they would overcome a much more dangerous threat, a "monstrous Slave Power" that intended to seize the West, add to its power over the federal government, and wreak further havoc on the liberties and aspirations of northern white men and women.

Yet, despite the different story line, the Van Burenites also shared much with those who came out of rival political traditions. In forging the new Free-Soil Party in 1848, they had to work hand in hand with old enemies, who not only had denounced the Slave Power for years but also had characterized Van Buren as the North's worst doughface. It was an awkward situation, to say the least. Nonetheless, at the Buffalo convention, the Little Magician's followers made one former enemy, Seth Gates of Wyoming County, their candidate for lieutenant governor. They made another, the son of their old nemesis John Quincy Adams, the presiding officer of the convention. They also ended up making him their vice presidential candidate.

That they backed Adams and Gates was partly political necessity. Although troubling to many Van Burenites, it was also fairly

Jr., ed., *A Collection of the Political Writings of William Leggett,* 2 vols. (New York, 1840), preface, 2: passim; idem, *Thoughts on the Proposed Annexation of Texas* (New York, 1844); "What Shall Be Done for the White Men?" *New York Evening Post* 27 April 1848; "Address of the Democratic Members of the Legislature of New York, April 12, 1848," in Martin Van Buren Papers; and "Letter of John M. Niles to the Free Soil State Convention of Connecticut," in *The Barnburner,* 12 August 1848.

The same themes were also popularized outside New York and New England. See, for example, the speech of Senator Thomas Morris of Ohio in *Congressional Globe,* 25th Congress, 1st session, 1838–39, appendix: 167–75; B. F. Morris, *The Life of Thomas Morris* (Cincinnati, 1856), 176–202; Salmon P. Chase and Charles Dexter Cleveland, *Anti-Slavery Addresses of 1844 and 1845* (Philadelphia, 1867); Salmon P. Chase, *Reclamation of Fugitives from Service; An Argument . . . in the Case of Wharton Jones v. John Van Zandt* (Cincinnati, 1847); and "Free Soil Platform of 1848," in *National Party Platforms, 1840–1960,* comp. Kirk H. Porter and Donald Bruce Johnson (Urbana, Ill., 1961), 13–4.

easy to do, for they now echoed many of the sentiments of their old enemies. Now they also insisted that the additional weight of three-fifths representation and Senate parity, coupled with the sectional solidarity wrought by the "black strap of slavery," enabled a declining and small minority of slavemasters to run roughshod over the "plain republicans of the North," corrupt their leaders, and effectively rule the nation.

7 | Pennsylvania and the West

In reformulating the Slave Power thesis, the Van Burenites gave the word *doughface* a new twist. They shifted the focus onto their Hunker rivals and Democrats from Pennsylvania and the West. And for special condemnation they singled out Lewis Cass of Michigan. Cass, so they argued, was especially culpable in leading northern Democrats away from their roots and into the hands of the "slaveocracy." In his "desperate leap for the *White House*," as one keynote speaker put it, he had turned traitor to the North and to freedom and had "become a soldier under the black banner of Aggressive Slavery."[1]

A onetime New England schoolteacher, Cass had moved to the Northwest Territory in 1801 and become one of the West's most aggressive expansionists. He wanted to annex Canada and hated the British for getting in the way. He provided the intellectual justification for Jackson's Indian removal policy, and as Old Hickory's secretary of war he was largely responsible for the Trail of Tears, the eight-hundred-mile forced march that killed off nearly one-fourth of

1. Speech of George Rathbun to the Utica Convention, February 1848, in O. C. Gardiner, *The Great Issue* (New York, 1848), 94–6.

the entire Cherokee nation. Later, as minister to France, he vehemently denounced a proposed five-power treaty that obligated the United States to work with Great Britain in suppressing the African slave trade. Did that mean that the British now had the right to search American vessels? Cass thought it did, and he appealed to anti-British sentiment across the United States. In so doing, he became the darling of the states' rights and proslavery factions in the Democratic Party.[2]

In their effort to block Van Buren's nomination at the 1844 Democratic convention, most of these states' righters and proslavery men threw their weight behind Cass. On the first ballot, fifty-seven of the seventy-five Deep South delegates voted for the Michigan Democrat. In contrast, only fifteen of forty-nine delegates from Cass's home base of the Old Northwest initially supported his nomination. He picked up several additional western votes on the second and third ballots. And on the eighth ballot, when his vote peaked, he had the backing of twenty-six western delegates. Only the Ohio men, who staunchly supported Van Buren, refused to cross over to Cass's side.

Cass never got two-thirds of the western vote, let alone the two-thirds of the convention vote needed for nomination. Denied the 1844 presidential nomination, Cass was quickly elected to the Senate. There he allegedly was the western Democracy's foremost spokesman on national issues and, in the eyes of the Van Burenites, a traitor to the hallowed traditions of the original Jackson party.

The Van Burenites of course were guilty of special pleading. Cass was hardly the monster they made him out to be. Nor was he able to deliver the western vote. And until the 1840s, western Democrats had never matched the Little Magician's northeastern followers in providing southern party whips with crucial votes. Nor had Pennsylvania and New Jersey Democrats. Only in the Senate, where it was relatively easy for southern leaders to fashion a majority, had these men been real assets. In the House, where winning always took more effort, it was a far different story.

That became clear at the time of the Indian Removal Act.

2. For details on Cass, the standard source is Frank B. Woodward, *Lewis Cass: The Last Jeffersonian* (New Brunswick, N.J., 1950). For a slightly different emphasis, see also Willard Carl Klunder, *Lewis Cass and the Politics of Moderation* (Kent, Ohio, 1996).

Andrew Jackson, despite his enormous popularity in Pennsylvania, had a tough time selling Indian Removal to his followers in the Keystone State. He threatened, he cajoled, he used patronage. Yet in the end, he managed to get only one-third of his Pennsylvania supporters to back the Removal Act. And in the Old Northwest, where there were still tribes of some stature, he did even worse. Despite the help of Cass, who was widely hailed as the nation's foremost expert on Indian affairs, Old Hickory managed to get only three of the eleven Jackson men to support the Removal Act .

By the time of the gag rule, party discipline had improved and putting together a majority was easier. New Jersey Democrats voted against the first gag, but twice as many Pennsylvania and western Democrats voted for the gag as voted against it. These numbers, however, hardly compared with the help provided to the South by New England Democrats, where the ratio was three to one, or New York, where it was as much as twenty-five to one. Until the new, tougher gag of 1840, southern party whips always found Democrats from the Ohio Valley, Pennsylvania, and New Jersey to be less responsive than those from the Northeast, especially those who looked to Martin Van Buren and the Albany Regency for guidance.

In 1840, when the New Englanders and the New Yorkers started having sober second thoughts about supporting "southern measures," there was for the first time a break in the pattern. New Jersey Democrats were still no help at all, since the state had been swept by the Whigs in the previous election, and every one of them voted against the gag. But Pennsylvania Democrats, although still lagging behind the New Englanders, now provided the South with more help than the New Yorkers. And among the Jacksonians from the Old Northwest, nearly as many now voted with the South as voted against.

By the mid-1840s, especially during the battles over Texas and the Wilmot Proviso, the changeover was complete. Northern Democrats still provided their southern colleagues with the necessary votes to win in the House, but the votes no longer came mainly from the New England and New York delegations. The most dependable doughfaces now represented Pennsylvania and the Old Northwest. In the battle over Texas and the subsequent battle over the Wilmot Proviso, not one New England or New York district backed the southern Democracy in both contests. In contrast, five districts

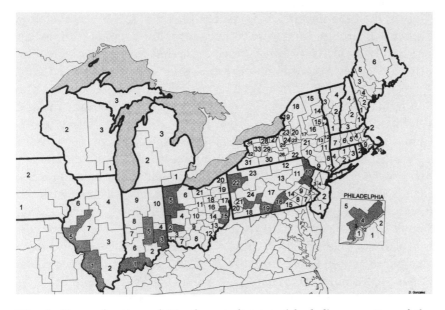

Map 1. Pennsylvania and Northwest districts (shaded) supportive of the southern Democracy

in Pennsylvania and eight in the Northwest sent to Congress men who never broke ranks with their southern colleagues.

Such remained the case until the Civil War, with Jackson men from Pennsylvania and New Jersey consistently providing the South with help, Democrats from the new frontier states to the west often providing the South with the most votes. But getting that support was no easy task. Southern Democrats and their northern allies had to work hard to put together the needed majority, much harder than they had had to work to secure Van Burenite votes.

Why was that the case? And why, in the 1830s, were Jackson men from the Ohio Valley, Pennsylvania, and New Jersey less responsive than their northeastern colleagues to southern demands and aspirations? Why the turnabout in the 1840s?

Two facts immediately stand out. First and perhaps foremost, these men were less likely to have strong ties to Martin Van Buren and his political fortune. Only the hard-money Ohio Democrats could be counted upon to support the Bucktail leader in a crisis.

Most of the others were fair-weather followers. As long as the New Yorker was on top, they were in his camp, but keeping him on top was hardly their first priority. Arguments that worked well with the Little Magician's hard-line followers thus failed to move them. They were less concerned about Van Buren's need to placate the South, his need to allay southern fears about a northern man in the White House, or his need to prove that he was not a closet abolitionist. Those were his problems, not theirs.

Some undoubtedly were Van Buren men in name only. Publicly in his corner, they were in reality just biding their time, looking for the right issue, the right man, and the right opportunity to break with the Bucktail leader.[3] Within the Democracy generally, there was a division of sentiment over tariff policy, with South Carolinians and cotton planters clamoring for drastic reductions and Pennsylvanians championing protection. Some westerners sided with the freetraders, others with the protectionists. Van Buren tried to straddle the gulf, which satisfied only those in the middle. Similarly, there were divisions over banking and currency questions. Here Van Buren was less vague. He was the acknowledged leader of the so-called radical wing of the party, which agitated for hard money and the divorce of the government from all banks. Conservative Democrats maintained that this scheme had to be thwarted. It endangered commerce as well as their self interests. They favored instead cheap paper currency and the use of local banks as federal depositories.[4]

Overcoming these and other divisions was no easy task. Jackson, despite his forcefulness and his popularity, never got either the Pennsylvanians or the westerners to close ranks behind the bugle horn of party. Typical of many was John Findlay of Cincinnati, who saw him-

3. For a full account of this group, see Michael A. Morrison, *Slavery and the American West: The Eclipse of Manifest Destiny and the Coming of the Civil War* (Chapel Hill, 1997), chaps. 1 and 2; and James C. N. Paul, *Rift in the Democracy* (New York, 1961), chaps. 2 and 3.

4. The divisions over currency and banking are more complicated than presented here. For the many twists and turns, see Bray Hammond, *Banks and Politics in America: From the Revolution to the Civil War* (Princeton, 1957), chap. 19; John M. McFaul, *The Politics of Jacksonian Finance* (Ithaca, N.Y., 1972); William G. Shade, *Banks or No Banks: The Money Issue in Western Politics, 1832–1865* (Detroit, 1972); James R. Sharp, *The Jacksonians versus the Banks: Politics in the States after the Panic of 1837* (New York, 1970); and Charles G. Sellers, *The Market Revolution: Jacksonian America, 1815–1846* (New York, 1991), 332–48, 355–9.

self as a staunch Jackson man, yet he voted with the administration only half the time.[5] Van Buren and his northeastern allies had better luck with the New England and New York delegations, essentially driving pro-bank Democrats like Boston's David Henshaw out of the party. But elsewhere, men who ignored the party leadership continued to hold prominent positions. While often standing in fear or awe of Jackson, they were generally less impressed with Old Hickory's hand-picked successor, the skillful, yet politically drab, Little Magician.

At first, this halfhearted commitment to Van Buren worked to the South's disadvantage. Later, however, it would work to the South's advantage. Indeed, in the battle over the two-thirds rule at the 1844 Democratic convention, half of the Pennsylvania delegation, and every member of the New Jersey, Indiana, and Illinois delegations would desert Van Buren, support the motion, and thus guarantee that someone more acceptable to the South got the presidential nomination.[6]

A more fundamental reason these fair-weather Van Burenites were initially only a secondary source of doughface votes was that most had little or no experience with party discipline. Unlike their northeastern colleagues, only a handful had been schooled in a system where political preferment depended on party loyalty and obedience to decisions worked out in a state party caucus. In achieving office, most had relied mainly on their own personal popularity, or on local cliques in their home districts, not on statewide parties. Indeed, their statewide parties tended to be fragile organizations, often little more than shifting alliances of men on the make, without the durability, structure, and discipline that characterized the Democracy in New York and New Hampshire. There were, in short, no Isaac Hills or Albany Regencies to lay down the law, to make or break political careers, to tell them to vote with the South or suffer the consequences. Whipping such men into line, getting a majority to vote with the South, was thus hard work.

5. Alvin W. Lynn, "Party Formation and Operation in the House of Representatives, 1824–1837" (Ph.D. dissertation, Rutgers University, 1972), 413 n. 9.

6. Congressional Quarterly, *National Party Conventions, 1831–1988* (Washington, D.C., 1991), 177; Richard C. Bain, *Convention Decisions and Voting Records* (Washington, D.C., 1960), appendix; James P. Shenton, *Robert John Walker: A Politician from Jackson to Lincoln* (New York, 1961), 44–6.

New Jersey was the exception. There, parties were tightly disciplined, but unfortunately for southern Democrats seeking doughface votes, the New Jersey party had the bad habit of losing every other election. In the 1830s that was partly because congressmen never ran for a specific seat in a specific geographical area. They ran at large and as a result had to win votes across the entire state. In practice, this meant that the Jacksonians either won every congressional seat in the state or lost every congressional seat. In 1834, for example, they won all six seats by roughly nine hundred votes. In the next election, they lost all six, only to win them back in the following election, only to lose them again in the next election.

In short, no Jacksonian congressman in New Jersey had a safe seat, and southern Democrats who rested their hopes on a New Jersey man invariably saw him go down to defeat in the next election. In 1842 New Jersey was forced by federal law to switch to the district system, and thereafter politicians ran for specific House seats in specific geographical areas. From the standpoint of southern Democrats, that should have been a better system, yielding steadier support. It might even have compensated for the fact that New Jersey lost a House seat after the 1840 census. But even under the district system, four of the five seats still kept swinging back and forth, first to one party, then the other.[7]

In Pennsylvania, the political pendulum swung less noticeably. Unlike New Jersey, Pennsylvania consistently followed the district system, and at least half the districts in the state were "safe districts," with one party or the other winning election after election. Unlike New England and New York, however, Pennsylvania never really developed well-organized, disciplined parties. The Democrats were the dominant party, but the state organization was loose and usually no one was certain who was in charge. Party discipline was rare and at times nonexistent. Party loyalty also left much to be desired, with many going their own way, supporting Jackson nationally while refusing to support the Democratic ticket in state politics. As a

7. Richard P. McCormick, *The History of Voting in New Jersey* (New Brunswick, N.J., 1950), 125–9; idem, "Party Formation in New Jersey in the Jackson Era," *Proceedings of the New Jersey Historical Society* 83 (1965): 161–73; Peter D. Levine, *The Behavior of State Legislative Parties in the Jacksonian Era: New Jersey, 1829–1844* (Cranbury, N.J., 1977), 27–39; *Congressional Quarterly's Guide to U.S. Elections* (Washington, D.C., 1975), 718–43.

result, Jackson outpolled Democrats running for statewide offices by some 20,000 votes.[8]

Pennsylvania, in fact, became Martin Van Buren's chief example of what was wrong with the early Jackson party. Especially outrageous, as he saw it, was the behavior of the state's congressional delegation. They ran for office on Jackson's coattails, yet when the Old General needed their help, they turned their backs on him. They failed to support him in the battle over Indian Removal. They failed to back his veto of the Maysville Road Bill. They opposed his war against the Bank of the United States. They fought him when he tried to lower the tariff. In short, they had not been "well instructed or very deeply imbued with the principles of the party they had joined."[9] Whipping them into line, teaching them what it meant to be good party men, was thus an uphill battle. Not even the greatest southern Democrat of them all had been able to accomplish that.

With respect to the new frontier states, the initial problem for southern Democrats was that these states had only a few seats in Congress. Illinois, for example, was entitled to only one congressman in the 1820s and only three in the 1830s. Indiana was entitled to three and then seven. Even if every one of these men had been an enthusiastic supporter of the South, these states could provide only four votes for the Indian Removal Act in 1830 and only ten votes during the battle over the Pinckney gag and its successors. Even in the 1840s, when reapportionment entitled Indiana and Illinois to ten and seven seats respectively, they still had only half as many votes in the House as New York.

On paper, to be sure, nearly all of these western men were "good" Jacksonian Democrats. In terms of the number of Jacksonians the two states sent to the House, one could even argue that they came close to matching New York. Yet party discipline in the West was much like party discipline in Pennsylvania. It left much to be de-

8. Philip S. Klein, *Pennsylvania Politics, 1817–1832: A Game without Rules* (Philadelphia, 1940); Charles McCool Snyder, *The Jacksonian Heritage: Pennsylvania Politics, 1833–1848* (Harrisburg, Pa., 1958); John M. Belohlavek, *George Mifflin Dallas: Jacksonian Patrician* (University Park, Pa., 1977); Philip S. Klein, *President James Buchanan* (University Park, Pa., 1962); *Congressional Quarterly's Guide to U.S. Elections*, 718–43.

9. *Autobiography of Martin Van Buren*, 2 vols., ed. John C. Fitzpatrick (Washington, D.C., 1920), 289, 314, 320, 325.

sired. Neither Indiana nor Illinois had anything approaching a statewide party organization. In Indiana the men who ran state politics, for all intents and purposes, never exercised any control over the men who ran for county and district offices. The latter simply nominated themselves for office, ran their own campaigns, capitalized on their own personal popularity, and tried to best their rivals at stump speaking.[10]

Even more disorganized was the early Jackson party in Illinois. The state grew so fast that politicians were always scrambling to keep in touch with the voters. The state constitution required that each county have an assemblyman, and between 1820 and 1840 the number of counties needing a man in the statehouse skyrocketed from nineteen to eighty-eight. Out of nowhere, it seemed, new men jumped into politics and captured the limelight. None of these men even considered looking to the state party for its blessing. They just ran for office, sometimes on their own, sometimes with the help of the local elite. Then in the mid-1830s, transplanted Yankees like Stephen A. Douglas tried to create order out of the chaos, by putting together local and statewide organizations that could make binding nominations and stop one reliable Democrat from running against another reliable Democrat. By 1840 Douglas and his colleagues were largely successful, overcoming the resistance of many independent local chieftains and securing complete dominance in statewide elections until 1856. Yet, even though they succeeded in putting together a statewide party, no one claimed that it matched the discipline and durability of the Bucktails.[11]

Without statewide party discipline and without a compelling need to make Van Buren acceptable to the South, these western and Pennsylvania Democrats initially posed a problem for southern party whips. At the same time, however, they were less likely to

10. Logan Esary, "The Organization of the Jackson Party in Indiana," *Proceedings of the Mississippi Valley Historical Association* 7 (1913–14): 220–43; Adam A. Leonard, "Personal Politics in Indiana, 1816–1840," *Indiana Magazine of History* 19 (1923): 1–56, 132–68, 241–81.

11. Theodore C. Pease, *The Frontier State, 1818–1840* (Chicago, 1920); idem, ed., *Illinois Election Returns, 1818–1848* (Springfield, Ill., 1923); Charles Manfred Thompson, *The Illinois Whigs before 1846* (Urbana, Ill., 1915); Robert W. Johannsen, *Stephen A. Douglas* (New York, 1973), chaps. 2–5.

swing in the opposite direction and vehemently oppose the South. Not only did they come out of a different political world than their northeastern colleagues—one in which there were no Isaac Hills and no Albany Regencies whose backing they had to cultivate—but the vast majority represented districts with few if any antislavery organizers in their midst. Thus talk about a domineering Slave Power endangering northern liberties was less common, and so were antislavery newspapers that lambasted doughfaces for voting with the Slave Power.

Indeed, during the heat of the controversy over the American Anti-Slavery Society's pamphlet and petition campaigns, Garret Wall of New Jersey claimed that in his travels through his home state he had never met an abolitionist. Three days later, James Buchanan insisted that the same had been his experience in Pennsylvania.[12] There were of course abolitionists in Buchanan's Pennsylvania, just as there were in Wall's New Jersey and in every other northern state. But neither Buchanan, nor Wall, nor any other Democratic Party official from the tier of states running from New Jersey west faced the predicament of Van Buren's New York and New England followers.

Consider, for example, the plight of Lemuel Stetson of upstate New York. A staunch Van Burenite who represented several dozen small communities bordering Lake Champlain, Stetson knew that Van Buren and the Bucktail leadership needed the backing of the South in presidential politics. But he also knew that the Bucktails had to win districts like his own to control New York politics. He had the advantage of being a native son, having grown up in the village of Champlain, just a few miles south of the Canadian border. He also had the advantage of representing many French Canadians, who overwhelmingly supported the Jacksonian ticket.

But by the time Stetson got into politics, there were two antislavery societies in his hometown, one with 200 members, the other with 40 members. The nearby town of Peru also had two societies, a men's group with 200 members and a women's group with 476 members. The latter had been in operation since December 1833, and while the women could not vote, they clearly had an impact on their husbands and sons and probably their fathers, uncles, and nephews as well. They also had bombarded Congress with peti-

12. *Congressional Globe,* 24th Congress, 1st session, 1835–36, appendix: 134, 182.

tions calling for the end of slavery in the nation's capital and opposing the annexation of slaveholding Texas.[13]

Altogether, Stetson had fifteen antislavery societies in his district and represented several thousand constituents who clearly despised southern slavery. In 1843 over seven hundred of the men in his district voted for the Liberty Party's gubernatorial candidate, and in 1844 over six hundred voted for Liberty Party's congressional candidate. Only a handful of legislators represented more abolitionists than Stetson did, and most of these legislators were Whigs.[14]

Once the issue of Texas heated up, Stetson had no doubt what the Bucktails must do. As he told Azariah Flagg, a member of the Albany Regency's inner circle, they had to distance themselves from the South. They had no choice. Just being known as the party that voted with the South was a drawback. The Bucktail leadership agreed with him. By their reckoning, Stetson's district was just one of ten where abolitionists now held the balance of power.[15]

Had Stetson lived in Pennsylvania or the Old Northwest, he may have thought differently. Certainly William J. Brown and William Watson Wick of Indianapolis, who represented the Fifth District of Indiana, never faced the same problems Stetson did. Nor did Stephen A. Douglas, the transplanted Yankee who represented the Fifth District of Illinois. In their districts the Texas issue had largely escaped eight years of antislavery condemnation. Antislavery women bearing anti-Texas petitions were a rarity.[16] So were abolitionist news-

13. D. H. Hurd, comp., *History of Clinton and Franklin Counties* (Philadelphia, 1880); American Anti-Slavery Society, *Fifth Annual Report* (New York, 1838), 138–44; and Index of Petitions, RG 233, National Archives.

14. American Anti-Slavery Society, *Fifth Annual Report*, 138–44; Lee Benson, *The Concept of Jacksonian Democracy: New York As a Test Case* (Princeton, 1961), 262; *The Whig Almanac, 1844*, 44–5; *The Whig Almanac, 1845*, 43–4.

15. Stetson to Flagg, 31 December 1844, Azariah C. Flagg Papers, New York Public Library; and John M. Niles to Gideon Welles, 12, 24, 25, 31 January 1845, Gideon Welles Papers, Library of Congress.

16. Beginning in 1835–1836, the American Anti-Slavery Society sent over a half million petitions to Washington against the annexation of Texas. Up until 1839 the petitions were regularly filed, after that, sporadically. Many were subsequently destroyed. Only a small minority of those in existence came from Indiana and Illinois. See Index of Petitions, RG 233, National Archives; Edward Magdol, *The Antislavery Rank and File: A Social Profile of the Abolitionists' Constituency* (Westport, Conn., 1986), chap. 5; and Gilbert Hobbes Barnes, *The Anti-Slavery Impulse, 1830–1844* (Harbinger reprint; New York, 1964), 266 n. 40.

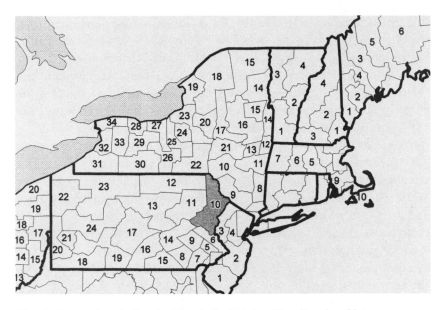

Map 2. Pennsylvania district (shaded) of Richard Brodhead and his successors

papers that harped on the fact that Secretary of State Calhoun, among others, had branded annexation a proslavery measure. Their entire states had fewer antislavery societies than Stetson had in his district. None of their constituents even had the opportunity to cast votes for Liberty Party congressional candidates, and only a handful cast votes for the Liberty Party's presidential candidate. Not one of these western politicians followed Stetson's lead of distancing himself from the South. On the contrary, all three wholeheartedly supported the annexation of slaveholding Texas and all three opposed the Wilmot Proviso.

The same situation prevailed in much of Pennsylvania. Although one Whig district had more antislavery societies than Stetson's district, and a few had almost as many, in much of the Keystone State the antislavery movement was woefully weak. That was even true in the region around Easton, one of the northeastern districts of the state, lying roughly on parallel with New York City (see map 2). Indeed, from a southern perspective, the representatives of that district, Richard Brodhead and his successors, came close to being perfect Democrats. If they shared any of Stetson's concerns, they rarely displayed them. Although Brodhead supported the repeal of the gag rule in 1844, he voted in favor of Texas the following year and against the Wilmot Proviso in the showdown vote in 1847. Later, as a United States senator, he voted to repeal the Missouri Compromise. His successors in the House—first Milo Dimmick, then Asa Packer, and then William Dimmick—followed in his footsteps, supporting the Fugitive Slave Act in 1850, the repeal of the Missouri Compromise in 1854, and the admission of Kansas as a slave state in 1858.

Not only did most of these western and Pennsylvania Democrats have fewer ties to Van Buren and fewer worries about the antislavery vote, but some undoubtedly would have found it hard to follow Stetson's advice and distance themselves from the South. A handful had southern roots, and more than a handful represented districts that bordered the South, districts that had many transplanted southerners and more than casual contact with the slave states.

For many years historians have assumed that such men provided the South with significant support. That was true in the Senate, less so in the House. In the Senate, where just one or two votes made a big difference, men with deep southern roots often played a telling role. Such was the case when Ninian Edwards and Jesse Thomas represented Illinois, Augustus Caesar Dodge and George Wallace Jones represented Iowa, and William Gwin represented California. All but Jones spent their formative years in the South and came from families that had acquired social status in the South. Jones, while born in the North, was educated in Kentucky, and it was there and later in Missouri where he formed lifetime friendships and rose in social prominence.

All five of these men, moreover, were either slaveholders or former slaveholders. William Gwin, as already noted, owned slaves in Mississippi for the entire decade he represented California in the Senate. But he was not the only free-state senator to have a vested interest in the productivity of Mississippi slaves. So did Stephen A. Douglas, whose first wife inherited a Mississippi plantation of some 2,500 acres and over one hundred slaves. In accordance with his father-in-law's bequest, Douglas himself managed the property, keeping in close touch with the overseer who directed the slaves and the New Orleans merchants who sold the cotton crop, and he received 20 percent of the plantation's annual income.[17]

17. Johannsen, *Douglas*, 211.

None of these men, of course, would have reached the Senate without the backing of their state legislatures. And in several of the frontier states, southern men in the state legislature clearly made a difference. That, as historians have frequently pointed out, was especially true in Indiana and Illinois. In both states the southern tier of counties frequently sent men to the statehouse who backed southern sympathizers for the Senate. Some were born and raised in slave country, like Ninian Edwards and Jesse Thomas. Others were northern-born men who sided with the South, like Indiana's three-term senator Jesse Bright, who despite being born and raised in New York, came to own Kentucky land and slaves and so enthusiastically backed southern causes that he was expelled from the Senate during the Civil War. In this respect, it is also well to remember that the man Lincoln regarded as the doughface of doughfaces, Stephen A. Douglas, owed his victory in the 1858 Senate race largely to legislators from southern Illinois. So, when it came to the Senate, men with deep southern roots and districts that bordered the South had considerable impact.

In the House, however, their impact was always less significant. Again, it was largely a matter of numbers. Whereas in the Senate one or two votes made a big difference, in the House one or two votes came far short of tipping the balance. Historians have made much of the fact that southern Indiana and southern Illinois repeatedly sent men to the House who were fiercely loyal to the South. That undoubtedly was the case, but how many of these men sat in the House at any one time? Usually no more than two or three.

And how deep were their southern roots? That was often debatable. In 1844, for example, Illinois sent two southern-born men to the House, and so did Indiana. But one had left the upper South when he was one year old, another when he was three years old. Their kinfolk were southerners, and they were undoubtedly indoctrinated with some of the ways of the upper South, but they were raised on the nonslaveholding frontier. The other two men spent the first twenty-five years of their lives in the South and knew slavery well, but only one voted with the South. The other was a Whig, and like other northern Whigs, he consistently voted against the South.

In addition, not all southern-born House Democrats were cut from the same cloth as their Senate counterparts. In an age when only a handful of southern men went to college, and less than one-quarter of southern white families owned slaves, all the senators were both college graduates and slaveholders. That was not the case with men who served only in the House. Most came from a different social class. As a group, they had more plebeian backgrounds and thus more in common with nonslaveholding whites who moved out of the upper South into southern Indiana, southern Illinois, and points west. In some cases, one gathers, their families had left the South gladly—to get away from the stigma of being designated "poor whites." As a rule, these men had no use for either the abolitionists or the planter aristocracy. They regarded the abolitionists as just a bunch of sanctimonious Yankee busybodies and pernicious Englishmen. And, from personal experience, they felt that the planters looked down on them and intended to oppress all nonslaveholding whites. Some had little patience with southern ways; others, however, were fiercely loyal to the upland South.[18]

As a group, transplanted southerners never made much of mark on the House. They were too few in number, never more than a handful in any one Congress. But for what it is worth, their voting habits followed the general pattern of the northern Democrats. In the 1830s, when the Van Buren wing provided the South with most of its needed votes, they were less supportive of southern measures than their northeastern colleagues. Later, when support among the

18. Cf. Henry Clyde Hubbart, "'Pro-Southern' Influence in the Free West, 1840–1865," *Mississippi Valley Historical Review* 20 (June 1933), 45–62; Silbey, "Pro-Slavery Sentiment in Iowa," 289–318; Morton M. Rosenberg and Dennis V. McClurg, *The Politics of Pro-Slavery Sentiment in Indiana, 1816–1861* (Muncie, Ind., 1968); *Biographical Encyclopedia and Portrait Gallery . . . of Ohio*, 3 vols. (Cincinnati, 1883–1895); William W. Woolen, *Biographical and Historical Sketches of Early Indiana* (Indianapolis, 1883); Newton Bateman and Paul Selby, eds., *Biographical and Memorial Edition of the Historical Encyclopedia of Illinois*, 2 vols. (Chicago, 1915). For the political culture of upland southerners who settled in the Old Northwest generally, see also John D. Barnhart, *Valley of Democracy: The Frontier versus the Plantation in the Ohio Valley, 1775–1818* (Bloomington, 1953); Richard Lyle Power, *Planting Corn Belt Culture: The Impress of the Upland Southerner and Yankee in the Old Northwest* (Indianapolis, 1953); and Nicole Etcheson, *The Emerging Midwest: Upland Southerners and the Political Culture of the Old Northwest, 1787–1861* (Bloomington, 1996).

Van Burenites lessened, they played a more prominent role. That was especially true during the decade following the annexation of Texas. But even then their support of the South tended to be sporadic. Four out of four, for example, followed their party's leadership and voted for the annexation of Texas, but only one out of five voted against the Wilmot Proviso. After the Kansas-Nebraska Act, their support for southern measures lessened.

Overall, party leaders got more consistent help from Democrats who represented districts that bordered the South than from transplanted southerners. Eleven out of thirteen, for example, voted for the annexation of Texas, five out of nine against the Wilmot Proviso. But not all these districts were Democratic strongholds. In some, Democrats faced strong Whig competition, and whenever the Whigs won the district, the South usually gained a potential enemy. It usually mattered not in the least whether the new Whig congressman was a New Englander by birth, a Pennsylvanian by birth, or a southerner by birth. In the mid-1840s not one border district Whig voted with the South. Nor did any southern-born northern Whig. All joined the Whig majority in opposing the annexation of Texas. All backed the Wilmot Proviso.

There were, to be sure, a few border districts that rallied to the southern cause time and again. The most notable was the First District of Indiana, located in the southwest corner of the state. The only northern Whig to vote for the 1840 gag, George H. Proffit, came from that district. A native of New Orleans, Proffit was also one of the few northern Whigs to support President John Tyler, and in 1843 he gave up his House seat to become the Tyler administration's emissary to Brazil. But the Senate refused to confirm his appointment and he had to return home the following year.

Once Proffit was out of the way, the Democrats carried the First District in nineteen out of the next twenty elections, and in the years before the Civil War it sent one doughface Democrat after another to Congress. In terms of background, these men had little in common. Two had southern roots, one was a product of New York's "Burned Over District," another was a Connecticut Yankee and a Yale graduate, and the most famous of all, Robert Dale Owen, was a Scottish immigrant whose father had founded the utopian community at New Harmony. Yet when they got to Congress, their her-

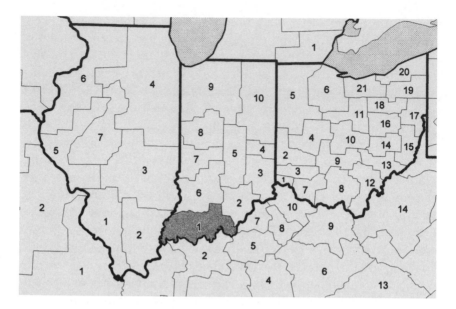

Map 3. Indiana's First District (shaded)

itage seemingly made no difference. They all voted with the South, again and again and again.[19]

Such unanimity, however, was rare. Neither Robert Dale Owen's district in southern Indiana nor Richard Brodhead's district in northeastern Pennsylvania was typical of Jacksonian strongholds. Most Democratic districts never came close to having a perfect doughface record. Most swung back and forth, sometimes electing a congressman who supported the South, sometimes electing one who did not.

More consistently supportive, however, were the men from Pennsylvania and New Jersey. At first, that worked to the South's advantage because, of the western states, only Ohio had much strength in the House. By the 1840s, however, the Jacksonians in-

19. The standard biography of Owen is a bit defensive in explaining how the great reformer and freethinker handled the slavery issue. The author presents Owen as basically an antislavery man yet clearly realizes that Owen repeatedly voted with the South against every antislavery measure except the gag rule. See Richard William Leopold, *Robert Dale Owen: A Biography* (New York, 1969), 76, 207–11, 240–1, 247–51.

variably won more seats in the West than in Pennsylvania and New Jersey. At the time of the Texas bill, for example, they had twenty-nine seats in the West, fifteen in Pennsylvania and New Jersey. Five years later, at the time of the Fugitive Slave Act, the ratio was thirty-two to ten. Four years after that, at the time of the Kansas-Nebraska Act, it was thirty-nine to twenty.

Had western Democrats been as supportive of the South as Pennsylvania and New Jersey Democrats, their numbers clearly would have worked to southern advantage. But just as more westerners voted with the South, so too did more cast votes against the South. And proportionately, when the roll call was finally tallied, they were always less supportive, sometimes by just a few percentage points, but sometimes by a significant margin. In the case of the Texas bill, for example, the difference was minute; in the case of the Wilmot Proviso, however, it was considerable. The table below shows the percentage voting with their southern colleagues on four of the most divisive bills in the late Jackson period:

	Penn.-Jersey Democrats	Western Democrats[a]
For annexing Texas (1845)	87%	83%
Against Wilmot Proviso (1847)	64%	31%
For Fugitive Slave Act (1850)	70%	47%
For Kans.-Nebr. Act (1854)	65%	57%

[a] At the time of Texas annexation and the Wilmot Proviso, the western free states were Ohio, Indiana, Illinois, and Michigan. Iowa and Wisconsin had been added to the Union by the time of the Fugitive Slave Act, and California by the time of Kansas-Nebraska.

In the 1840s and 1850s, moreover, no western leader capable of delivering the western vote emerged. Not even the two men who were widely hailed in their time to be the voice of the West, first Lewis Cass of Michigan and then Stephen A. Douglas of Illinois, could bring western Democrats into line.

The notion that Cass was the voice of the West, in fact, was largely make-believe. He opposed the Wilmot Proviso, spoke against it, and was one of five free-state senators to side with the South in the crucial showdown vote in 1847. In doing so, he ignored the sentiments of Michigan Democrats and the Michigan legislature, which had instructed him to vote for the proviso.[20] Furthermore, his stand had virtually no impact on western Democrats in the House. Shortly after the Senate voted down the proviso, it came up again in the House. Less than one-third of the western Democrats followed Cass's example. And not one House member from Cass's home state voted with Cass. Two voted for the proviso; one missed the vote.

Shortly thereafter, Michigan Democrats chose an outspoken Proviso Democrat to run for governor. No sooner had they gotten him elected than they turned their attention to getting Cass, the state's leading opponent of the proviso, elected president. They failed, but not because they failed to make an all-out effort at the Democratic convention or failed to get out the vote in Michigan. The following January, the same men rammed through the state legislature a resolution backing the proviso. Indeed, the resolution stated that Congress had a duty to prohibit slavery in the land taken from Mexico. In both houses, the resolution passed by enormous majorities. Yet the same legislature, after a two-week struggle, reelected Cass to the Senate. Obviously, for some Michigan Democrats, having a favorite son in the White House, or at least in the national party's inner circle, and thereby acquiring additional patronage and power, came well before intellectual and political consistency.[21]

In the Senate, the reinstated Cass continued much as before. He played a leading role in fashioning the Compromise of 1850 and tried to shepherd it through the Senate. He lashed out against those who had labeled him a doughface. He accused them of chastising him simply because he was unwilling to "cover the country with blood and conflagration to abolish slavery."[22] He supported an early version of the Fugitive Slave Act. As a lawyer, he insisted that it

20. *Congressional Globe*, 29th Congress, 2d session, 1846–47, p. 540; Klunder, *Cass*, 166–7.

21. For information on Michigan politics, I am heavily dependent on Floyd Streeter, *Political Parties in Michigan, 1837–1860* (Lansing, 1918), 83–143; and Ronald P. Formisano, *The Birth of Mass Political Parties: Michigan, 1827–1861* (Princeton, 1971), 207–12. For details on Michigan elections, I have relied on *Congressional Quarterly's Guide to U.S. Elections.*

22. Lewis Cass, *Senate Speeches on the Dissolution of the Union and the Constitution of California, February 12 and February 20, 1850* (Washington, D.C., 1850); *Congressional Globe*, 31st Congress, 1st session, 1849–50, p. 399.

was in keeping with the nation's most sacred legal guarantees in that it provided the accused fugitive with the right of habeas corpus and a jury trial in his home state. In committee he insisted on the jury trial provision, saying it was crucial, and it was included in the bill that went before the Senate. But in the amendment process, that provision, along with the right of habeas corpus, was stripped from the bill.

The final bill gave federal commissioners the authority to summarily decide the fate of the accused and provided an extra five-dollar fee if they decided in favor of the claimant slaveowner. It left northern blacks at the mercy of venal tribunals, with no legal protections whatsoever. It also imposed heavy fines on northern whites who hid fugitives or helped them in any way. All in all, it was a tough measure for even a northern doughface like Cass to support. In the end three northern Democratic senators voted for the bill, but Cass was not one of them. He could not bring himself to vote for the amended bill, but he did not vote against it either. Along with eight other northern Democrats, he conveniently missed the crucial vote. Once the bill became the law of the land, however, Cass endorsed it and sang the praises of the Compromise of 1850.

This time his position was more in keeping with western Democrats in the House. When the final bill came before the House, they split virtually down the middle, with fifteen supporting the measure, thirteen in opposition, and four following Cass's example and missing the vote. And as usual they were collectively less supportive than New Jersey and Pennsylvania Democrats, who cast not one vote against the bill. Seven voted in favor, three abstained.

Back home in Michigan, however, Cass was still out of touch with many Democrats. They vacillated in the state legislature, rescinding earlier instructions to support the Wilmot Proviso, yet refusing to approve his glowing endorsement of the 1850 compromise. Cass then put his reputation on the line and campaigned hard for the lone Michigan congressman who supported the Fugitive Slave Act, only to see his candidate lose by a whopping margin, some 1,500 votes more than any other Michigan congressional candidate. The next year, the party chose for governor a man who was virtually Cass's exact opposite, Robert McClelland, who vehemently opposed the annexation of Texas, strongly endorsed the Wilmot Proviso, and had a reputation for being extremely hostile to the South. He won by a landslide, capturing over 58 percent of the vote.[23]

By this time Cass, who was approaching his seventieth birthday, had to share the honorific of being "the voice of the West" with Stephen A. Douglas, the Little Giant from Illinois, who was nearly thirty years his junior and far more energetic. It was Douglas, not Cass, who came to the rescue of Henry Clay's Compromise of 1850, divided the omnibus bill into separate parts, and worked diligently to get northern Democrats to either absent themselves on the crucial Fugitive Slave vote or vote with the South.

Douglas had much in common with his older colleague. He too was a product of northern New England who had taken off for the West as a young man. And he too was an aggressive expansionist. At first, however, he had to work harder to gain national attention, losing his first bid for Congress in 1838 by 35 votes. He won five years later with a 441-vote margin but with less than 51 percent of the total vote.[24] Once in Congress, he too developed a record as a staunch supporter of the South, voting for the Texas bill in 1845 and against the Wilmot Proviso in both 1846 and 1847. Elevated to the Senate, he too ignored instructions from his state legislature to back the proviso. And he too missed the crucial vote on the Fugitive Slave Act.

Unlike Cass, however, Douglas did not intentionally miss the controversial and decisive roll call. He was off in New York City settling a debt, apparently expecting the debate to last another two weeks. Once he heard the vote was to be taken, he hurried back to Washington, although not at the breakneck speed he later contended. Arriving after the roll call, he went out of his way to declare his support for the Fugitive Slave Act and indicated that had he been in Washington he would have joined the three northern Democrats who voted for the bill.

Overall, Douglas's tenure as "the voice of the West" differed from Cass's in only one respect. Generally, he was more in tune with House Democrats from his home state. Only the Chicago Giant, Long John Wentworth, consistently canceled out his vote.

23. *Congressional Quarterly's Guide to U.S. Elections,* 747, 509.
24. Ibid., 726, 734; Johannsen, *Douglas,* 63–72, 117–23.

And while Douglas failed to get the majority to join him in voting against the Wilmot Proviso, he did get three of the seven House Democrats to abstain. In his struggle to get votes for the Fugitive Slave Act, five of the seven followed his lead.

With rank-and-file Democrats back home, however, Douglas had the same problems as Cass. He too put his reputation on the line and campaigned hard for a doughface congressman who had voted for the Fugitive Slave Act. And, as in Cass's case, his man lost badly, winning a thousand fewer votes than in the previous election and thus becoming the only incumbent to go down to defeat. Throughout northern Illinois, moreover, the press and public meetings lambasted Douglas for supporting the Fugitive Slave Act. In his hometown of Chicago, the city council not only denounced the bill, characterizing him as a traitor, but they even excused the police from enforcing the new law. Douglas immediately struck back. In a three-and-one-half-hour speech at Chicago's city hall, he confronted his critics and rallied his forces. The next night, the council repealed its resolutions, and a few weeks later the state legislature rescinded its Wilmot Proviso instructions and lauded Douglas and the Compromise of 1850. Three months later, in January 1851, a Democratic meeting in Jo Daviess County suggested Douglas for president. Shortly thereafter, Democrats in other Illinois counties followed suit. But all was not well. Wentworth and his Chicago Democrats hardly jumped on the bandwagon. Indeed, they portrayed Douglas as a candidate of the last resort, and he had to work hard to win even their token support.[25]

That he achieved by the 1852 Democratic convention. Yet, in his initial bid for the party's presidential nomination, Douglas found himself with a worse problem than Cass had in 1844. Not only did he have limited western support, he lacked the backing of the South. Michigan and Indiana were still with Cass. Only Illinois, half of the Iowa delegation, and a minority of the Wisconsin and Ohio delegations were truly in Douglas's camp. The South backed Pennsylvania's James Buchanan to offset other northern candidates. Thanks to the two-thirds rule, the convention became hopelessly deadlocked. Cass, Douglas, and Buchanan successively took the

25. Johannsen, *Douglas,* 298–303, 345, 351; *Speech of the Hon. Stephen A. Douglas on the "Measures of Adjustment," Delivered in the City Hall, Chicago, October 23, 1850* (Washington, D.C., 1851); Don E. Fehrenbacher, *Chicago Giant: The Biography of "Long John" Wentworth* (Madison, Wisc., 1957), 102, 117–8.

lead, but none came close to capturing a majority, much less the two-thirds needed for nomination. Finally, after forty-eight ballots, the exhausted delegates turned to a dark horse, Franklin Pierce of New Hampshire, a dependable doughface who was known to the public only as a brigadier in the Mexican War.

It was during Pierce's administration that Douglas became the undisputed congressional leader of northern and western dough-faces. He had an advantage over all his predecessors in that he had more northern Democrats to work with. The party had scored smashing victories in state after state in the 1852 elections, and as a result ninety-three northern Democrats now sat in the House, nearly forty more than at the time of the Fugitive Slave Act. He needed them. He needed every edge he could get to win support for the hotly disputed Kansas-Nebraska Act, the most divisive piece of legislation that Congress passed before the Civil War, and perhaps the most divisive in the entire history of the nation.

As it was, Douglas had to work for months to whip northern Democrats into line, to get the necessary majority to repeal the Missouri Compromise and open the northern half of the Louisiana Purchase to the possibility of slavery. Douglas argued that the possi-bility was remote—indeed, nonexistent—and that all he was doing was giving the South a fig leaf. He grossly underestimated the opposi-tion to the repeal and treated with contempt all those who disagreed with him. To his angry opponents, the Missouri Compromise was not a trivial matter. It was a sacred compact. Initially, it had benefited the South. Now, just as it was about to benefit the free states, the South wanted to renege on the bargain. It was considered a breach of faith on the South's part.

These sentiments, Douglas predicted, would dissipate in a few weeks. He was dead wrong. Erstwhile supporters joined the revolt. Some feared that Kansas-Nebraska would upset the settlement of 1850, which allegedly had put the slavery question to rest. Others regarded it a violation of a sacred covenant. Over the objections of Douglas's friends, the Connecticut Democratic convention offi-cially went on record against the bill and the Pennsylvania Demo-cratic convention refused to endorse the bill. In Chicago Douglas's friends called a rally and found it jammed with the bill's enemies. Resolutions in support of the bill and the Little Giant were hooted down. Even the *Chicago Democratic Press* turned on Douglas and accused him of committing an unpardonable political error.[26]

Had it not been for the three-fifths rule, Douglas probably would have failed. He would have had to get forty-nine northern Democrats to vote with the South. As it was, he needed twenty-seven northern votes. Not all potential supporters, however, responded to his herculean efforts. The news from back home had convinced many that Douglas's bill was a political disaster and that the storm over Kansas-Nebraska would destroy all before it. The last thing they wanted to do was confront the onslaught, but they had no desire to buck the party leadership either. They wanted an indirect way out, one that would enable them to kill the bill without being blatant about it.[27] In early March a doughface Democrat from New York City, Francis B. Cutting, provided them with the mechanism.

The New Yorker had nothing against Douglas's bill. He was staunch member of New York's Hard Shell faction, and the Hards had already strongly endorsed the bill. But even more important to the Hards was getting even with the Pierce administration. As they saw it, Pierce had cut them out of patronage and given it to their Soft Shell enemies. Particularly aggravating was Pierce's decision to make William L. Marcy secretary of state and deny Daniel S. Dickinson a cabinet post. Even more irritating was the administration's decision to dismiss Greene C. Bronson as collector of the port of New York. That position controlled over seven hundred jobs, more patronage than any post in New York, maybe more than any in the federal system. The Hards called for a congressional investigation of Bronson's dismissal, but they failed to get it. They also demanded that free-soil Democrats be stripped of federal patronage and tried to drive a wedge between the Softs and Pierce's southern supporters, but so far they had not succeeded. Now a handful of

26. *New York Evening Post,* 21 February, 31 March 1854; *Hartford Daily Times,* 17 March 1854; *Philadelphia Daily News,* 5 June 1854; *Chicago Democratic Press,* 16 February, 24 May 1854; Allan Nevins, *Ordeal of the Union: A House Dividing, 1852–1857,* 2 vols. (New York, 1947), 2: 146–9.

27. See, for example, the letters to William L. Marcy, January–February 1854, William L. Marcy Papers, Library of Congress; the letters to Horatio Seymour, January–February 1854, Horatio Seymour Papers, New-York Historical Society; and John Dix's correspondence, January–April 1854, John A. Dix Papers, Columbia University Library.

Hards decided to make Pierce squirm, to deny him a victory in Kansas-Nebraska until he mended his ways, and to kill Kansas-Nebraska if he didn't.[28]

The opportunity came in early March. To get Kansas-Nebraska on a fast track, Douglas's floor manager in the House, William A. Richardson of Illinois, moved that the bill be referred to his territorial committee. Immediately, Cutting countered with a motion to send the bill to the committee of the whole, where it would be the fiftieth bill on the calendar. Richardson accused him of trying to kill the bill by "indirection." Cutting, in turn, pretended that he was just advocating "full, frank, and candid discussion" so that the bill would be brought to the "proper shape" and the anxious northern electorate would appreciate its virtues. Immediately, all those who wanted to kill the bill—northern Whigs, Free-Soilers, and dissident Democrats—rallied behind Cutting's proposal. So did the handful of Hards who wanted to make Pierce's life miserable. As a result, Cutting's motion prevailed, 110 to 95.[29]

Douglas and Richardson thus needed help to overcome this strange combination of forces and bring Kansas-Nebraska up for a vote. They got it from the Pierce administration and its control of federal patronage. The Hards could be bought, but what about the others? Using patronage to swell doughface numbers had worked in the past. Jackson had used it on a limited scale to win approval for Indian Removal. The Polk administration had used it more extensively in the battle against the Wilmot Proviso. But would it work this time? The Pierce administration in 1854 pulled out all the stops. Cabinet members worked the halls of Congress, dangling jobs

28. *New York Evening Post*, 4–5 January, 28–30 March, 2 May 1854; *Albany Argus*, 9–10, 12, 14, 18 January, 8 February 1854; *Congressional Globe*, 33d Congress, 1st session, 1853–54, pp. 190–4; Leonard D. White, *The Jacksonians: A Study in Administrative History, 1829–1861* (New York, 1954), 177–8; Mark L. Berger, *The Revolution in New York Party Systems, 1840–1860* (Port Washington, N.Y., 1973), 17–31.

29. *Congressional Globe*, 33d Congress, 1st session, 1853–54, pp. 701–3. The comment on the bill's opponents and the Hards is based on an analysis of who voted for the motion, who voted against it, and how they voted on subsequent motions. With the exception of the Hards, most northern politicians revealed where they truly stood on this motion. Not all Hards, moreover, were guilty of double-dealing. At least five—James Maurice, Andrew Oliver, Jared V. Peck, Rufus W. Peckham, and John Wheeler—genuinely opposed the bill. See *Albany Argus*, 1, 3 June 1854. Maurice missed the final vote on Kansas-Nebraska; the other four voted against it.

before hesitant Democrats, while the administration's official newspaper promised doughfaces that they would be "sustained by every means within the power of the party."[30]

The sustenance consisted mainly of small favors, such as letting William Marcy Tweed of New York replace a postmaster, providing several New York districts with hefty shipbuilding contracts, and paying a Milwaukee newspaper to print federal mail contracts. But such favors added up. At one point in the long struggle over free soil in the West, Caleb Cushing calculated the dollar value for Massachusetts Democrats: If they decided to enhance their power in state politics by joining forces with the free-soilers, they would gain a mere $75,000 in state jobs; if they sided with the administration and the South, they would gain $1,000,000 per annum in federal patronage.[31]

At the same time, cabinet members threatened to cut free-soilers off from the spoils. The Hards, in one crucial sense, thus got their way. The old notion of healing party wounds through patronage, championed by their enemy William L. Marcy of New York and other pragmatists, lost ground to the demand by Daniel Dickinson of New York, Edmund Burke of New Hampshire, and other Hards for total proscription of all "administration traitors." Even free-soilers who kept a low profile, never blatantly challenging the leadership, were cut off from the spoils.[32]

In the end, the combination of presidential pressure, federal patronage, and Douglas's hard work paid off. By early May, most of the Hards were aboard and so were a handful of dissident Democrats. Sixteen men who had supported Cutting's motion now sided with Richardson or made themselves scarce when it came time to vote. Thus Richardson had the votes to dispose of one bill after another in the committee of the whole and on May 8 succeeded in laying aside

30. Mark W. Summers, *The Plundering Generation: Corruption and the Crisis of the Union, 1849–1861* (New York, 1987), 211ff.

31. "Notes on Party Spirit," Caleb Cushing Papers, Library of Congress.

32. William L. Marcy to S. M. Shaw, 7 September 1851, WLM to Horatio Seymour, 3 April, June 1852, WLM to Horatio Seymour, John B. Skinner, and Erastus Corning, 24 May 1852, Seymour Typescripts, New-York Historical Society; Daniel S. Dickinson to Edmund Burke, 5 December 1853, 24 March 1854, Edmund Burke Papers, Library of Congress; John R. Dickinson, ed., *Speeches, Correspondence, Etc., of the Late Daniel S. Dickinson*, 2 vols. (New York, 1867), 1: 394–406; Morgan Dix, *Memoirs of John Adams Dix*, 2 vols. (New York, 1883), 1: 261–78; William E. Parrish, *David Rice Atchison of Missouri: Border Politician* (Columbia, Mo., 1961), 132–8.

the last eighteen bills that preceded Kansas-Nebraska. He then moved to substitute the Senate version of the bill, which had passed in early March, for the measure before the House.[33]

Three weeks of stormy debate followed. Douglas worked alongside Richardson, whipping dissident Democrats into line. Indeed, in the eyes of many dissidents, the two men from Illinois behaved like dictatorial, insolent "slave-drivers." Finally, on May 22, Richardson's motion to substitute the Senate bill prevailed and immediately thereafter Kansas-Nebraska passed the House, 113 to 100. Back in Illinois, Douglas and Richardson's supporters greeted the victory with a 113-gun salute.[34]

How did the West respond? At first southern Democrats got just as much support from western Democrats as they did from their Pennsylvania and New Jersey colleagues. But in the two-month battle to get Kansas-Nebraska enacted, a smaller proportion of western Democrats switched sides. Most stuck with Richardson throughout or opposed him from beginning to end. He had the backing of fifteen of thirty-seven in his battle against Cutting's motion. Six more came over to his side in the next two months. Also switching sides were five Pennsylvania and New Jersey Democrats, and as a result a larger proportion of the Pennsylvania and New Jersey delegations voted with the South.

The biggest shift in votes, however, occurred within the New York delegation. Only one New York Democrat voted with Richardson against Cutting's motion. By the time the final bill came up for a vote, Richardson had the support of nine New Yorkers. Here, in percentages, is how the New Yorkers compared with other northern Democrats:

	Against Cutting's Motion	For Kansas-Nebraska
Western Democrats (N = 38)	41%	57%
Penn.-Jersey Dems. (N = 20)	40%	65%
New England Dems. (N = 13)	23%	23%
New York Dems. (N = 22)	5%	41%

Of the eight New Yorkers who switched sides, three were from upstate, five from the City. The most conspicuous was Francis B. Cutting.[35]

33. *Congressional Globe,* 33d Congress, 1st session, 1853–54, pp. 1130–33.
34. Johannsen, *Douglas,* 434.
35. *Congressional Globe,* 33d Congress, 1st session, 1853–54, pp. 703, 1254.

All in all, eleven men who had voted for the Cutting resolution, along with six men who had abstained, came over to Richardson's side and voted for the Kansas-Nebraska Act. Five more who supported the Cutting resolution made themselves scarce when it came time to cast the final, decisive vote. These twenty-two men made the difference. Without them, Kansas-Nebraska would have gone down to defeat.

What did they get for it? Only one, George Vail of New Jersey, was reelected to Congress. Six were defeated. The other fifteen either chose not to run again or were not given the nomination. Two died within a year or two of the vote. But most fared well in the coming years. One later became governor of Illinois, another senator from Kansas. Two received jobs from the Pierce administration, one as attorney general of the Minnesota Territory, the other as clerk of the United States District Court for northern Ohio. Two others later received jobs from the Buchanan administration, one as consul to Scotland, the other as consul to India. Another was offered a post by the Pierce administration but turned it down. Still another, a part owner of a Philadelphia newspaper, received lucrative printing contracts from both the Pierce and Buchanan administrations. And the most notorious of them all, William Marcy Tweed, got the chance to make appointments in his district.

The others simply retired from public life and returned to their civilian occupations. Most were lawyers. Of these the most notable was Francis B. Cutting, a graduate of Litchfield Law School. He already had a lucrative practice in Manhattan. He went back to it, almost full-time, and prospered.

All of this, however, was largely ignored by the press and the public at large. The 113-gun salute in Illinois was hardly in honor of Cutting and the men who joined him in switching their votes. It was in honor of Stephen A. Douglas. And he was quick to take the credit. "I passed the Kansas-Nebraska Act myself," he later boasted. "I had the authority and power of a dictator throughout the whole controversy in both houses. The speeches were nothing. It was the marshaling and directing of men, and guarding from attacks, and with a ceaseless vigilance preventing surprise."[36] And so the story came to be told.

36. As quoted in Johannsen, *Douglas*, 434.

8 | Collapse of One Pillar

The twenty-two northern Democrats who switched their vote during the battle over Kansas-Nebraska never received the honors that Douglas did. Nor were they credited with changing the course of American history. And except for William Marcy Tweed they have been largely ignored by historians. Indeed, who has heard of Francis B. Cutting? Or Norman Eddy? Or Frederick Green? Yet, despite their obscurity, nearly all of these men achieved a modicum of success after Kansas-Nebraska.

That was not the case with their party. In the fall elections following passage of the Kansas-Nebraska Act, the Democrats lost twenty-one of the twenty-two districts that these vote switchers represented. The single exception was New Jersey, and even there the incumbent's victory margin fell from 3,000 votes in 1852 to 450 votes in 1854. Elsewhere all the incumbents lost, sometimes by just a few percentage points, sometimes by landslide margins. One Indiana incumbent got just 45 percent of the vote, another 44 percent. In Wisconsin, James Macy saw his public support plummet from 55 percent of the total vote in 1852 to 39 percent in 1854.

Of the party's fifteen replacement candidates, only four came close to winning. Most lost by huge margins. Tweed's replacement in New York's Fifth District, running in a four-man race, finished third with 25 percent of the vote. Cutting's replacement in New York's Eighth District finished second in a three-man race, with 31 percent of the vote.

The biggest loser, however, was Frederick Green's replacement in Ohio's Ninth District. The Ninth bordered Lake Erie and was the Democratic stronghold in the northern part of the state. Indeed, for the past decade the party had won the district handily, never capturing less than 57 percent of the vote. It also had sent a string of congressmen to Washington who voted against the South. At first, Green was no exception. Winning 92 percent of the vote in 1850 and 74 percent in 1852, he was in step with his predecessors when he supported the Cutting resolution in March 1854. In the next two months, however, he broke with local tradition and backed the Kansas-Nebraska Act. Rather than run for reelection, he accepted a patronage job from the Pierce administration in the United States District Court in Cleveland and moved out of the Ninth District. The local party was thus left to defend his "treasonous" record against the newly fashioned Republican Party. Their choice to replace him got clobbered, winning only 40 percent of the vote in a two-man race.

What happened in Green's district and in the districts of the other vote switchers was unusual. The Democrats did not lose twenty-one out of twenty-two seats across the entire North. But the total losses were staggering—fifty of remaining seventy-one seats. Entering the 1854 election holding ninety-three northern seats in the House, the Jacksonians emerged with only twenty-two.[1]

Stephen A. Douglas refused to accept the blame for this debacle. It was not Kansas-Nebraska, he argued, that led to his party's demise. It was the rise of anti-Catholic and anti-immigrant fervor.

1. Some accounts indicate that the Democrats started out with ninety-one seats and ended up with twenty-five. The disparity in the tallies stems largely from discrepancies in the sources and the turmoil that characterized the 1854 election. Not only did Whigs and Free-Soilers run under a host of new labels, and some under two labels, but five incumbent Democrats switched parties, ran against the Democracy, and won. I have counted these reelections as losses for the Democratic Party, but they have sometimes been counted as Democratic victories even though the party's official candidates were defeated. Another source of confusion is that some documents list two incumbent Democrats as Free-Soilers before the Kansas-Nebraska de-

The Little Giant undoubtedly had a point. Nearly three million immigrants had poured into the United States since 1845, totaling about 13 percent of the nation's population, and the vast majority had settled in the North. Well over one million of these newcomers were Catholic Irish. Not only were the Irish poor and desperate, their church had long been anathema in Protestant circles. Thousands of Protestant families had copies of Foxe's *Book of Martyrs* in their homes. Hundreds of thousands of northerners had learned at their mother's knee about the "whore of Babylon," the Spanish Inquisition, the Gunpowder Plot, and the "awful disclosures of Maria Monk." For years Protestants had attacked convents and fought with Catholic workers on the streets of Philadelphia, New York, and Boston. And for years most northern Whigs had catered to Protestant animosity and helped drive Catholic newcomers into the Democratic Party.

In 1852 these new Democrats made a difference. They undoubtedly helped Franklin Pierce win the presidency and tipped the balance in scores of races for congressman, assemblyman, and alderman. And some of the Democrats they helped elect, like Mike Walsh of New York, were not only proslavery but blatantly so.

Whig strategists knew that they had a problem. The Irish vote, growing by the thousands every day, had to be nullified or the Whig organization would be destroyed at the polls. Some Whigs wanted to compete against the Democrats for Irish support. Others wanted to make it harder for the Irish to vote, calling for a residency requirement of twenty-one years for naturalization, and launched a drive to make the Whig Party into a nativist party. Many were also convinced that their alliance with southern Whigs was in hopeless disarray, that their old national party was dead or dying, and hence were eager to form a new alliance if one could be arranged.

But should the new alliance be basically a nativist alliance or an antisouthern alliance? On the one hand, hundreds of thousands of northern voters indiscriminately blamed the "Irish menace" and "popery" on the northern Democracy. Temperance reformers also singled out "drunken Irishmen" and their political protectors for

bacle, while others list them as Democrats. I have counted them as Democrats, which was their party affiliation in the 1852 election. For the discrepancies in the sources, see Kenneth C. Martis, *The Historical Atlas of Political Parties in the United States Congress, 1789–1989* (New York, 1989), 380–90.

special censure. But hundreds of thousands of northern voters also indiscriminately blamed all northern Democrats, doughfaces and free-soilers alike, for the repeal of the Missouri Compromise. A few spoke about the moral evils of slavery. More railed about the possible expansion of slavery and southern power. Douglas, as usual, underestimated their resentment.

In this general tumult, ninety-three Democratic House seats were at risk in the fall of 1854. The challengers were not just the old familiar Whigs and Free-Soilers. Also confronting the Democracy were newcomers and old foes who ran under new labels, sometimes two labels at the same time. Along with nativists who usually called themselves Know-Nothings, there were antislavery nativists who called themselves Know-Somethings, opponents of the new Kansas-Nebraska Act who called themselves Anti-Nebraska men or Republicans, as well as a smattering of Temperance men, Maine Lawites, and Silver Gray Whigs. Then, to make the retention of Democratic seats even harder, the Democratic Party itself was divided between Rum Democrats, Hard Shell Democrats, Soft Shell Democrats, and Half Shell Democrats.

Did Kansas-Nebraska cause the 1854 debacle? It was hard to tell.[2] Some seats were lost to men who ran as Know-Nothings, some to Anti-Nebraska men, and many to men who had a foot in both

2. The cause of the northern Democracy's decline is a matter of much debate. Some historians blame the turn of events mainly on bungling politicians. Others claim that antislavery and antisouthern sentiment overwhelmed the existing parties and created the new Republican Party of Abraham Lincoln. And still others point to underlying changes in local politics, the demise of the old economic issues of Jackson's day, and the rise of ethnocultural issues such as temperance and anti-Catholicism. Cf. Avery Craven, *The Coming of the Civil War*, 2d ed. rev. (Chicago, 1966); Eric Foner, *Free Soil, Free Labor, Free Men* (New York, 1970); David M. Potter, *The Impending Crisis, 1848–1861* (New York, 1976); Stephen E. Maizlish, *The Triumph of Sectionalism: The Transformation of Ohio Politics, 1844–1856* (Kent, Ohio, 1983); Tyler Anbinder, *Nativism and Slavery: The Northern Know Nothings and the Politics of the 1850s* (New York, 1992); Michael F. Holt, *The Political Crisis of the 1850s* (New York, 1978); Paul Kleppner, *The Third Electoral System, 1853–1892* (Chapel Hill, 1979), 59–74; Joel H. Silbey, "'There Are Other Questions Beside That of Slavery Merely': The Democratic Party and Antislavery Politics," in *Crusaders and Compromisers: Essays on the Relationship of the Antislavery Struggle to the Antebellum Party System*, ed. Alan M. Kraut (Westport, Conn., 1983), 163–6; and William E. Gienapp, *The Origins of the Republican Party, 1852–1856* (New York, 1987).

camps. In addition, some seats were lost because the local Democratic Party split in two and ran two men for the same office. Among the twenty-two seats that the party managed to retain were fourteen doughface seats. Two years later, when the party's fortunes revived in some districts, thirty-one of the fifty-three northern Democrats elected to Congress were doughfaces. But doughface politicians received a larger share of federal patronage, and in close elections federal spoils undoubtedly made a difference. Moreover, the Know-Nothing Party, whose program skyrocketed in popularity at the Democrats' expense in 1854, collapsed in late 1856 almost as fast it had risen. More viable was the new Republican Party, which also rose in the unstable atmosphere of the 1854 elections, stumbled for a year or so, and then soared in the 1856 elections.

Whatever the cause of the Democratic debacle, the northern wing of the Jacksonian coalition barely survived the 1854 election. And with fewer Democrats in Congress, the number of doughfaces in Congress also plummeted. The two, as always, went hand in hand.

The doughfaces' new rivals, moreover, had a decisive advantage over their old Whig rivals. Northern Whigs, even though they repeatedly voted against the South, had to cooperate with their southern colleagues to win national elections. The new Republican Party had no such restraints. Based entirely in the North, the party had no need, much less desire, to maintain a working arrangement with the great slavemasters of the South. On the contrary, the stock-in-trade of the Republicans was to attack the political influence of the plantation aristocracy. The Slave Power, contended one Republican after another, had long ruled the nation, and now it was conspiring to expand its power by annexing Cuba, capturing the West, and extending slavery into the free states.

The main victims of this thrashing were northern Democrats, especially men like Frederick Green and Norman Eddy, who allegedly had sold their souls to the Slave Power. Such men were no longer characterized as northern men with southern principles. They were not given credit for having any principles. They were deemed men of no principles, men who were easily bought by the Slave Power.

The South thus lost the power to get things done. Thanks to its hold on the Senate, it could stop legislation from being passed. But getting favorable legislation through the House was a different story.

The problem for the South was largely a matter of numbers. Not enough northern Democrats were elected to tip the balance in favor of the slave states. Half the northern Democrats still voted with the South. Indeed, the overall percentage voting with the South barely changed at all. But with far fewer northern Democrats in the House, the support of half was just not enough. That became crystal clear in the spring of 1856 when Congress split into two warring camps over the caning of Charles Sumner.

During that incident, about half the northern Democrats in the House sided with the South. That was not an easy choice, even for men who believed that the Massachusetts senator had it coming. Making a case against Sumner, to be sure, was not difficult. In his two-day "Crime against Kansas" speech, the Massachusetts orator un-doubtedly went out of his way to insult three senators, Douglas of Illinois, James Mason of Virginia, and Andrew P. Butler of South Carolina. Particularly disparaging were his remarks about Butler, an ailing three-term senator who was back home in South Carolina.[3] Yet what happened three days later was hard to justify. Representative Preston Brooks, a nephew of Butler, entered the Senate chamber and with a cane beat Sumner senseless as the latter sat at his desk. So heavy were the blows that the gutta-percha cane, which was pur-posely selected because it would not break, snapped in two. So badly injured was the Massachusetts senator that he would not return to the Senate until December 1859.[4]

In the South, Brooks became something of folk hero, but in the North huge rallies in virtually every city protested the assault and demanded that "Bully" Brooks be punished. Not only were the crowds vast, but the speakers came from all parties, and to many it seemed as if past political differences had been obliterated. News that southerners hailed Brooks as a conquering hero, endorsed his action, and even sent him gold-headed canes, only added to the

3. For the text of Sumner's speech and the negative reaction of other senators, see *Congressional Globe*, 34th Congress, 1st session, 1855–56, appendix: 529–47.

4. For the attack by Brooks and its aftermath, the most important source is *House Reports*, "Alleged Assault upon Senator Sumner," 34th Congress, 1st session, 1855–56, no. 182. For detailed scholarly accounts, see David Donald, *Charles Sumner and the Coming of the Civil War* (New York, 1960), 288–311, and William E. Gienapp, "The Crime against Sumner: The Caning of Charles Sumner and the Rise of the Republican Party," *Civil War History* 25 (September 1979): 218–45.

anger. So did news from Kansas that "Border Ruffians" from slave-holding Missouri had joined proslavery forces in Kansas in sacking the town of Lawrence, burning down the Free State Hotel, and destroying the presses of two free-state newspapers, the *Herald of Freedom* and the *Kansas Free State.*

Wasn't that proof that Sumner was right? Wasn't the "slave oligarchy" guilty of the rape of Kansas as the Massachusetts senator claimed? Weren't "Bleeding Kansas" and "Bleeding Sumner" just two parts of the same story? Astute observers predicted that the caning, as exploited by the Republican press, would cost the Democratic Party some 200,000 votes in the upcoming election.

In Washington, Congress had to respond. Even at a time when legislators frequently carried knives and guns, many fought duels, and some periodically whipped inferiors, beating a senator senseless was not accepted parliamentary procedure. Henry Wilson, the other Massachusetts senator, left it up to the older members of the Senate to "redress the wrongs of a member of this body, and to vindicate the honor and dignity of the Senate."[5] A committee was then appointed, and it concluded that Brooks was not within the Senate's jurisdiction and could only be disciplined by the House. Meanwhile, in the House, an investigative committee began taking testimony from Sumner and twenty-six other witnesses. Passions quickly got out of hand, and members of both houses began threatening one another, first with words, then with challenges to duels. In June the House committee recommended the expulsion of Brooks and the censure of two of his colleagues.

After more bitter argument, more threats, and challenges to duels, the motion to expel finally came to a vote in mid-July. The motion failed. The majority voted against Brooks, 121 to 95, but the necessary two-thirds majority was lacking. Every southern congressmen but one voted against expulsion, and every northern Whig, Know-Nothing, and Republican but one voted for expulsion. What did northern Democrats do? Six voted for expulsion, eleven against, and five abstained.[6] In terms of percentages, those numbers were in accord with the past. The trouble, from a southern perspective, was that northern Democrats were now outnumbered by

5. *Congressional Globe*, 34th Congress, 1st session, 1855–56, p. 279.
6. Ibid., 1628.

nearly five to one. Thus the South would have gone down to defeat had the motion required a majority vote.

The South's predicament improved slightly with the 1856 fall elections. Contrary to earlier predictions, northern Democrats regained some of their lost seats. Most of the gains occurred in Pennsylvania and the West, but the party also did well in New York City and the Hudson River counties, where the Hards and Softs reached an uneasy truce, agreeing to stop running candidates against each other, and settled on one Democratic candidate for each district. These successes, however, could not hide the fact that elsewhere the party was badly beaten, that it was routed even in districts that at one time had been Jacksonian strongholds. Men like Horatio Seymour and David Ogden of New York were mortified by the results. They had sent their "best speakers and most active men into the field" only to be "swept away" on Election Day.[7]

Nationally, doughfaces now seemed to be the rulers of the roost among the Democratic factions. At the Democratic convention in Cincinnati, they were the Democracy's only viable candidates. Southern Democrats favored first Pierce and then Douglas, the two men most responsible for the Kansas-Nebraska Act. But northern Democrats opposed them for the "irreparable harm" they had caused the northern wing of the party. Finally, on the seventeenth ballot, both sides agreed on James Buchanan of Pennsylvania, a candidate who was known to be a northern man with southern principles, but who had been in London as minister to Great Britain at the time of the Kansas-Nebraska controversy and thus had avoided the wrath of the thousands of Democrats who despised Douglas's measure.

Buchanan, in fact, was the consummate doughface.[8] A sixty-four-year-old veteran of many political wars, who had represented Pennsylvania in both the House and the Senate and had served as Polk's secretary of state, his close associates in Washington were generally southerners or men with deep southern connections. He

7. Seymour to William L. Marcy, 12 November 1856, Ogden to Marcy, 30 November 1856, Marcy Papers, Library of Congress.

8. The standard biography of Buchanan is Philip S. Klein, *President James Buchanan* (University Park, Pa., 1962). His interpretation, needless to say, differs from mine, but I have drawn on his fine book for many details.

roomed for many years with Senator William King of Alabama, a fellow bachelor. His chief advisers included Governor Henry Wise of Virginia, Senator John Slidell of Louisiana, and Robert Tyler of Virginia. Even his most trusted northern advisers had southern ties: Representative J. Glancy Jones of Pennsylvania, an ardent dough-face, had been a southern preacher and lawyer, and Senator Jesse Bright of Indiana, another ardent doughface, owned land and slaves in Kentucky.

Ideologically, Buchanan also had much in common with the southern wing of his party. He was, in most instances, a strict constructionist with regard to the Constitution. He detested abolitionists and "Black Republicans." He opposed slavery only in the abstract. For all practical purposes, he saw no great wrong in its continued existence. He assumed that most slavemasters were humanitarians at heart and dismissed all those who argued the contrary. He thought most slaves were well treated and downplayed the slave pens and slave auctions in the nation's capital which told a different story. He sympathized with southern expansionists who hungered for Cuba and wanted to add slave territory to the United States.

Indeed, while not closely tied to Kansas-Nebraska, Buchanan had been a conspicuous supporter of the southern drive to annex Cuba with its half-million slaves. He had been secretary of state in 1848 when the Polk administration tried to buy Cuba from Spain for $100 million. And in 1854, while minister to Great Britain, he had joined the ministers to Spain and France in issuing, under orders from President Pierce, the Ostend Manifesto. That document urged the United States to immediately buy Cuba from Spain at any price up to $120 million. It also proclaimed that if Spain refused to sell and its possession of Cuba should seriously endanger the "internal peace" of the slave states, then the United States would be justified in seizing Cuba "upon the very same principle that would justify an individual in tearing down the burning house of his neighbor if there were no other means of preventing the flames from destroying his own home."[9]

News of this saber-rattling manifesto had horrified most northern Democrats. They knew that their political enemies would condemn

9. For excellent accounts of the Ostend Manifesto, see Amos Aschbach Ettinger, *The Mission to Spain of Pierre Soule, 1853–1855: A Study in the Cuban Diplomacy of the United States* (New Haven, 1932), 339–412; Robert E. May, *The Southern Dream of a Caribbean Empire, 1854–1861* (Baton Rouge, 1973), 67–74.

the "burning house" rhetoric as just an excuse to steal additional slavery territory and expand southern power. They had paid dearly for Kansas-Nebraska. They had no intention of being hammered again. Even such a staunch doughface as Lewis Cass denounced the manifesto,[10] while northern Democratic newspapers joined the chorus in branding its authors "brigands" and "highwaymen." The Pierce administration also ran for cover, disavowing the proposal and letting the "three wise men of Ostend" fend for themselves. The harsh barbs hardly hurt Buchanan with zealous expansionists and southern Democrats. They were delighted with him and had little trouble supporting his presidential candidacy.

Without these southern backers, Buchanan would have lost the 1856 presidential election. He won only five free states, losing eleven to the Republican candidate, John C. Frémont, who was twenty-two years his junior and a western folk hero with little political experience. In the free states the election brought out a whopping 83 percent of the eligible voters, and the vast majority voted for someone other than the Pennsylvania bachelor. Among lifelong Democrats in the northern tier of free states, probably one in five voted against the party's nominee, in the lower tier, maybe one in ten. In contrast, in the fifteen slave states, Buchanan won handsomely, losing only Maryland to the Know-Nothing candidate, Millard Fillmore. All in all, the slave states provided the Pennsylvania Democrat with nearly two-thirds of his electoral votes.

Southern Democrats, needless to say, never let Buchanan forget these facts. Nor was he able to forget that the Democratic majority in both the House and the Senate was dominated by southerners. In forming a cabinet, he chose four southerners, three doughfaces. Omitted entirely was anyone who understood, much less represented, the free-soil element of his party. Checking the growing sectional bias of the Democracy was thus next to impossible.

Two days after Buchanan's inauguration, the Supreme Court in the Dred Scott case declared the Missouri Compromise unconstitutional, thus opening all federal territories to slavery. The Buchanan administration's official organ, the *Washington Union*, immediately joined southerners in singing the praises of the Court. So did

10. *Congressional Globe,* 33d Congress, 2d session, 1854–55, p. 827; Cass to William L. Marcy, 9 April 1855, Marcy Papers.

Caleb Cushing of Massachusetts, Pierce's attorney general, who insisted that Chief Justice Taney was "the very incarnation of judicial purity, integrity, science and wisdom."[11]

The Republicans, in contrast, not only denounced the decision but blamed it on Buchanan. Had Frémont been elected president, David Dudley Field told a New York convention, the Supreme Court would not have dared to violate "the principles we have received from our forefathers."[12] Was this an exaggeration? Not as much as it might at first seem. The southern judges, historians later discovered, had wanted all along to issue a proslavery decision, but they knew that the authority of such a decision would be weak if they had only a one-vote majority and no northern judge was on their side. They set about to persuade one of the northern Democrats on the Court, Robert C. Grier of Pennsylvania, to join them. Unbeknown to his Republican critics, Buchanan helped them in this effort, and his intervention undoubtedly contributed to Grier's decision to join the southern majority in declaring the Missouri Compromise unconstitutional.[13]

The Republicans also raised the question, "What next?" David Dudley Field and his fellow delegates to the New York Republican convention had no doubt about the answer. They assumed that the Court's next step would be to declare that under the Constitution slaveholders could live with their slaves in the free states. For how long? To most Republicans it hardly mattered. One month would lead to two, one year to a second year, one decade to another decade. Republicans in the New York Assembly noted that Dred Scott had lived for two years in the free state of Illinois, and under the Court's decision that had not dissolved "the relation of master and slave." What then would? The answer, they assumed, was "nothing." The Court was determined to "bring slavery within our borders, against our will, with all its unhallowed, demoralizing, and blighting influences."[14]

This was not just paranoia. In November 1857 the *Washington*

11. *Washington Union*, 6, 11, 12, 21, 28 March 1857; Caleb Cushing, "Speech . . . at Newburyport, Massachusetts, October 31, 1857," Caleb Cushing Papers, Library of Congress.

12. *New York Tribune*, 7, 9–12, 21, 25 March, 23–25 September 1857; Don E. Fehrenbacher, *The Dred Scott Case: Its Significance in American Law and Politics* (New York, 1978), 417–48.

13. Philip G. Auchampaugh, "Buchanan, the Court, and the Dred Scott Case," *Tennessee Historical Magazine* 11 (1926): 231–40; Fehrenbacher, *Dred Scott*, 311–2.

14. *New York Tribune*, 23–25 September 1857; *Congressional Globe*, 35th

Union, the administration's official organ, declared that the abolition of slavery in the North was clearly an unconstitutional attack on private property.[15] And New York Republicans were well aware of a case in their own court system that might provide the Supreme Court with the opportunity the justices allegedly desired. In 1852 a New York judge had ruled that eight Virginia slaves had become free the moment their owner brought them into the Empire State. It mattered not in the least that the owner was just passing through, waiting for a ship to take them immediately to New Orleans. New York no longer recognized a slavemaster's right of transit or temporary sojourn. A middle-level court had upheld the judge's decision, but the state of Virginia had challenged the New York freedom law and appealed to New York's highest court.[16] What if the state's highest court upheld the New York freedom law? Would the Taney court override the New York decision? Republican lawyers had no doubt that it would.

Meanwhile, in Kansas, proslavery lawmakers were adding fuel to the fire. Knowing that Congress would not pass legislation enabling them to form a state, they decided to force the issue. Over the governor's veto, they passed legislation calling for a census, the election of delegates to a constitutional convention, and a convention in the fall of 1857. The free-state forces, assuming with good reason that the census would be rigged, boycotted the entire affair. As predicted, the census was rigged. In over half the counties, proslavery officials either never took a census or never bothered to register voters. All in all, half the eligible voters never had a chance to register, and the eight counties bordering slaveholding Missouri ended up with two-thirds of the delegates.[17]

At this point, Buchanan appointed Robert Walker territorial governor. A Pennsylvanian who had made his name in Mississippi pol-

Congress, 1st session, 1857–58, p. 665; *New York Assembly Documents*, 80th session, 1857, no. 201.

15. *Washington Union*, 17 November 1857.

16. *Lemmon v. The People*, 20 New York 562 (1860); Paul Finkelman, *An Imperfect Union: Slavery, Federalism, and Comity* (Chapel Hill, 1981), 285–338.

17. Of the many fine studies of the Kansas controversy, I am indebted especially to Kenneth M. Stampp, *America in 1857: A Nation on the Brink* (New York, 1990), chaps. 10–12; Robert W. Johannsen, *Stephen A. Douglas* (New York, 1973), 576–631; Fehrenbacher, *Dred Scott*, chap. 19; and James A. Rawley, *Race and Politics: "Bleeding Kansas" and the Coming of the Civil War* (Philadelphia, 1969).

itics, Walker had earlier blocked Van Buren's attempt to get the 1844 Democratic nomination and had become Polk's secretary of the treasury. He had also advocated the acquisition of both slave-holding Texas and slaveholding Cuba. He had, in short, strong southern credentials. But he was not foolhardy. He estimated that Democrats in Kansas outnumbered Republicans by two to one, but more than half of them would go over to the Republicans if the Democracy tried to turn Kansas into a slave state. In his view, Kansas was bound to be a free state, and his party simply had to accept that fact. Otherwise, they would lose the people of Kansas to the "abolitionists." He set about to have honest elections in Kansas and get the free-state majority to participate.

Despite Walker's pleas, the free-state men refused to take part in the election to choose constitutional delegates, and thus the proslavery forces prevailed easily. At Lecompton, they drafted a proslavery constitution. It proclaimed that "the right of property is before and higher than any constitutional sanction, and the right of the owner of a slave to such slave and its issue is the same and as inviolable as the right of the owner of any property whatever." It also prohibited any constitutional amendment for seven years and declared that even after seven years had passed "no alteration shall be made to affect the rights of property in the ownership of slaves."[18]

Knowing that their handiwork would be rejected if submitted to a fair vote, the delegates first decided to send the document straight-way to Washington without a referendum of any kind. But, on sober second thought, a majority decided that such a move was just too brazen to succeed. The delegates then worked out a bogus referendum, whereby the voters would not have the opportunity to vote down the fundamental constitution, just the opportunity to choose between two alternative clauses—one that would legally permit additional slaves to be brought into Kansas, another that would legally bar the future importation of slaves. But here again there was a rub. The election was not to be conducted by Governor Walker, but by officials named by the convention, the same men who had rigged the constitutional convention. That further convinced free-state men that the whole constitutional movement was a sham.

Walker set off for Washington to enlist Buchanan's support against

18. Daniel W. Wilder, *The Annals of Kansas* (Topeka, 1875), 140, 146.

the Lecompton constitution. But before he got there, Buchanan, who had wavered for nearly half a year, came down on the prosouthern side. Pressured by his cabinet and his proslavery friends in Congress, he threw his full weight behind the Lecompton constitution. Was it a gut-wrenching decision? Probably not.[19] Buchanan shared his friends' hatred of abolitionists and Republicans and saw no great wrong in extending slavery into Kansas. He also knew that he had enough votes to get the admission bill through the Senate, and he was confident that with executive pressure he could bring enough northern Democrats in line to get the measure through the House.

Once the *Washington Union* announced Buchanan's decision,[20] many northern Democrats panicked. The administration, as they saw it, had handed the Republicans another issue with which to beat down any chance they had of recapturing lost northern districts. They were already being lambasted for the Supreme Court's action in Dred Scott. Now they were expected to defend fraudulent elections in Kansas as well as a proslavery constitution which even the territorial governor, a one-time Mississippi slaveholder, deemed unacceptable. Rather than blame the president directly, however, many pretended that the editor of the *Union* was speaking for himself.[21] This fiction was hard to sustain, and a few weeks later, when the president's message was read to Congress, it became an impossible challenge.

The president delivered his message in early December 1857. The next day, Douglas rose in the Senate and attacked the administration's Kansas policy. A few days later Walker resigned in protest. A few days after that, the referendum called by the Lecompton convention took place. With most of the free-state men abstaining, the official results showed some 6,000 votes for Lecompton with additional slavery and some 500 for it without additional slavery. Of the proslavery votes, nearly 3,000 came from areas along the Missouri border that had yet to be settled. Towns with six buildings and forty settlers had over four hundred voters. Two weeks later, there was

19. Historians are sharply divided on this issue. Many say that Buchanan caved in to southern pressure. This of course implies initial resistance on his part. Others think the resistance was at best minimal. Cf., for example, Allan Nevins, *The Emergence of Lincoln: Douglas, Buchanan, and Party Chaos, 1857–1859*, 2 vols. (New York, 1950), 1: 239–47, and Stampp, *America in 1857*, 283–5.

20. November 18, 24, 29, 1857.

21. *Washington Union*, 24 November, 1, 3 December 1857.

another election in Kansas, this one called by the state legislature. This time the proslavery men abstained and Lecompton was voted down by over 10,000 votes.

Buchanan nevertheless pushed ahead. Denouncing the actions of free-staters in Kansas and announcing that "Kansas is . . . at this moment as much a slave State as Georgia or South Carolina," he sent the Lecompton constitution to both houses for adoption.[22] What followed was a dramatic contest, with long sessions, filibusters, and fist fights on the floor. Much attention was focused on the Senate, where the Little Giant of Illinois led the revolt against the Buchanan administration. Douglas's actions perplexed some. Others concluded that he had no choice: Lecompton's rigged convention and fraudulent votes had made a mockery out of "popular sovereignty."

But the Senate was never in doubt. The president had the votes he needed—and then some. His problem was the House, where he needed another fifteen to twenty votes. He had plenty of weapons and used every one of them. He made conspicuous examples of those who crossed him, firing several of Douglas's allies, including the Chicago postmaster, the state mail agent in Illinois, and the federal marshal of northern Illinois, replacing them with "good" Lecompton Democrats. At the same time, he had his underlings work the halls of Congress, promising patronage awards to the faithful: supply contracts for firms tied to House members, shipbuilding contracts for firms in which congressmen owned shares, an overseas appointment for a close friend of Garnett Adrian of New Jersey, and a similar appointment for a friend of John B. Hickman of Pennsylvania. And then for some there were less traceable favors—wine, women, and cash. All of these enticements came into play again and again in the battle to get Lecompton through the House.[23]

Yet, in the end, Buchanan failed to get the votes he needed. His opponents introduced a substitute motion to resubmit the entire

22. James D. Richardson, ed., *A Compilation of the Messages and Papers of the Presidents,* 20 vols. (New York, 1897), 7: 3010.

23. For Buchanan's use and misuse of presidential power, see *House Reports,* 36th Congress, 1st session, 1859–60, no. 249; *House Reports,* "The Covode Investigation," 36th Congress, 1st session, 1859–60, no. 648; Mark W. Summers, *The Plundering Generation: Corruption and the Crisis of the Union, 1849–1861* (New York, 1987), 252–60; and David E. Meerse, "James Buchanan, the Patronage, and the Northern Democratic Party, 1857–1858" (Ph.D. dissertation, University of Illinois, 1969).

Lecompton constitution to a popular vote in Kansas. The amended bill passed the House, 120 to 112, on April 1, 1858. For the first time in memory, the South had suffered a crushing defeat.

The administration immediately scrambled to mask defeat and deny the anti-Lecompton forces outright victory. The result was a "compromise" bill that deliberately subordinated the Lecompton constitution and highlighted a secondary issue, the fact that Kansas had asked for twenty-three million acres of public land grants, about six times the norm for new states. The administration proposed cutting the land grant to about four million acres and asking the voters if they would accept statehood with the reduction. If they ratified this proposal, then Kansas would immediately be admitted as a slave state under the Lecompton constitution. If they rejected it, Kansas would have to wait until it had a population of 90,000 before it could become a state. In short, rejection meant the death of the Lecompton constitution and the postponement of statehood for several years.

Republicans railed against these stipulations, saying they amounted to a bribe and a threat. Some Democrats agreed. Douglas at first wavered and then at the last moment joined the protesters. But there seemed to be little doubt that the Kansans, given the opportunity, would use this dodge to kill the Lecompton constitution. And the administration gave anti-Lecompton Democrats every inducement to see the "compromise" bill from this perspective.

Having lost the real battle, Buchanan and his southern cronies went all out to save face and win a procedural victory. There was an army contract for the brother of John Ahl of Pennsylvania, five thousand dollars for the roommate of Lawrence Hall of Ohio, a township of land for Joseph McKibben of California (which he refused), the same township for John Haskin of New York (which he also refused). Then there was the threat to fire McKibben's father from his job as a Philadelphia naval agent. As a result, a handful of anti-Lecompton Democrats joined forces with the administration, and on the last day of April the face-saving "compromise" passed the House, 112 to 103, and the Senate, 31 to 22.

A few months later the voters of Kansas did what most everyone had expected. They rejected Lecompton by a six to one margin.

The defeat of the Lecompton constitution left an unusually large residue of hatred and bitterness. Southern senators spoke of the "treachery" of northern Democrats. The *Washington Union* repeatedly denounced Douglas as a "traitor." And the Pennsylvania president gained a reputation as a corrupt bungler.

Why did Buchanan and his southern cronies fail? Never before had any president so flagrantly used his patronage power to reward "good" congressmen and punish the recalcitrant. The White House, lamented one Illinois Democrat, had bought congressmen "like hogs in the market." Yet Garnett Adrian of New Jersey resisted the overtures of the White House. So did John Hickman of Pennsylvania. And so did Joseph McKibben of California.

Resistance, however, was hardly new. Not every northern Democrat thought like William Marcy Tweed or Caleb Cushing. Not everyone was willing to trade his vote for presidential favors. Some undoubtedly found it insulting. Others had little to gain. Many represented districts that followed the yearling policy, whereby a man was sent to Congress to serve for two years—or at best four years—and then was replaced by another party member regardless of the circumstances. For such men, a long-term political career, especially a long-term career in Washington politics, was usually a secondary concern. Getting patronage for their home districts was important, but still more important was staying in the good graces of the people back home.[24]

Even some nonyearlings were caught in a bind, pressured from both sides. Such was the case of William English, the man who actually introduced Buchanan's face-saving "compromise" bill. The representative of Indiana's Second District, English had spent most of his thirty-six years in his home district. His parents were the small town of Lexington's most distinguished pioneers. He had grown up there and opened a law practice there. In the 1840s he had taken a job in the

---

24. The number of Jacksonian congressmen who accepted lucrative federal appointments for voting the "right" way is open to debate. At one time scholars thought the Jacksonians were as venal as the opposition press made them out to be. Years later, historians "proved" that the opposition press had grossly exaggerated the extent of the Jacksonian spoils system. By how much? One study concluded that of some four hundred Jackson men who served in Congress between 1825 and 1837, "only" about twenty "were rewarded with appointive offices." (See Alvin W. Lynn, "Party Formation and Operation in the House of Representatives, 1824–1837" [Ph.D. dissertation, Rutgers University, 1972], 260.) What about the Jackson men who served later? Most scholars portray them as much more venal than their predecessors. (See especially Summers, *Plundering Generation.*)

state house for one year and a job in the Treasury Department in Washington for four years. But after the Democrats lost the White House in 1848, he had returned to Lexington. Four years later, he ran for Congress and won handsomely with 55 percent of the vote. He supported the Kansas-Nebraska Act, barely survived the 1854 election, and by the time of the Lecompton constitution was serving his third term. He had no desire to buck the president. Indeed, he was a protégé of Senator Jesse Bright, one of Buchanan's closest doughface advisers, and he supported the Lecompton constitution. The trouble was that his constituents were on the other side and they gave him no peace. What did English do in the showdown vote, the one that really counted? He rejected the White House's overtures and voted against the president.

The impact of spoils politics and presidential pressure thus had its limits. That had been true at the time of Jackson's Indian Removal Act, Pinckney's gag rule, the Wilmot Proviso, and Kansas-Nebraska. Yet on each of those occasions the southern wing of the party had prevailed. It usually took a lot of work, weeks of rounding up the necessary votes, but in the end the southern wing prevailed. Now, after the rout of the northern Democracy in 1854, winning the House was much more difficult.

Douglas's rebellion undoubtedly added to the difficulty. Indeed, from the standpoint of both the Buchanan administration and Douglas's biographers, he was the chief cause of the South's defeat. Yet the southern wing of the Democracy had had to cope with prominent northern defectors before. And in 1844, when the Van Burenites revolted, the number of defectors was not only far greater but also included the most disciplined members of the party. At that time, however, the southern wing of the party quickly recovered and mustered enough votes from other northern Democrats to annex Texas and defeat the Wilmot Proviso.

Why, then, did they fail to offset the Douglas rebellion in 1858? The Little Giant worked diligently to get western Democrats to break with the administration and vote against Lecompton. But how many men actually followed him? Probably no more than a half dozen.[25]

25. Fourteen western Democrats voted against the South. Some of these men would have done so even if Douglas had supported the Lecompton constitution. Others, like Indiana's William H. English, while friendly with Douglas, took their cues from other northern Democrats, mainly men in their home districts.

And Douglas had virtually no success with eastern Democrats. Indeed, in the showdown vote, Buchanan proved that he had far more political muscle than Douglas, getting a larger percentage of northern Democrats to cast doughface votes than at the time of Kansas-Nebraska four years earlier. In 1854, despite all Douglas's hard work and Pierce's horse trading, only 48 percent of the northern House Democrats voted with the South. In 1858, even with Douglas leading western Democrats into rebellion, 59 percent of the northern House Democrats sided with Buchanan and the South.

The difference in 1858 was largely a matter of numbers. In the past there had always been enough northern Democrats in the House to turn a southern minority position into a majority political position. That had been the case with Indian Removal in 1830, with the gag rule between 1836 and 1844, with Texas in 1845, with the Wilmot Proviso in 1847, with the Fugitive Slave Law in 1850, and with Kansas-Nebraska in 1854. In 1858 the numbers simply were not there.

Buchanan and the South thus faced an entirely different situation than Douglas and Pierce faced four years before. At the time of Kansas-Nebraska there were ninety-three northern Democrats in the House, more than at any other time before the Civil War. Forty-four of these men were persuaded to support the South. By the time of Lecompton, even with the gains of the 1856 election, the party had only fifty-three northern seats. And even though thirty-one of these men sided with the South, that was not enough votes. The northern wing of the Democracy had been decimated, and as a result, the day of the doughface had passed.

Following the Lecompton debacle, the number of northern House Democrats plummeted once again. The northern Democracy went into the 1858 fall elections with fifty-three seats in the House. They came out with only thirty-four. This time doughface Democrats suffered the most. That had never been the case in the past.

For years doughface Democrats had one advantage over their colleagues. They had always been more likely to get federal spoils. The Jackson administration began this policy on a limited scale in 1830 to marshal support for Indian Removal. The Polk administration carried it further in the 1840s. The Pierce administration at the time of Kansas-Nebraska was blatant about it. And the Buchanan administration, as we have just seen, dished out patronage to loyal followers without restraint.

Such largesse, one suspects, not only affected votes in Congress but also the outcome of close elections. Initially the reelection rate for doughfaces was worse than that of other northern congressmen. Following the Missouri crisis of 1820, only three of seventeen House doughfaces were reelected, less than half the northern average of 42 percent. Four were defeated and ten retired. How many were forced to quit is, unfortunately, uncertain. But few House members served more than a term or two, and what really mattered was whether the party won or lost the district. By this standard, their parties lost five of seventeen seats, which was twice the average.

All this changed, however, in the Jacksonian era. With doughface districts getting a larger share of federal spoils, the Jacksonians had less trouble retaining doughface seats than other northern seats.[26] This was true even after the Kansas-Nebraska Act, when the party paid dearly at the polls, losing 68 percent of its doughface seats and 81 percent of its other northern seats.[27] It was not until 1858, following Buchanan's attempt to steamroll Congress into accepting Kansas as a slave state, that the impact of federal spoils clearly reached its limit.

In the 1858 congressional elections, the Buchanan administration went after "disloyal" Democrats with a vengeance.[28] The president's men packed local conventions with government officeholders and had them vote against the incumbent. In the Illinois Senate race, they

26. This generalization is based on career-line studies of northern House members who voted on the Missouri bill of 1820, the Pinckney gag of 1836, the 1840 gag, the Three Million Bill of 1847, the Fugitive Slave Act of 1850, the Kansas-Nebraska Act of 1854, and the Montgomery-Crittenden amendment of 1858. Information on reelection rates was compiled from several sources but mainly the U.S. Congress, *Biographical Directory of the American Congress, 1774–1971* (Washington, D.C., 1971) and the *Congressional Quarterly's Guide to U.S. Elections* (Washington, D.C., 1975).

27. In the 1854 election, there were five incumbent Democrats who switched parties, ran against the Democracy, and won. I have counted these as losses for the party.

28. For details on what the Buchanan administration did during the 1858 election, I am dependent on the following sources: *House Reports*, 36th Congress, 1st session, 1859–60, no. 249; *House Reports*, "The Covode Investigation"; *Congressional Globe*, 36th Congress, 1st session, 1859–60, pp. 2938–50; Summers, *The Plundering Generation*, 254–60; and Meerse, "James Buchanan."

ran a candidate of their own against Douglas and forced federal office-holders to contribute to his campaign. At the same time, three of the president's closest advisers—J. Glancy Jones, John Slidell, and Jesse Bright—instructed federal workers in Illinois to defeat legislators committed to Douglas's reelection, even if that meant supporting Lincoln.

Along with Douglas, nine House Democrats were singled out for special attention.[29] Among them were John B. Haskin of New York, who earlier had been offered a township to mend his ways, and Joseph C. McKibben of California, who had not only been offered a township but had been ordered to support the president's Kansas policy or his father would be fired. These men had proved to be stubborn to the end and thus earned a spot on the administration's special hit list. In the case of Haskin, the president's men made sure someone else got the party's nomination. Haskin went over to the Republicans and won reelection by thirteen votes. McKibben won reelection in 1858, but Lecompton Democrats in California changed the election laws and invalidated his reelection.[30]

Even more time and money was spent in behalf of the faithful. To help Thomas Florence hold onto Pennsylvania's First District, more than 1,700 "colonists" were moved to Philadelphia and added to the navy yard's job rolls on the condition that they vote Democratic. Florence won reelection by 331 votes. To help William Maclay in New York, 2,700 "colonists" were temporarily hired at the Brooklyn Naval Yard. Maclay won easily. So blatant was the secretary of navy in awarding shipbuilding contracts to inflate the Democratic work force that the next two congresses felt compelled to investigate.

Nonetheless, the impact of federal patronage clearly had reached its limit. Even though the Buchanan administration bribed news-

29. David E. Meerse, "The Northern Democratic Party and the Congressional Elections of 1858," *Civil War History* 19 (June 1973): 125, 128.

30. *Congressional Quarterly's Guide to U.S. Elections,* 760. The *Biographical Directory of the American Congress* mistakenly reports that McKibben was defeated in 1858. He was actually defeated the following year when he had to run a second time. See *New York Tribune Almanac, 1859,* 63; *Tribune Almanac, 1860,* 58; Winfield J. Davis, *A History of Political Conventions in California, 1849–1862* (Sacramento, 1892), 86–111; and David A. Williams, *David C. Broderick: A Political Portrait* (San Marino, Calif., 1969), 188–229.

papers and colonized voters in behalf of loyal congressmen and singled out some anti-Lecompton Democrats for punishment, doughface Democrats for the first time had a harder time on Election Day than other northern Democrats. All in all, the party lost 70 percent of the its doughface seats as compared to 26 percent of its other northern seats.[31]

One pillar of the old order thus gave way in the 1850s. To the Buchananites, it was the fault of Douglas, who, like Van Buren before him, was a traitor to his party.[32] To Douglas, who survived the 1858 election, it marked a severe blow to the "nationality" of the Democratic Party and hence the survival of the Union. To Seward and Lincoln, it meant that decades of slaveholder domination might finally be coming to an end.

In the newly elected House, the new Republican Party now had more than a three to one advantage over northern Democrats. Even New Hampshire, once the banner state of the Democracy, had become solidly Republican. In 1853 the Jacksonians had won every district in the state by at least 1,200 votes; four years later they lost every district in the state by 1,000 or more votes. In 1859 they failed to make a comeback and lost every district again.[33]

Even longtime New Hampshire doughfaces went over to the new party. Benjamin Brown French, for example, had been a staunch

31. In "The Northern Democratic Party and the Congressional Elections of 1858," 119–37, David Meerse attempts to minimize the impact of the Lecompton controversy. In doing so, he makes some valid points. He correctly points out, for example, that historians have exaggerated the voters' reaction to Buchanan's Kansas policy, that many congressional contests were extremely close, and that the Buchanan Democrats lost some districts because of local issues. But the election returns and his evidence also indicate that the nine House Democrats who consistently opposed the administration's Kansas policy, and thus made the administration's hit list, collectively did better than the men the administration supported. According to my calculations, six men on the hit list ran for reelection (one as a Republican), and all six won. Three men chose not to run again, and in each instance their replacements won. The Democracy thus held onto eight of the nine seats, while losing two-thirds of its other northern seats.

32. *Washington Union,* 6, 14 November 1858.

33. For the effectiveness of the Republican's crusade against the Slave Power in New Hampshire, see Thomas R. Bright, "The Anti-Nebraska Coalition and the Emergence of the Republican Party in New Hampshire: 1853–1857," *Historical New Hampshire* 27 (Summer 1972): 57–88.

doughface since the days of Isaac Hill. A quintessential party operative, he had worked in the clerk's office of the House from 1833 to 1847 and then as commissioner of public buildings in the 1850s. Good-natured and convivial, he liked planters, envied their lifestyle, and shared their views. He regarded antislavery resolutions as "impudent & uncalled for" and censured abolitionists for attacking "in spirit, the Holy Word of God." He insisted that the Bible ordained slavery and cited the usual verses to prove his claim. He also insisted that Maryland house slaves dressed better than New Hampshire women and that Maryland field hands were so well off that "Freedom to them would be ruin."[34]

Nonetheless, in the 1850s French switched parties. He first flirted with the Know-Nothings, then the Anti-Nebraska men. The turning point apparently came when his brother vehemently opposed the Kansas-Nebraska Act. President Pierce hauled French into his office, chastised him for his brother's actions, and then asked him to write a letter to a New Hampshire newspaper justifying the bill. French first consented, then refused. Thereafter, he had nothing but harsh words for his old friend Pierce and within months joined the Republicans.[35]

Had southern Democrats been more yielding, maybe they could have held onto a man like French. As late as 1859 he still had one foot in the Democratic camp and had high hopes that Stephen A. Douglas would find an answer to the vexing slavery question. But nothing was done to reunite men like French with their old party. Not only were northern Democrats now the minority party in the North, they were also the minority wing of their own party in both houses of Congress. In 1852, when French was still a party stalwart, they had twenty-six more seats than their southern colleagues in the House. Now they had only half as many seats. Even worse, they were made to feel it.

In the past, when southerners had been so dominant, they had usually downplayed the slavery issue. They tried desperately to keep it out of politics, tolerated some dissent from their northern

---

34. Benjamin Brown French, *Witness to the Young Republic: A Yankee's Journal, 1828–1870*, ed. Donald B. Cole and John J. McDonough (Hanover, N.H., 1989), especially 220–1.

35. French, *Witness to the Young Republic*, 260–3.

brethren, and shared some of the spoils of office. That was not the case, however, when the new Congress met in December 1859. The state of Virginia had just hanged John Brown for criminal conspiracy to incite a slave rebellion, and southern Democrats wanted to ferret out all those who supported Brown's raid on Harpers Ferry. They were in no mood for compromise. Offering an olive branch to men like French was clearly out of the question. Indeed, with the South fully in control and Buchanan still calling for vengeance against anti-Lecompton Democrats, the caucus stripped the northern wing's foremost politician, Stephen A. Douglas, of his chairmanship of the Committee on Territories. They also kicked California senator David Broderick out of the caucus because of his vociferous opposition to the Lecompton constitution. And they went on record in favor of a federal slave code for the territories.

The southern wing also took a hard line in the 1860 presidential election. In the recent past they had always supported a doughface for president and, through him, controlled presidential politics. Now in 1860, with the decline of the northern Democrats and the rise of the new Republican Party, the southern wing refused to support Douglas's nomination for president, bolted the national convention, and nominated a southern candidate. With the defeat of their candidate and Lincoln's election, they lost control of the presidency. In Lincoln they now had a president who was committed to the "ultimate extinction" of slavery and truly believed that an unscrupulous Slave Power had controlled the nation's history. And for the first time they were now governed by a northern president who owed nothing to the South. Indeed, the Republicans were not on the ballot in ten southern states, and Lincoln captured only 26,000 votes in the slave states, compared to 1,800,000 in the free states.

William H. Seward had predicted that the long domination of the Slave Power was coming to an end. The North, he told the Senate during the heated Lecompton debate, would "take the Government" and end the rule of the South.[36] Hotspurs in the lower South, longing for secession, now said that Seward's prediction had come to pass. To counter them, Alexander H. Stephens and other Unionists called on the South to consider its domination of the federal government since

36. *Congressional Globe*, 35th Congress, 1st session, 1857–58, p. 943.

the founding of the Republic, to play democratic politics and try to regain power in the next election. There was no reason to panic, they said. Lincoln would have a rough time governing. He had come far short of winning a majority of the nation's vote. His party controlled neither Congress nor the Supreme Court, and it lacked the organizational means to distribute patronage and carry out routine services in the slave states.

Oddly enough, James Henry Hammond, the South Carolina firebrand, fully agreed with this position. He had carried the battle against Seward in 1858. In words that were repeated as far west as San Francisco, he had told northerners that they dared not make war on cotton, that no power on earth dared make war on cotton, that cotton was king, that every society had a "mud-sill" class to do the menial work, and that the South had found a people ideally suited to such work in its black slaves. But on one point he had agreed with his northern nemesis. He had agreed with Seward's claim that slaveholders ruled the Republic. He was proud of it. He regarded it as "the brightest page of human history."[37]

Privately, however, Hammond dismissed as wishful thinking Seward's prediction that the North would take the government and end the rule of the South. He also dismissed the notion that Lincoln's election meant the end of southern dominance. Lincoln's election was just a setback. The North, as Hammond saw it, lacked staying power, and thus the South, if united, would continue to dictate national policy. The notion that the South had only two choices—either to secede or accept an inferior position in the national government—was nonsense. Secession was not only foolish but self-destructive. Indeed, it reminded him of "the Japanese who when insulted rip open their own bowels."

Yet, what did Hammond do in the winter of 1860–1861? He got swept away by the "epidemic." Upon learning of Lincoln's election, his South Carolina colleague James Chesnut resigned from the Senate. So too did Senator Robert Toombs of Georgia. And South Carolina's Andrew Gordon McGrath resigned from the United States District Court. Once Hammond heard of these resignations, he followed suit. It was impulsive, he told his brother. Indeed, all of them had acted like "great asses." Yet once it was done, there was

37. Ibid., 962.

no turning back. So he hid his private thoughts and enthusiastically endorsed the crusade for southern independence.[38]

In a sense, then, it was men like Hammond who finally destroyed the Slave Power. Thanks to their leading the South out of the Union, seventy-two years of slaveholder domination came to an end. Many think that it would have happened anyway, that Lincoln's victory marked a real change in the nation's politics, and that the South would have lost its hold on the Democratic Party, the Senate, and the Supreme Court. Maybe they are right. Maybe southern power in Washington was more precarious on the eve of the Civil War than Hammond recognized.

But the fact remains that Hammond had lived nearly sixty years in a republic in which slaveholders had exercised extraordinary power, and secession soon brought that to an end. The formation of the Confederacy by South Carolina and ten other slave states gave him a brief respite from Lincoln, Seward, and "Black Republicanism." It enabled him to live a few more years under a government in which slaveholders clearly ruled. But he dreaded the future. He had no desire "to look beyond the veil" and live under any other form of government. He never had to. He died before Sherman's "grand army of Mud-sills" reached South Carolina, demolished everything in their path, and destroyed forever the last vestiges of slaveholder rule.[39]

38. For this and the preceding paragraph: Drew Gilpin Faust, *James Henry Hammond and the Old South* (Baton Rouge, 1982), 357–61; James Henry Hammond to Marcus C. M. Hammond, 12 November 1860, in *The Hammonds of Redcliffe*, ed. Carol Bleser (New York, 1981), 88; Lawrence T. McDonnell, "Struggle against Suicide: James Henry Hammond and the Secession of South Carolina," *Southern Studies* 22 (Summer 1983): 109–37.

39. Bleser, *Hammonds of Redcliffe*, 18.

Index